The Complete Idiot's Refere

Sixteen Basic Topics That Must Be Ev

1. Banking—Where to get the most cost-effective service?
2. Mortgage—Can you afford to purchase a home?
3. Mortgage—Do you have the best deal possible?
4. Credit—How is your credit report and credit rating?
5. Credit—Retire all your consumer credit and save big time!
6. Financial Plan—Calculate your net worth.
7. Financial Plan—Evaluate your cash flow.
8. Financial Plan—Cost of a College Education.
9. Financial Plan—Retirement Plans.
10. Financial Plan—Social Security.
11. Financial Plan—Life, Disability, and Health Insurance.
12. Estate Plan—Review your will, trust, power of attorney for health and financial matters.
13. Taxes—Plan for minimizing the taxes you pay.
14. Taxes—Do it yourself or use a professional.
15. Computerize your financial life—you will not regret this investment.
16. Read and learn—financial pages, TV shows, professional financial advisers and lawyers, talk to your friends, talk to their friends.

Five Reasons Women Need to Invest Now

1. Self-reliance and self-determination come from learning to invest on your own.
2. While you might find someone to do this for you during most of your lifetime, women live longer than men.
3. Women own and manage over half the small businesses in this country, and are gaining ground in more traditionally male professions, so go forth, be confident, and conquer.
4. Women are frequently the head of household, and need to teach their children, by example, how to be an investor.
5. It is time to focus on you and your financial future.

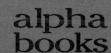

alpha books

Five Important Ingredients for Stock Selection

1. Understand what the company provides to our world.

2. Do your homework. Investigate the management of the company by reading the annual report and news releases, as well as analysts' opinions to insure continuity in performance of the stock price.

3. Only purchase companies you can see owning for the long haul.

4. Be smart in choosing the price you are willing to pay for quality.

5. When working with professionals, be sure that they answer your questions and are courteous—don't give *your* money to *rude* people!

Five Important Things to Do Before You Begin

1. Evaluate where you are right now, financially.

2. Get organized; establish a filing system and a way to keep track of your progress.

3. Clean up your debt picture.

4. Review your benefits from your employer and how they fit into your overall financial picture.

5. Choose your advisors carefully.

Five Common Errors to Avoid

1. Don't refinance too often.

2. Don't sign *anything* you don't understand.

3. Don't forget to pay the credit card bill on time.

3. Don't be impatient. Plan your work, work your plan.

4. Do not simply delegate this to even a most trusted advisor. Keep your hand in the decisions at all times.

5. Measure twice, cut once. Carefully and thoroughly consider any changes before you make them.

Three Questions to Ask an Advisor or Broker

1. What is your experience and background?

2. What is your investment philosophy and style?

3. How are you compensated for your advice?

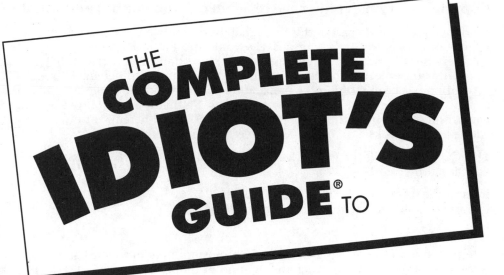

THE COMPLETE IDIOT'S GUIDE® TO

Investing for Women

by Jennifer Basye Sander, Anne Boutin, and Jim Brown

alpha books

A Pearson Education Company

For marketing and publicity, please call: 317-581-3722

The publisher offers discounts on this book when ordered in quantity for bulk purchases and special sales.

For sales within the United States, please contact: Corporate and Government Sales, 1-800-382-3419 or corpsales@pearsontechgroup.com

Outside the United States, please contact: International Sales, 317-581-3793 or international@pearsontechgroup.com

Alpha Development Team

Publisher
Kathy Nebenhaus

Editorial Director
Gary M. Krebs

Managing Editor
Bob Shuman

Marketing Brand Manager
Felice Primeau

Editor
Jessica Faust

Development Editors
Phil Kitchel
Amy Zavatto

Production Team

Development Editor
Alexander Goldman

Production Editor
Tammy Ahrens

Copy Editor
June Waldman

Cover Designer
Mike Freeland

Photo Editor
Richard H. Fox

Illustrator
Brian Hoffner

Book Designers
Scott Cook and Amy Adams of DesignLab

Indexers
Cheryl Jackson

Layout/Proofreading
Mary Hunt
Daniela Raderstorf
Cheryl Moore

Contents at a Glance

Contents

Foreword

Seven out of ten of us will at some point be alone in our lives. Ensuring our financial well-being is as essential as safeguarding our family's health. While many women take the time to thoroughly educate themselves on subjects such as nutrition and a host of other topics related to parenting, they feel paralyzed when it comes to long-term financial planning. Reviewing options for retirement plans proves too burdensome for many women who, unable to cope with the paperwork involved, keep postponing their decision until the harsh reality of life sinks in far too late.

The sad truth is that the average median income for a woman over the age of 65 is approximately $9,000 per year. Those not sufficiently prepared for what should be the "golden years of life" find themselves living in abject poverty. Preparing for those years is not a luxury for any of us. It is mandatory.

That's the bad news. Yet the good news may surprise you: A number of recent studies indicate that women who do choose to handle their own financial matters actually fare better than men—both individually and collectively. According to the National Association of Investment Clubs, women's investment clubs consistently outperform their male counterparts. Another study conducted by two professors at the University of California at Davis shows that women investors outperform men on an individual basis as well. The reasons cited vary from study to study, but the bottom line is that when women are educated enough to understand the financial options available to them, they can and do excel at the task.

While I cannot promise that all readers of this book will become millionaires, I can guarantee that those of you who enrich yourself with knowledge about financial matters will be much better off in the long run. Those who are young and begin to invest while in their 20s can easily achieve a comfortable lifestyle for their later years. In fact, a simple IRA backed by sound investment choices each year can actually be worth a million dollars at retirement. Would you rather take the time now to ensure a retirement of security for your loved ones, hobbies, and other enjoyable pursuits, or perhaps even world travel, or face an alternative of a day-to-day struggle to survive?

The choice is clear, and—no matter what your age—*The Complete Idiot's Guide® to Investing for Women* is an excellent road map and practical guide. At the very least, you will soon realize how much money you literally throw away each year just by using credit. Those who learn about the hidden costs associated with credit cards and simple banking transactions will soon save enough money to not only reimburse the cost of this book but also afford to buy additional copies for valued friends and loved ones. Clearing up past credit problems and breaking poor financial habits provide a solid foundation of wealth creation. My father often quoted the familiar adage, "A fool and his money are soon parted." We all have been financially naive (if not downright foolish) at one point or other in our lives—myself included! Your purchase of *The Complete Idiot's Guide® to Investing for Women* may well prove to be the smartest money you've ever spent.

As a speaker, I have recently traveled the country addressing various groups of women about their finances. A number of women have confessed to me privately that they actually become dizzy in the company of their brokers or financial consultants. Believe it or not, most of what you will learn by reading this book is not rocket science, and any "idiot" among us can easily grasp the fundamental concepts. It takes only a couple of hours to become acquainted with the terminology and various aspects of asset allocation, for example. Yet all too many women have been intimidated into giving up their say in financial decisions to the men in their lives—husbands, boyfriends, or brokers—who have, in turn, taken advantage of this naivete. Just to relay the major horror stories that I've heard would fill the pages of several books this size. Suffice it to say that countless hardworking and trusting women have been totally wiped out by unscrupulous advisors. One must never be trusting when it comes to matters financial. Knowledge and discipline are mandatory. I learned the lessons of Wall Street the hard way, rising up the ranks from my first job as secretary to achieving substantial success in my field and a personal fortune in the millions. Yet I'll be the first to admit that I largely neglected my own financial goals in the process. Throughout the 20 years I spent working on the Street, my first priority was always the needs of my clients. In this respect, I am a typical woman, casting myself in the traditional role of caregiver. It's time for us all to rearrange our priorities, especially when it comes to our financial well-being, and learn to take care of ourselves. We can no longer rely on the company for which we work to provide for us in the later years of life via an adequate retirement or pension package, nor can we depend on Social Security to be there when we need it most. Corporate America, and even America itself, keeps its eyes firmly focused on the bottom line. We are the only ones looking after our own interests, and we would be total idiots not to realize that!

Starting down the road to financial security is not difficult. You must take the time to understand the various options available to you and be able to recognize the many con artists and frauds who lie in wait along the way. Those who amass a working knowledge of financial matters will never become victims. And many of you will discover that you have a natural flair for choosing stocks and other investments, amassing great wealth in the process.

Reading a book such as this is by far the best way to obtain an unbiased view on planning for a secure financial future. Once you learn a few basic principles, the subject matter will no longer make you dizzy. And more than a few female "idiots" may outsmart all the male financial geniuses in the process!

Marlene Jupiter

Author of *Savvy Investing for Women—Strategies from a Self-Made Wall Street Millionaire*

New York City

October 1998

Introduction

Money. Everyone thinks about it, everyone talks about it, and worse yet, everyone worries about it. Everyone, regardless of her or his income or net worth, worries about money. Do I have enough? How much is enough? Just what is the best way to make it grow?

And you as a woman, a thinking woman, have been much targeted lately—that is, you and your money have been targeted. Financial advertisements abound in women's magazines, and the television airwaves are cluttered with ads focused on financial services.

So how do you start to invest your money wisely? And if you have already begun to invest, how do you move to the next level? Where do you turn for financial advice? Do you ask your husband, your neighbor, or your mom? Any one of those folks might be perfectly capable of giving you solid advice but, unfortunately, equally capable of steering you in the wrong direction. And asking questions might make you feel like…well, kinda like an idiot. So why don't you skip those folks and give us a chance to help you understand the world of investing. Soon enough, you'll be the one giving financial advice!

Within the pages of *The Complete Idiot's Guide® to Investing for Women*, we, Anne and Jennifer, have combined our knowledge, experience, and expertise to clearly present the information you'll need to maneuver in the financial world. We start by establishing just what your current financial picture is, move on to establishing your investment goals, and then tackle the question of how you can actually begin to achieve those goals.

How to Use This Book

We have divided the investment process into six parts. If you take them one at a time, through each part of this book, you will learn everything about investing your money: from the basic steps of assessing your net worth to the more complex steps of increasing it!

Part 1, "Focus on Your Finances—*Now!*," gives you the push you need to wade out on your own into the world of money. We start by examining why women must be involved in investment decisions—regardless of their marital or financial status—and move on to looking at how well some women are doing now in the big, bad world of investing. Then it is a lesson in the basics: sorting out your finances, understanding how much you are making on the money you have now, deciphering some of that stuff you get in the mail, and finding out where you can turn for help in handling it all.

Part 2, "I Owe, I Owe, It's Off to Work I Go," helps you get a further handle on things. You figure out just exactly what your net worth is, take a close look at the different types of debt in your life, and turn a cold eye on how much your car is costing you.

Part 3, "Get Rich Like Bill Gates Did!," launches you into the nitty-gritty of investments. You learn how to get rich just like Warren Buffett did (with stock), tunnel your way into the bond market, and find a mutual fund to your liking. When you are ready to shift into a higher financial gear, we talk about the wild and woolly worlds of options, futures, commodities, and more.

Part 4, "So Much Money, So Little Time," helps you decide whether you really want to handle your money on your own or would prefer professional advice and guidance. Learn also about popular software packages and online investment tools that can help you manage your finances.

Part 5, "When I Am an Old Woman, I Shall Wear Purple Cashmere," takes a clear-eyed look at what happens when women reach retirement age. You learn what to expect, and how to plan for the unexpected. These chapters examine all types of retirement plans, from 401(k)s to KEOGHs and everything in between. Start now to ensure that your retirement years are enjoyable and free of financial stress.

Part 6, "Everybody Dies—Why Not Have a Plan?," tackles the uncomfortable subject of death and inheritance. Yours, unfortunately. From why you need a will now to the steps you can take to reduce the tax bite for your heirs, estate planning truly is a topic that you shouldn't avoid.

In addition, to make sure that you don't get lost in investment lingo, we've included a glossary that contains all the words and terms you need to handle yourself in any financial conversation.

Want to know how to read a financial report? We've included that in the back of the book, too. We've also included a basic description of just how the stock market works, how to decipher the financial pages, and a lengthy list of magazines and newspapers that we think you should read.

Extras

Brief asides and comments sprinkled throughout the chapters contain extra bits of information that we think you should know.

Wise Women Know

These anecdotes from our friends and colleagues provide real advice from real financial professionals.

Wealth Words

Check these boxes for definitions of investment terms, from the very basic to the extremely obscure.

Cash Cautions

Warning! Warning! We have included a number of things that you should avoid at all costs: the biggest mistakes you could make, the pitfalls you have to watch for along the way, the dangerous (but oh-so-tempting) missteps to which novice investors might succumb.

Acknowledgments

First and foremost, Anne would like to thank Angela Goettinger for her encouragement to become a financial advisor. Finally, Anne is grateful to all her clients who are too numerous to mention, as without clients, none of this would be possible.

Jennifer would like to thank all of the positive money role models she has had in her life, from family to friends—their influence has been vast. Thanks, too, to her husband, Peter, who is always ready to answer a financial question or two or three.

We would both like to thank our alma mater—Mills College. Attending a women's college gave us the inspiration, encouragement, and environment in which to grow and succeed.

Special Thanks to the Technical Reviewer

We would also like to thank our technical reviewer, Daphne Philipson, a Managing Director at a large private equity firm in New York.

Part 1
Focus on Your Finances—*Now!*

Investing? Sure, you've thought about it, but do you really need to handle it yourself? The short answer is—yes. In this opening section, we present a harsh reality or two about what lies ahead financially for most women. But we also offer a bit of sweetener—lots of information on the vast number of successful women who have already made the plunge into the financial world: women who run major brokerage houses, women whose very words can make the stock market move!

Once we've pumped you up about the possibilities, we begin to take you through some of the preliminary steps you need to get your financial house in order before you begin to invest.

Chapter 1

What, Me Worry?

In This Chapter

➤ But I know that my husband (father, children, pension) will take care of me!

➤ Taking charge of the rest of your financial life

➤ Making it on your own—a small dose of financial reality

➤ You are not alone in this—plenty of women are plunging in to the world of investing

➤ Plan your work, and work your plan

Hmmmm…a book on investing for women…now why on earth would you need that? How can investing be any different for women than it is for men? After all, a stock is a stock, a bond is a bond, and despite the fact that you will probably have to pay your dry cleaner more to clean your shirt than the man in line behind you will have to pay for his, the bank will pay you both the same amount of interest on your money!

But I'll Be Taken Care of…Won't I?

And besides, you have a husband who worries about the family financial stuff. It all looks so dull and dry, all those numbers, all those percentages. Why would you want to choose a stock on your own, only to lie awake at night worrying that the stock you chose might go down instead of up?

Not to mention that you are certain that dear old dad will remember you very generously in his will. That money should come your way close to when you are old enough to retire, so why worry about saving for retirement on your own?

No rich husband, no rich daddy? Then perhaps you are hoping that your own kids will help take care of you financially in your old age. After all you did for them—hundreds of homemade cookies and thousands of peanut butter sandwiches and uncounted late-night glasses of water—surely they will pitch in to make certain that their beloved Mom lives a life of comfort and ease.

And don't forget about Social Security! In those few moments when you weren't making sandwiches and cookies and fetching glasses of water, you were hard at work. Every one of your paychecks had a little line at the end that told you how much money had come out of your paycheck and into Social Security—that must be a pretty hefty sum after all those years on the job!

Cash Cautions

How secure is Social Security? Well...it should still be around when your turn to retire arrives, but the age bar might well have been moved from the current 62 to even older. And keep in mind that the average monthly benefit ranges from a low of $473 to a high of only $1,210. Can you live on that?!

Wealth Words

Investing—Using money to purchase securities or property, or anything that will increase in value and/or produce income.

Bursting Out of Your Financial Cocoon

So...which of these thoughts is in the back of your mind? Be honest now, don't we all expect someone else (anyone else!) to rescue us at the last minute? Well, are you ready for the cold, unvarnished financial truth? Take it from us, not only is Prince Charming not coming, but your husband might secretly be as uncomfortable with investing as you are. And chances are your dad will spend all of your inheritance on Alaskan cruises, and your children will have to pony up hefty sums to pay for their own children's education. And as for all that money you paid into Social Security, sorry sister.

It is high time (heck, it has been for awhile!) for women across the nation to assert themselves financially—to conquer the fear of finances, master the art of investing, and scale the dizzying heights of financial freedom! Come on now, here we go!

Uh, Did We Lose You Already?

Oh, you aren't getting in line, fired up and ready to march forward into the wonderful world of Wall Street. Ah, still uncertain about whether you should really try to master the big, bad investment world? Okay, ladies, sit down and pour yourself a nice glass of wine. We want to give you a few of the statistical wake-up calls that women face with their money.

Taking Charge of the Rest of Your Life

Why do we insist that you take charge of your own financial future? Because of the following grim statistics:

➤ Fifty percent of all marriages end in divorce—and divorced women experience up to a 26% decline in their standard of living as a result of the divorce.

➤ Twenty percent of all adult women living in America are single, either because they have never married or because of widowhood or divorce.

➤ Not only do women outlive men, but men are more likely to become disabled. Married women must prepare themselves for having a husband suffer an unexpected illness or long-term disability. Not the best time to have to suddenly learn all that you can about your finances and how to run them.

➤ Of the category of Americans referred to as the *elderly poor,* 75% are women.

Scary stuff, indeed. But we don't want to scare you into taking the plunge and investing on your own. Scared and panicky investors seldom make the right decisions. We think you should begin to invest on your own because you are confident that it is something that you will learn to master; because you are certain that it is important to your future; because you are ready to take charge.

Money Motivators

Handling money—particularly the large sums of money that we hope you will eventually acquire through investing—is an extraordinary feeling. A feeling of power, of competence, of courage and strength. So much is said and written about how to raise one's self-esteem. Well, we've got the real answer! How much higher can you raise your self-esteem than to track how well your own investments are doing? Talk about an ego boost!

And not only can it boost your ego and stiffen your spine, but there will also be a dramatic change in the way you relate to the folks in your life. Once you master the world of money, you will find that it affects the way you operate in your personal relationships. You might become more assertive about expressing your opinions (particularly in discussions about the stock market!). You might become impatient with people who condescend to you. And you might actually shake up a few areas in your life that could use a change!

Married...With Children

Although many single women have made peace with the idea that they are ultimately responsible for their own finances, many married women have not. Despite decades of advances in the lives of women, deep down we married women really do believe that our husbands should be in charge of the money problem. Some women may actually have married in order to spare themselves the trauma of dealing with money on any level.

Glance back up at the list of women's financial realities. Divorce, widowhood, lower incomes, longer lives. All are circumstances that, sadly, any married woman might find herself in someday. As married women ourselves who plan long and happy marriages, we wish the very same for you. We do not wish your marriage any ill, but we do want you to be as capable as possible when it comes to dealing with investment matters.

Just How Do We Do It?

What are our lives like? Anne, a longtime stockbroker, married John, a bone surgeon, when they were both in their early 20s, just out of college. As their careers evolved and Anne acquired financial training and developed a high comfort level with money (not to mention that John was a medical student with little free time), she began to handle all of the finances, taxes, and investments for her family.

Jennifer, a financial writer, married Peter when they were both in their mid-30s. They both arrived in the marriage with investment experience and accounts of their own, and both are active investors. Peter (who has been investing in the stock market since junior high school) still handles his own investment accounts. He keeps Jennifer informed of most of his major trades, but not all of the daily ups and downs. Jennifer manages her own (alas, much smaller) investment account, as well as the various and sundry retirement accounts she has picked up over the years. Peter is the primary person when it comes to paying bills and figuring taxes. Their breakfast table discussions frequently revolve around what is going on in the stock market or what was in that morning's *Wall Street Journal*.

Anyone Else?

Not all married women have lives just like ours. Here are just a few of the ways that some married couples deal with their finances:

➤ In some marriages, both the husband and wife are equally involved in all financial decision making, from budgets to investments and everything in between.

➤ Some husbands make all decisions pertaining to the household's finances, investments, and taxes.

➤ Some wives handle the household money—paying bills, making bank deposits, balancing the checkbook—but the husbands handle the investments.

➤ And in some marriages, like Anne and John's, the wives handle all the cash!

In a perfect world for married women who are interested in investing, all marriages would be just like the first one on the list above—where the husband and wife are equally involved in all financial decision making. But this world is far from perfect, and sadly, most marriages are far from perfect, too!

What is important here is, How does *your* husband feel about your getting involved with investment decisions? And how do *you* feel about the way he feels? It is a scary topic to broach. But for the sake of your own financial security, you must. Even if you are worried about how your husband will respond to your newfound interest in investing (and your desire to be involved in the decision making about investing), this matter is far too important to put off simply to avoid an argument. If it means you might rock your marital boat, unpack the life preservers, because you will have to rock it.

Ah...the Relief Team Has Finally Arrived!

Your husband's reaction may well surprise you—he might be enormously relieved! Imagine the terrible burden that he bears making all of the financial decisions, carrying all of the worry and stress. Why wouldn't he want to share that? Why wouldn't he welcome your participation? And who knows, he might even secretly hope that you will be interested enough to eventually relieve him of the whole load and take it on yourself!

Tax Time

In addition to being involved in financial and investment decisions, married women must also be fully aware of their family's tax situation. Blindly sign a joint tax return? Don't do it! Congressional hearings into IRS reform were held in the summer of 1998. Standing up to testify was a sad little parade of women who had done just that—and ended up paying dearly for it. Reforms are in the works to change how "innocent spouses" will be treated in the future; nevertheless, many divorced women's lives are in financial ruin because they once signed a tax return that they didn't understand.

No Shrinking Violets!

Leery as you are about causing a fuss with your husband, look once again at the list of women's financial realities—which is scarier? You must become involved in your family investments!

But enough about married women. Let's look at the lives of a few other women and the many circumstances we all find ourselves in.

Single, But Maybe...

You're single now, but don't plan to always be single? This is a perfect time to start to handle your own investments, build financial skills, and increase your assets. That way, when the time is right for you to marry, you will bring valuable investment knowledge to your marriage and start off on an equal footing with your husband. Make sure that you and your future spouse discuss how you plan to handle family finances and investing *before* the wedding.

Wealth Words

Asset—Any possession that has monetary value (can be bought or sold).

There are, of course, just as many single women who aren't involved in their finances as there are married women. Some single women have yet to begin their saving and investment plan, either because they hope to someday find a man who has or because money is just too frightening a topic to tackle.

And some women might always be single. "By the time I was in my mid-30s, I felt that it was likely I would never marry, so I needed to start thinking about financial stability, retirement, and the future," a self-employed single woman in Chicago told us. "I'd always been careful with my money, but hadn't really begun planning for the future. Even though there were retirement plans available from some of the companies I'd worked for, I didn't join them."

What do we have to say to single women who are reluctant to take charge of their investments? Get your head out of the clouds, girlfriend, and get going with your financial education.

On Your Own...Again

Divorced women have been thrust into the position of handling their own money. Whether you are the sole breadwinner or are still receiving alimony and/or child support, it is up to you to handle that money.

Cash Cautions

There is no correlation between education and financial savvy. Madeline, a Phi Beta Kappa graduate of a women's college and partner in a large law firm, was so little interested in money matters that she even allowed her husband to allocate her 401(k) contributions. Now in the midst of a divorce, she vows never to ignore her money again!

"All of a sudden it happens—boom, you are in charge of the money!" Sherry Crum, a recent divorcee, shared her feelings about the transformation: "During my marriage, I wasn't motivated at all about financial matters. My husband took care of it all. But now it is a completely different story, I know that it is up to me to preserve and increase the money that I'll get in my settlement. And I am really looking forward to educating myself. Even if I someday marry again, I will never lose the knowledge that I acquire now."

Not only must divorced women think about investing to preserve their own financial future, but they must keep in mind the education needs that loom on the horizon. Some divorced women might have to shoulder the kids' college costs alone, some might anticipate help from the ex-spouse, but all must think about and plan for it.

Alone...and Grieving

Every estate attorney can tell you a tale about the grieving widow who admits that not only did her late husband make all the financial decisions but that she doesn't even know where he kept the information about their investments.

Is this a position that you want to find yourself in someday? We don't think so. Is this a position that you have already found yourself in? Then this is the book for you!

In our chapter on investment clubs, you'll meet a recent widow who joined a women's investment club not to build up the substantial investment portfolio that she was suddenly charged with managing, but for a simpler reason. She was fed up with the way that her financial advisors treated her.

"They talk to me as if I am a child, and a poorly educated child at that!" Many elderly women meet with this same sort of attitude in the financial world, a sort of pat-her-on-the-shoulder-and-speak-softly-to-the-old-dear kind of approach.

Widows have unique financial concerns, first and foremost to get a handle on just what their financial situation is. Many financial experts agree that the very first year of widowhood is the worst time to make investment decisions. Grieve first and then educate yourself on just what investments your husband has left you. And then when your mind is a little clearer, start to tackle the matters at hand and take a more active role in the financial decisions.

Graduating to the Real World

And what about young women just starting out in life—when should they start thinking about their investments? Now! Women in their early twenties have so much ahead of them to plan for, things like buying a car, taking an exotic vacation, or even buying a house of their own. And sometimes these same young women have so much behind them that they have to work on clearing up! Student loans that need to be repaid, maxed out credit cards from a lean senior year, or post-college moving costs.

Larissa Phinney is 3 years out of college and well into her second real job. Working for a high-tech company in the Silicon Valley, she is sometimes shocked by the way her peers behave. "Not enough of the other young people in my office, both women and men, are taking advantage of what is out there. Some don't participate in the 401(k) or the company's stock option plan. They don't seem to realize that, by starting now rather than in 10 or 15 years, they will be that much farther ahead in the future."

Having been raised by a single mom who handled all of the money matters, Larissa tells us that she "feels pretty confident about handling my money. It's important to me to be a woman who has her own money." And by starting to plan so early, Larissa should easily achieve that goal! Young women need to educate themselves about investing and handling money and start to take steps to clear up debt and avoid acquiring more of it!

Cash Cautions

Thinking that your life would be great if only you were single again? Guess again—after divorce, women experience up to a 26% decline in their standard of living.

9

Wise Women Know

According to Tracy Gary, the founder of the San Francisco–based educational organization Resourceful Women, "Learning about money—managing it, talking about it with our loved ones, using it to bring about social change—is as important today as it was for our mothers to learn to drive and our grandmothers to secure the right to vote."

Get With the Program!

You can see that your work is really cut out for you. Regardless of your own personal and financial circumstances, there is a universal need to make a financial plan. You need to plan your work and then work your plan.

This approach is not nearly as dull and dreary as it sounds. In the following chapters, we walk you through all the steps you need to take to clearly assess your financial picture—everything from what your net worth is to whether you are paying too much for your checking account. Once this money picture becomes clear, we move on to the real matter at hand—learning to invest, and learning to carefully consider all your financial moves in the context of your ultimate financial goals. Oscar Wilde once observed: "There is only one class of people that thinks more about money than the rich, and that is the poor. In fact, the poor can think of nothing else." Once you master the art of investing and confidently handling your money, you can spend your time thinking about other things!

Anne likes to tell her clients that investing and financial planning is an ongoing process, not a destination. "Life happens along the way. Things happen that will cause you to change your plan. The government may make tax law changes, your children may make changes to their education plans, your health may change. And your financial goals will need to change along with them."

Ready to Make the Plunge?

Are you still a little uncertain about going it alone? Hang in there, we have included one whole chapter to pump you up—page after page of facts and figures about women's money, famous women in the financial world, and well-known wealthy women who have successfully managed large sums of money. So read on and see just how much money women already have now, and how much we are likely to handle in the coming years!

The Least You Need to Know

➤ Chances are that you will be on your own financially at some point in your life—so you'd better be prepared for it!

➤ Social Security will probably still be around when you need it, but the monthly benefits are depressingly low.

➤ Married women should never cede total control of the family investments to their husbands.

➤ Husbands might be relieved that their wives are finally taking an interest in money matters.

➤ Many single women are also uninvolved in money matters, to disastrous effect.

➤ A financial plan is a fluid thing that must change over the years according to your financial needs.

Chapter 2

Gosh, Will They Let Me In? Isn't Investing a Boy's Club?

In This Chapter

➤ Women's wealth is on the move

➤ Outreach programs from major brokerage houses

➤ Wall Street women who make a difference today

➤ Well-known women of wealth

➤ Women of really independent means

So, still worried about making investing decisions on your own? Or intimidated by the attitudes that you might bump into the first time you saunter through the big, etched-glass doors of a brokerage firm? Managing money seems so...manly. And it seems like the world of money is mostly filled with men, too. Not too many faces out there with lipstick on, mostly just faces with a five o'clock shadow. Guys who look like Michael Douglas in the movie *Wall Street,* striding around with starched shirts and suspenders. Is that the ways things are? Let's look closer, and see what the real truth is today. We think you will take great comfort in knowing not only just how much money the women of America really control now, but also just how many of the faces on Wall Street really do wear blush. We'll also give you a look at some of the women who managed their own money successfully earlier in the century—back when it really was a boy's club!

Women's Wealth Is on the Move—Up!

Women's wealth is on the move up. In the great strides that we have all made personally and professionally, our incomes and net worths have increased accordingly.

Cash Cautions

With so many good programs to choose from, why settle for anything that makes you feel crummy? Stay away from any broker or program you feel is condescending. Everyone wants your business, so look around and choose the best for you!

"Money is the measuring rod of power," the billionaire Howard Hughes once said, and as women's power in the workforce has grown, so too have our incomes. More women are working, and they are staying on the job longer. Sure, we all know that women still make less than men make (76.4% of what the average man earns, but who's counting?), but check back in another 10 years!

Because women tend to outlive men, the grim fact is that women inherit money more often than men. According to the research of OppenheimerFunds, 9 out of 10 women will be solely responsible for managing their own finances at some point in their lives. Sooner or later, we do get a chance to run the financial show, so you'd better be prepared for it!

Who Decides Now?

A recent U.S. Department of Labor survey reveals that in 32% of American households with investments, women make the investment decisions on their own. In 21% of households, women share in the financial decision making with their husbands.

Later in the book, you'll learn more about the popularity of investment clubs—what they are, why they are, and how to form one. What they definitely are is popular with women! According to the National Association of Investors Corporation, (the organization that helps coordinate the clubs) 65.3% of its 700,000 members are women.

Impressive numbers, indeed, and they are only going to increase in the coming years. Women's increasing economic power has caught the attention of business. From car manufacturers to home improvement stores, everyone is after the money we control. And Wall Street investment firms are leading the pack. Let's see what kinds of programs have been developed to help ease women into the investment world.

They Like Us, They Really Do!

Let's take a look at june-one company OppenheimerFunds. The first mutual fund company to develop an outreach program for women investors was OppenheimerFunds. The movement to start a special program to educate women was lead by CEO Bridget Macaskill, who recognized a real need for an educational campaign. Cathleen Meere, the manager of OppenheimerFunds' Women & Investing program told us: "We launched this program back in 1992 because we saw a need.

We'd interviewed 1,000 men and 1,000 women about their investment knowledge and habits, and there was a huge gap. Women were not involved to the degree that they should be. We checked again in 1997 and found that improvement had occurred, but that the improvement was only incremental. There is still a great need for this program." Check out the OppenheimerFunds Web site at www.oppenhiemerfunds.com, and click on the section for women. It includes several interesting profiles of women in different life stages (with different investment needs) and also includes financial worksheets you can use.

Wise Women Know

"Our Women & Investing program is by no means a marketing conceit," says the woman who runs OppenheimerFunds, Cathleen Meere. "As a matter of fact, we like to tell people that the goal of our program is to put ourselves [the program] out of business! We hope that there comes a day when we no longer need to have an outreach program for women investors!"

Beyond the efforts of the large companies, many savvy individual stockbrokers and financial consultants are organizing seminars, luncheons, and special newsletters to try to target women as clients. More clients, more business, more commissions! A San Mateo–based stockbroker with Smith Barney, Lori Whitney, had great success mounting a mother-daughter investment luncheon with her clients. "I've been a stockbroker for 14 years, and this has by far been my most successful outreach program," she told us. "A pleasant surprise was the energy in the room that day, as a group the women in the room really connected with one another. They felt comfortable asking questions and showed much greater confidence and self-esteem than they might have in other, mixed-sex, circumstances." Sun America and many others have special women's programs, too.

Wealth Words

Commission—The fee charged by a broker or brokerage house to process a customer's stock purchase or sale.

The Women of Wall Street

Yes, women are being heavily targeted as customers by both individual brokers and the large investment houses. But is there a corresponding increase in the numbers of women who work on Wall Street? You bet there is! And these women are powerhouses. Let's meet some of the most powerful and influential women in the world of money:

Abby Joseph Cohen

As chief strategist (and now a partner) for Goldman Sachs, what Abby Cohen says on any given day can greatly influence the direction of the entire stock market. She has been famously bullish on the stock market, even calming the waters and bringing the market back up during a short plunge during the summer of 1998 just by publicly restating her bullish stance.

Muriel Siebert

At age 63, Siebert is busier than ever—busy expanding her discount brokerage house Muriel Siebert & Company. Since 1967 when she became the first woman ever to buy a seat on the New York Stock Exchange. Siebert has been a financial trailblazer.

Mary Farrell

Managing director at PaineWebber, Farrell is a well-known commentator on the ways of Wall Street and is frequently a panelist on the PBS financial show, *Wall Street Week with Louis Rukeyser*.

Bridget Macaskill

President and CEO of OppenheimerFunds, Bridget Macaskill got her start in England marketing orange juice before coming to America and working (quite reluctantly, at first) on Wall Street.

Gail M. Dudack

Managing director and chief investment strategist, UBS Securities, LLC, Gail Dudack is also a regular on Louis Rukeyser's PBS show. She is well-known for her insightful analysis of the financial world.

Elizabeth Bramwell

Elizabeth Bramwell manages some $400 million in assets with her own invest-ment management company, Bramwell Capital Management. She also runs the Bramwell Growth Fund.

Elaine Garzarelli

The president and CEO of Garzarelli Management, Elaine announced on CNN's *Money Line News Hour with Lou Dobbs* on October 13, 1987, that, despite what everybody else believed, the market was due for a terrible crash. A scant 2 weeks later, she was proved right.

In addition, a number of women hold powerful positions on the Securities and Exchange Commission, known in the business as the SEC. The SEC is an independent government agency that is charged with regulating the financial industry. Elaine Cacheris is the regional director of the Pacific region for the SEC, Karen Buck Burgess is the associate general counsel, and Lori Richards is the director of the Office of Compliance.

As you will learn in later chapters, pronouncements from the Federal Reserve Board (referred to as the Fed) can greatly influence what happens on the stock market. A men's club? Not any longer—while Alan Greenspan is well-known (and much feared) as the chairman of the Federal Reserve Board, the vice chair is a woman named Alice M. Rivlin.

Wealth Words

Bull market, bear market—A bull market is a long period of time when stock prices are on the rise. A bear market is a long period of time when stock prices are on the decline. Either kind of market can last for months or even years.

And even the New York Stock Exchange (NYSE) has a few powerful women at the top. For example:

Sheila Blair

As senior vice president of government affairs, Blair is the chief lobbyist for the NYSE in Washington, D.C.

Anne E. Allen

As vice president, floor operations, Allen is in charge of the trading floor's order-processing systems; she has other responsibilities as well.

Regina C. Mysliwiec

As vice president of enforcement and sales practices, Mysliwiec heads the investigation and prosecution of violations of the securities laws and exchange rules.

The Face in Front of the Camera

So yes, more than just a few token women wield genuine power and influence on Wall Street. The media is constantly seeking out these women for their opinions on financial matters. And in many cases, the reporters who are asking the questions are women, too! Many well-known financial reporters like Deborah Marchini on CNN's *Business Day* and Maria Bartiromo on CNBC and anchors like Sue Herera on CNBC's *The Money Wheel* and *Market Wrap* and Cassie Seifert on PBS's *Nightly Business Report* are familiar sights to well-informed investors.

Wise Women Know

Two of the best-known financial programs on TV are *Wall Street Week with Louis Rukeyser* and *The Money Line News Hour with Lou Dobbs*. But what happens when either of these guys wants to take a vacation? They call in a woman to take over! A frequent stand-in for Louis Rukeyser is PaineWebber's Mary Farrell. And when Lou Dobbs is away, he turns the show over to Jan Hopkins.

Wealth Words

Seat—A seat on an organized securities exchange like the New York Stock Exchange or the American Stock Exchange. A seat on the exchange entitles the owner to trade stocks directly instead of through a broker.

The Women With the Pen

Women have long been a force in traditional financial journalism. Recognize the name Sylvia Porter? Financial columnist Sylvia Porter had to use the byline S.K. Porter when she began covering the world of money back in 1935. In the 70-plus years that her name has been associated with solid financial information, she has published many influential money books.

Also dating back to the '30s was an influential publication called *Magazine of Wall Street*. For many years the publisher was listed on the masthead as C.G. Wycoff, and one of the contributors was Charles Benedict. In fact, both were actually Cecilia Wycoff, who owned and operated the magazine for many years during its heyday.

Well-known Women of Wealth

Now that we've reassured you that women are well-entrenched behind the scenes (or in some cases actually creating the scene themselves) in the financial world, what about women who possess and control their own wealth? Who are the rich, smart women who are making all the right decisions on their own? Let's read a few inspirational stories:

Dorothy Grossbaum

You might not recognize the name, it was her influence that caused her son, Benjamin Graham, to become well-known. As a young widow, Dorothy ran a boardinghouse to support her family, and speculated in the stock market; her young son began to track the family investments as well. Thanks to mom, he went on to build a career based on what he called "value investing," the strategy his disciple Warren Buffett uses.

Caroline Rose Hunt

The youngest member of the Hunt family of Texas (oil baron H.L. Hunt), Caroline watched from the sidelines as her brother Bunker Hunt tried to corner the world silver market in 1980. After he lost most of his money, she not only refused to bail him out with her money, but wisely separated her investments from her family. She leaves her money in real estate, hotels, real estate investment trusts (REITs), and savings and loans.

Irene Wells Pennington

A member of *Forbes* magazine's list of the 400 richest folks, the *Forbes* 400, at age 97 Irene Wells Pennington controls a $600 million fortune in stocks, bonds, and other tax-planning ventures.

Women of *Really* Independent Means

The statistics are everywhere—women are starting their own businesses at an astonishing rate. Experts estimate that by the year 2000, women will control 40% to 50% of all companies in America. (They controlled 36% of all businesses in the country in 1998.) What a remarkable statistic! Eight million women from California to Maine now own and operate their own businesses. These women account for a stunning 80% of all new jobs that have been created recently.

What does this information mean to you? It means that once again, women's economic power and status in the business world is increasing. And as an investor, it also means that there will be more and more great opportunities to invest in women-owned companies! *Working Woman* magazine recently compiled a list of 37 publicly traded companies in which women have a majority equity stake. Among those who made the list—the discount broker, Muriel Siebert, and the head of the Washington Post Company, Katherine Graham.

Now Let's Start on You!

Now that we have you excited about just how much money women already control and how many businesses are interested in helping us to invest it wisely, you're ready to examine your own situation. Starting with the next chapter, we get down to nickels and dimes, so go get your purse. Soon you will know exactly where you stand and, better yet, exactly how to get to where you want to be financially.

The Least You Need to Know

➤ The world of investing is no longer a men's club, but is actively seeking to encourage women's participation.

➤ Women control more and more of the money in the country thanks to our increasing salaries and our tendency to live longer than men.

➤ Wall Street is the address for more than a handful of powerful and important women in the financial world.

➤ Women are also very involved in regulating the financial world.

➤ Women make financial news and report on it.

➤ Great role models exist of women who control large private fortunes and make their own investment decisions.

➤ By the year 2000, women will control 40% to 50% of the businesses in the country.

Chapter 3

The Money Under Your Mattress

In This Chapter

➤ Unscrambling the nest egg

➤ How do you rate?

➤ Money in, money out

➤ Passbook paralysis

➤ More money, maybe

➤ Lumping it all together

The Cash Stash

Admit it, does this sound like you? Many women sleep easier knowing they have some of their "safe" or emergency money under their mattress. All right, so maybe it isn't actually under your mattress, but in some secret place nearby (Jennifer will blush and confess to keeping a wad of cash in a wooden cigar box). This stash would better be described as "mad" money because of the lunacy of thinking cash is safe in your possession. Money is in fact merely a tool we use to barter for our time and for our worldly possessions.

Hiding it anywhere in our home may keep that money convenient for emergencies that arise while we are at home, but what about the emergencies in all the places we really spend our day: at work, on errands, in stores, and in other places of business? Have you ever stopped to wonder why the short and fast-moving lines at the grocery stores are the cash-only and less-than-20-items checkout lines? Most people pay with credit cards or checks, not cash. The old saying "carry only as much cash as you can afford to lose" is certainly valid in today's world.

Even your government, responsible for printing that currency you have under the mattress, is going to make you take your lumps because the largest face value it now creates is the $100 Benjamin Franklin! Think about it: Inflation is still running in the 2% area, and you have one hundred $1 bills under your mattress—two of those greenbacks become worthless to you each year. For all of these reasons, it pays to pull all your spare cash together and at least start earning interest. Let's get started doing just that.

Unscrambling the Nest Egg

The easy part of improving your financial life is pulling it all together. Over your next Saturday morning cup of coffee, sit near the desk where you pay the bills and start looking for bank statements, passbook savings account statements, and any investment securities statements you might already have. Put all the statements you find into one large pile. Now go through your stack, one page at a time:

Wealth Words

Interest—Payment for the use of borrowed money. When you put money in a bank, you are literally loaning it to the bank. The bank, in turn, uses your money to make investments from which it hopes to make a profit.

➤ Look for the line on the statement called "ending balance" and circle that number with a brightly colored pen.

➤ Look for any indication of the rate of interest the institution might have paid and for the service fees it might have charged to you. Circle those numbers, too.

➤ Make a clear list of what you find, with account numbers, balances, and fees tallied.

Returns to Lender

This list will help you compare the returns on your money from the various places you squirrel it away. Yes, you should count the money under the mattress, in the coffee can, or in the freezer as well. If you find you hold money in more than two places, ask yourself why. There is not one good reason, but many understandable reasons to not have your eggs in one basket.

Now that you know where your money is and how much you are earning on it, do you really need all of these accounts? No. Select the service that gives you the best rate of interest, with the most reasonable service fees, and put all these monies in the place you select. It is much easier to keep tabs on your spare money by reading one statement each month.

Is That All There Is?

Still have the sneaking suspicion that there must be more money somewhere? After that long cup of coffee, if you feel there *must* be more than you were able to identify, pull out last year's tax return. Check the entries of interest and dividends sent to you on 1099 forms. Any financial institution that pays you interest or dividends must send you a 1099 form in January; this notice summarizes the money the institution paid you for the use of your money. Therefore, as you are pulling together all those totals, this is one net the income you earned from your money cannot slip through. Incidentally, even if your mailbox was destroyed for the month of January each year, if you failed to report this income on your taxes, not to worry; the IRS will send you a letter letting you in on your mistake immediately. It gets a copy of all your 1099s from the same people who are required to send them to you.

Here is a second important project to help you get a handle on your money. The ugly truth about how much interest you pay must be revealed! So, dig into that drawer and pull out all your credit card statements.

➤ While you are collecting information on the interest you earn, review all your credit card statements to learn about any interest you have *paid*. What you owe is every bit as important as what you earn.

➤ Also, take the time to review your mortgage statement.

➤ And while you are at it, make a pile for any retirement account statements as well.

Once again, make yourself a new list with total balances, and the interest or increases from year to year, to track the numbers getting larger. If you find the interest you paid is larger than you imagined, do not be discouraged. We work on this problem in Chapter 6, "Evaluating Your Net Worth."

So, How Do You Rate?

The interest rate you earn is not always what it appears to be. That is why it is most important to look at the actual dollars earned, rather than to simply compare the interest rate numbers. Confusion usually arises over how frequently interest is *applied* to your account. As interest accrues, it creates a *compound effect*; that is, your interest earns interest. Compounding is a *very* powerful financial tool and should not be ignored.

Compound It!

Still need help understanding the power of compounding? Think of two piles of 100 pennies each. One bank offers 7% interest, compounded monthly. In other words, at the end of each month, for each 100 pennies, the bank adds 7, so that pile has 107 pennies at the end of January. The next bank offers 7% interest, but it compounds (adds interest) only once a year (annually). They add pennies to your pile only once each year. Obviously, the account that gets interest each month ends up with more pennies because the interest ends up earning interest. You do not have to understand more than this: what the interest rate is and how often interest is applied.

Attention Shoppers!

Shopping for the best interest rate may seem tedious, but the rule of thumb is that banks that exist for shareholders (that is, the banks that have stock that trades on an exchange) and have many branch offices, usually pay less interest than do credit unions, and savings and loans that tend to exist for members. This concept makes sense: the more interest a bank pays to you, the less of a profit it makes on your money. Banks that have common stock want to make a profit for their shareholders. In contrast, savings and loan institutions and credit unions want to keep their members happy and are willing to make modest profits.

Money In, Money Out

You've probably seen the bumper sticker "I can't be out of money, I still have checks!" and chances are you smiled knowingly. This statement, while very amusing, is really quite scary. Checks are only as strong as the money in the account to pay them. Many people find the process of balancing their checkbook each month too much of a hassle. So they periodically check the amount of money in their accounts and then write a check if they guess the balance can cover the check. The surprise comes when someone to whom you wrote a check holds it for many months and then cashes it. Banks make lots of profits off people who bounce checks. If you do not remember how to balance your checkbook, a simple review course follows. With your most recent bank statement in front of you, do this:

➤ Open to the part of your checkbook where checks are recorded.

➤ Compare the numbers on the checks you have written to the check numbers that have cleared on your statement.

➤ Make a list of any checks that have not cleared and tally the total value of the list. These are your *outstanding* checks.

➤ Deduct this amount from the closing balance of your bank statement; this number should match the number you show as available on your checkbook.

If the numbers don't match, you need to check your addition and subtraction. The lazy-lady method you can substitute is to put the lower number in your checkbook and not question the difference. If you always work with the lower number, at least your checks won't bounce.

Interesting Enough?

More important than making an account balance is being certain you earn interest on your checking account. Most people do not bother to do this, and many keep a lot of extra money in their checking account to avoid the embarrassment of bouncing a check. It is not difficult to earn as much as 5% on your checking account. If you are making less than this amount, ask yourself why. Many people believe they have *free* checking, that is, no fees are charged on their account. These same people often are not earning one penny of interest on their checking and have a minimum balance requirement of $1,000.

In this scenario, your bank is earning about $50 a year on your minimum balance requirement in exchange for not charging you for checks. This arrangement hardly sounds like a free account! You can usually earn that same amount on your checking account and still not pay any fees. It pays to comparison shop for these accounts. Many places run their checking accounts as fly traps—that is, they pay a good interest, without fees, to entice you to do other business with them. For example, most brokerage accounts work this way.

Cash Cautions

Free checking! Sounds great, but is it *really* free? Does the account pay the going interest rate? Do you have to maintain a hefty minimum balance? The bank might be making more off your money than you would pay in check charges elsewhere. Check it out.

Passbook Paralysis

Savings accounts usually entice you to leave your money in them longer than you do with checking accounts by offering a higher rate of interest. Savings accounts also do not give you as many checks or may impose a minimum size for the check. For most savings accounts, you have to take a "passbook" (which strangely resembles a passport) to the bank so the teller can manually record each entry into or out of the account. Some banks will accept your telephoned instructions to move money from your checking account that is paying no or low interest into your savings account that is paying low to reasonable interest. This cat-and-mouse game is certainly worth the effort, but there are places where it does not have to be this hard. You'll learn more in this chapter about a type of account called a *central asset account* that enables you to put everything in one bank and to move money between accounts with greater ease.

The most redeeming aspect of a savings account is that it causes people to *save*. Even at low interest, saving money is very important. Would it disturb you to know that in 1996, net household savings as a percent of disposable income was only 4.5% in the United States? This figure is very low compared to other developed countries like Canada (8.1%), the United Kingdom (9.6%), Germany (11.3%), France (14%), and Japan (16.3%). Therefore, the importance of passbook savings accounts is to put something in them. Save! Pay yourself first. Remember Ben Franklin's wisdom—a penny earned is a penny saved. Or was that a penny saved is a penny earned? Or does it matter what you do with your pennies? The idea is that to make your money work for you.

Save, Save, Save

It is never too early or too late to start saving. Any money you can put aside is better than not saving at all. A passbook savings account is a rudimentary method, but it's tried and true. So collect all that money under the mattress, in the coffee can, or in the freezer; take out your passbook; and fill out your deposit slip.

More Money, Maybe

Money market funds are one step beyond the savings account for committed savers. Money markets offer the highest rate of interest to the saver, without making any time requirement. They usually limit your access by requiring deposits to be more than $1,000 and withdrawals to be more than $500. The name *money market* is very descriptive. There is, indeed, a market place where businesses, banks, government entities, and other people shop for cash to use for their specific needs. You can lend your money to these people by using a money market fund.

Cash Cautions

Yes, you should have a savings account. But please do not put *all* of your money in it! A passbook savings account is not an investment plan. The rate at which your money will grow is far below what you might earn from other types of investments.

A *money market fund* is simply a pool of money operated by an investment company that raises money from shareholders (you own one share for each dollar you put in the fund). The fund invests in commercial paper, banker acceptances, repurchase agreements, government securities, certificates of deposit, and other highly liquid and safe securities and pays the interest averaged from this collection of investments. Sounds complicated, but the bottom line is, they make more money for your money!

Money market funds were launched in the mid-1970s and were especially popular in the early 1980s when interest rates and inflation soared. Interest is credited monthly, and you don't pay a sales charge to invest in such a fund. These funds are a marvelous way to get the highest, safest rate of return on your savings dollars. Banks, credit unions, savings and loans, and investment firms all offer money market funds. The minimum investment is usually $5,000, with future deposits required to exceed $1,000 and future withdrawals to exceed $500. Many funds allow you to write up to three free checks a month, which is a convenient method of withdrawal

Sounds great, but is there a downside? There is only one possible negative aspect of money market funds—they are not government insured. Bank and savings and loan deposits are guaranteed by the federal government (up to $100,000 per depositor) but funds deposited in money market accounts are not.

However, based on what the manager of the fund does with your dollars, that is, invest in very safe, highly liquid (something that can easily be sold) investments, no one has yet lost a penny in a money market fund.

Lumping It All Together

Getting back to the results of that Saturday-morning cup of coffee, where you reviewed all your statements. Did you ask yourself if there was an easier way to keep track of your various pockets of money? Well, the financial-services community is one step ahead of you. The central asset account is here to serve you.

Wealth Words

Money market fund—A type of mutual fund that can serve as a savings and checking account with a higher-than–normal interest rate. It usually has a high minimum balance and a limit to the number of checks you can write each month.

A Little Over Here, a Little Over There

Many women like to have several "pockets" of money, each serving as an emotional blanket. Perhaps you have an emergency fund, a savings account from every decade of your life, at a bank close to where you worked at the time. Perhaps you own one or two mutual funds, representing gifts made to you by well-meaning relatives to mark important occasions in your life. You might even have tucked away a few stock certificates that you inherited from dear old Auntie May. Finally, you might have a checking or savings account that you opened when the bank was giving away frequent-flyer miles. Now is the time to reclaim your free time and ease your mental stress. You need to select a central asset account and consolidate your various pockets of money into one place.

Central asset accounts assemble all information, from checking to savings, mutual funds to stocks, and credit cards to debit cards, onto one statement. Imagine the ease of having your entire monthly financial activity summarized on one statement. The numbers do not necessarily change; they simply appear in one place, delivered in one envelope, each month. Furthermore, these accounts offer automatic electronic bill-payment services, and you can often arrange for direct deposit of your paycheck into such an account. No more standing in line at the bank or waiting at the ATM. What a way to live! Does this sound too good to be true? Must there be a negative catch?

In fact, there is no negative catch, and many financial-service providers offer their version of such an account. Banks, brokers, investment firms, and even savings and loans offer central asset accounts. Furthermore, as you become more confident in the use of computers, most of these accounts offer online access so you can verify any account activity on a daily basis if you desire.

De-stress Tax Time

The benefit of such an account is never more obvious than at tax time. You receive a consolidated 1099 tax-reporting information statement. Instead of receiving several thin and odd-sized slips of paper in the mail in January, you get one statement, on a full-size piece of regular paper, on which all the numbers are organized for you. Many consolidated 1099 statements include detailed instructions about where to apply each subtotal number to your 1040 tax-filing form. It is a wonderful way to live.

And This Will Cost How Much?

What does such a life-changing service cost? The highest you should pay is $150 per year. If this sounds like a lot of money, stop to consider that many checking accounts cost $5 per month, or $60 per year. What services do you receive in return? Credit cards usually carry an annual fee of $10 to $25, and what services do you receive for that? Finally, your time is the greatest savings of all. If you could have this snapshot of your entire financial life arrive in the mail, in one envelope, once per month, imagine the time you would save!

One potential obstacle, though, with these accounts is that you usually need a minimum amount ($10,000 to $20,000) to even qualify to have one. This amount can sound daunting, but look back on the tally from your Saturday-morning cup of coffee. You might be surprised how those statements, and the money under the mattress, added up.

A Helpful Voice on the Phone

Some central asset account statements also come equipped with a real live person's name—someone you can call with any questions about activity on the statement. That person, defined as your account representative, financial consultant, or personal advisor, is prepared to give you advice on the full range of financial services offered by the place where you establish your central asset account.

The Least You Need to Know

➤ It doesn't pay to have cash stashed around the house, no matter how safe it makes you feel.

➤ Get a handle on how many accounts you have, how much money is in each, and what rate of interest you are earning.

➤ Get a handle on how much interest you are paying out—in mortgages and credit cards.

➤ Compounding interest is a powerful way for your money to make more money.

➤ Make sure you are getting the best deal for your checking account.

➤ Central asset accounts can make life much easier because all your financial information comes in on one statement.

Chapter 4

Junk Mail and Other Stuff You Will Receive

In This Chapter

➤ Do you really have to read all of this stuff?

➤ Some of this stuff really is junk mail

➤ Didn't records go out of style?

➤ All the glossy reports

➤ What the IRS wants you to keep

➤ Letting go...of your mail

Every day it is the same story—your mailbox is stuffed with catalogs, bills, charity fund-raising letters, offers for platinum credit cards, and a fistful of other official-looking mail. Is there a way to get on top of this paper blizzard, to efficiently manage all of this so that, once you start investing, you don't sink under the increased weight of even more mail? Yes, and we will quickly show you how.

What, You Mean I Have to Read This Stuff?

With all that mail in your box each day, how do you know what deserves your time and what to send straight to landfill?

➤ Open your mail the *same* day you receive it.

➤ Give yourself ample time (5 minutes should do) to make the first pass through the daily mail.

➤ Open anything that you immediately recognize. Keep the important contents and quickly toss the envelope and any filler advertisements.

But Isn't That Obvious?

You'd be surprised how many people keep decades-old envelopes, clinging to the notion that the postmark date is relevant and important. Business mail is always be clearly dated on the statement or bill. The time frame covered and the date the statement is printed are always present. They are usually not displayed prominently, but you can always find them.

Some of That Stuff Really Is Junk Mail

As for the mail you do not immediately recognize, open those items last, or learn to determine the contents without breaking the seal on the envelope. You know the kind of mail we mean. That endless stream of credit-line offers, home-refinance offers, change of telephone long-distance service offers, let me be your financial advisor offers, and join our cassette, tape, or book of the month club offers.

These are the mailbox items that clutter our houses and our minds. Sadly, the truth is that the volumes of junk mail actually allow the postal service to keep postage stamp prices at the veritable bargain of 32 cents. Kinda like volume discounts. They don't call it bulk mail for nothing.

Cash Cautions

All of that annoying bulk junk mail actually helps the post office keep down the price of regular postage. But that doesn't mean you need to read everything that any Tom, Harry, and David send to you.

After you have opened the relevant mail, kept the statements and payment envelopes, and thrown away all the internal advertisements and envelope stuffers, it is time to read your mail.

Scan every statement and bill to see that every entry, particularly expenditures, is correct. This first scan will give you the peace of mind to put the mail aside for a better read later. Set aside a regular time in each week to review all your bills and statements, arrange for payment, and file the documents you want to save in the file cabinet. File cabinet, you say? *Yes*, it is absolutely essential that you have a file cabinet. No organized, financially sophisticated woman should live without one.

From the Mixed-up Files of Mrs. Basil E. Frankwiler

Establish a file for the following categories:

➤ Monthly bills (give every type of bill its own file—one file for phone bills, for example)

➤ Tax records

➤ Personal records (birth, marriage, health, and wills!)

➤ Employment benefits

Keep records for the current year in this file cabinet, as well as key documents you might need on a moment's notice. Copies of birth certificates, your passport, and your Social Security card are examples of the kind of things which you might need occasional, but instant, access to. Furthermore, this file cabinet will come in handy as a flower vase holder. Yes, it is much sweeter to pay the bills with the fragrance of stargazer lily in the air.

But I Thought Records Went Out of Style

You will also need a closet or cabinet in the attic or garage for long-term permanent storage of items that are more than a year old, for example, tax records and financial asset records.

This storage area should not include newspapers, magazines, old books, and the like that fill the garages and attics of America.

How long must you hang on to this stuff? Here is your most important lesson—you must keep your tax records for 7 years.

In addition to saving the actual tax returns, you also need to preserve for 7 years any piece of paper that supports the numbers on your tax return. Sorry, but those envelopes stuffed with receipts need to stay put. You don't want to be caught without them, should the IRS come to call. Actually, the IRS's reach is limited to 7 years only if you accidentally made a mistake on your filing. If you intentionally made the mistake, the IRS can look back for a lifetime! But we'll tell you more about that later.

Cash Cautions

Hang onto any and all tax-related records for 7 years.

Don't get caught without your receipts, or both you and the IRS will be mighty unhappy.

Nontaxing Topics

How long should you keep the paperwork or billing notices for your private, non-tax-related records? This is where most people err on the side of keeping things too long.

Let's face it, if the utility bill was in error, you should call the company *immediately* to clear up the error. So, it makes sense that any utility bill that is correct and more than a few months old is no longer relevant. *Throw it away!* Of course, you could keep a specimen or two just for idle curiosity about the cost of such services in the past.

Show Me the Money

What about investment and savings statements? These must be reviewed each month for accuracy. And it is *imperative* that you review your financial holdings statements within a few days of receiving them. If you find any errors, or even an entry you do not fully understand, contact your service immediately. The one time that you skip this review process might be the one and only month a deposit is misplaced, or a trade, which you did not place, is accidentally posted to your account. Don't take that chance!

What kind of errors can occur in financial accounts? The most common and benign error is that a trade that belongs to someone else is accidentally placed in your account. You will be alarmed to see that the trade was paid from your reserve funds, and you will be short in your reserves. This problem is easily solved when the company moves the trade to the correct account and credits you the funds that were removed. This reversal is done "as of" the date of the error, so any interest or dividends you (and the genuine owner) should have received automatically move back into the correct accounts.

But I'm Sure I Bought Some More Stock!

The worst kind of error is when an order you placed *fails* to occur, and you do not notice. These kinds of errors must be corrected the day they are finally discovered. Usually, the sooner the better for you and your service provider. Although you might believe that placing the order *once* should be enough, it is important that you verify that the order was completed.

Wise Women Know

Immediately report any errors or discrepancies you spot on your financial account statements. If left unchallenged for a certain period of time, some errors are irreversible.

How do you address an error in your account? Call your financial service *immediately* to bring it to their attention. If you are not satisfied with the response you initially receive, ask to speak to the office manager. Write down the facts, in chronological order as best as you can recall, and ask that the error be corrected. Ask for confirmation in writing that your request is completed. Your credibility increases the closer you are to the day the error occurred. If you call several months to a year after the error occurred, the bank or stockbroker might refuse to reimburse you. This potential nightmare is why you must read your statements and trade confirmations within days of receiving them.

Trade Talk

What is a *trade confirmation*? We will soon dive headlong in to the investing scene, but it is important to mention this term now. A trade confirmation is the "bill of sale" you receive immediately after you make an investment.

Even when you already have the funds to pay for your purchase in your account, a confirmation of the trade is mailed the day you make the order. You must keep these confirmation slips to verify your cost basis for tax purposes when you sell the investment. In other words, when you declare your income, you need to prove the price at which you bought the stock as well as the price at which you sold it.

Wealth Words

Annual report—A firm's annual statement of operating and financial results.

Glossy Reports

Once you own investments, you will start to receive reports about them. The big, magazine-style books you receive *once* per year are called *annual reports*. They are basic descriptions of the business progress of the company or mutual fund you own. The law requires all publicly owned corporations to report to their shareholders annually, and companies spend thousands of dollars each year to create annual reports—to project an image of success.

Wise Women Know

The most-read annual report in the nation is General Electric's, and CEO Jack Welch writes it. In second place is the annual report that Warren Buffett writes for his company, Berkshire Hathaway. Why? Because financial folks think that these two men *really* know what they are talking about!

Quarterlies

Four times per year, a company presents a summary of its performance numbers and statistics in a *quarterly report*. These reports are usually on thin white paper; they typically have few words but lots of columns of numbers. These numbers are presented by the company or mutual fund and audited by a public accounting firm for accuracy.

It is easy to learn to read financial reports (see our appendix on this topic for additional information). The rule of thumb is that you like to see the numbers at the bottom line getting larger in value each year. It means that a company is growing its earnings, cutting its expenses, or both. Bigger earnings usually translate into a higher stock price eventually, which is why you decided to invest your money in this company or fund in the first place. Annual and quarterly reports are the way a company keeps you informed about its progress.

Proxy Syndrome

What is a *proxy*, and why should you care? In the bigger picture, as the national election draws near, do you feel your vote counts? A proxy is your vote regarding important business decisions that the company or mutual fund is making on your behalf. Although a proxy asks you to vote on important questions about how the company is run, more important is the invitation not to vote at all. You can give permission to the board of directors to vote your shares. So while you are looking at a voting ballot, it doubles as a proxy you could sign giving the board of directors the authority to vote your shares.

Wealth Words

Proxy—A proxy form authorizes someone to act in your stead, in this case to cast a vote at a shareholder's meeting.

Does the financial world collapse if you neglect to vote? No, they can run the company without your input. If you cannot sleep at night with these stacked up on your to-do pile, throw them away. If the company *really* cannot move forward on a matter without more votes, do not worry; it will ask again and again until it gets enough votes to move forward.

The Replacements

With your newfound commitment to throwing things away, you must be wondering, what do I do if I discover I threw away something I need? Replacing most records is challenging, but not impossible, in this age of computers. Most of your monthly bills can be reproduced or summarized for you by the utility, phone, or sanitary service company that sent it to you. And if it is financial records you seek, the investment company that holds them can also reproduce the statements you receive regarding your financial assets.

Many mutual fund companies actually send a statement that summarizes all previous months in the calendar year. Hence each statement repeats the data from the month before and simply adds the new number from this current month to the statement. So to keep that file manageable, throw away all statements except the newest.

Memories...

Even the IRS can provide copies of your previous year's filings! Its computer keeps a record of your entire filing and allows you to give permission to others to request copies. If you have ever applied for a Small Business Administration (SBA) loan, you know what we mean. You can sign a permission slip allowing the SBA to get copies of your previous 3 years' tax filings.

Most of your financial records can also be re-created from the computers that others maintain on your behalf. In addition, you can keep copies of things on your computer or on a floppy disk. If you want to be a high-tech record keeper, you can invest in a scanner, which will read and scan your documents and convert them to an image that your computer can store for you. Scanners are not *terribly* expensive, but this routine is probably a lot more work than most readers need.

And Your Point Is?

Our point here is that most of your valuable data is stored in many places in the world, on many different computers. Paper storage is only one way to keep records. Most of us keep far more paper then we really need. Most of us keep these records too carelessly for them to truly be of use to us. Most of us have many other things we ought to be doing with our time instead of meticulously filing and storing old bills and envelopes. Most of us feel some guilt at throwing things away without at least opening and reading them.

It is your mail, and you do not *have* to read any of it. You do not owe the marketing firm even 1 minute of your time to read its advertisement. You do not owe the marketing firm even 1 minute of your time to answer its phone call. If the item in the mail contains information that is very important to you, *believe* me, the company will send you another bill if you inadvertently throw away this one.

Take Back the Streets!

Take control of your mailbox! Seize power over your time in the day. Throw away those invitations to servitude that are disguised as platinum and titanium credit cards!

Why keep a 3-foot-high stack of mail-order catalogs with winter clothes when the thermometer in your window reveals summertime temperatures? Get your money's worth out of that garbage bill you pay each month.

Now that we have you throwing away everything, what harm can possibly come to you from the garbage can? Must you take special precautions in the way you dispose of things? Heavens, yes!

That titanium credit card offer needs to land in the landfill in at least two different pieces, never to be reunited again. People can steal your junk mail, pretend to be you, and steal your excellent credit rating. They usually go through your mail *before* you do, which is also against the law. But some thieves go through your discarded mail as it leaves your home on its way to landfill heaven. They won't be able to hurt you if you tear these offers in half or thirds before chucking 'em in the garbage.

Getting Started Again

Where to start? You know you have way too much paper. The great thing about keeping too much is it is easy to catch up. You do not need to do it all at once. Just start with today's mail. Throw away what you do not need as you are walking back to the house with a handful of mail. Then, later this week, as you pay your bills, look at that pile of paid bills that need to be filed and throw away the old utility bills, which you have resolved not to keep. Monday night, as you watch *Ally McBeal* or your husband watches *Monday Night Football,* throw away the old catalogs, the yellowed and wrinkled ones from last winter, or even last week! It is a liberating feeling!

Treat yourself to a beautiful storage cabinet. Linda's teakwood file cabinet matches the roll-top desk she uses to pay her bills. It is chock-full and needs its annual cleaning but is still a restful place to sit for an hour or two.

Auto Pilot

One way to make the paperwork even simpler is to arrange for automatic bill payments whenever possible. You will still receive bill statements, but they merely confirm that the bill has been paid directly out of your checking or savings account. The bill simply tells you how much the company took, and why. This works particularly well for the recurring monthly bills like mortgages, utilities, and even the phone bill. Once you get the confirmation that your bill was paid, and you verify that they did not add any extra zeros onto the end of your otherwise reasonable number, you can throw that slip of paper away as well.

But what about that shoebox full of checks you wrote way back when you were in high school! Still can't work up the nerve to throw those away? Many financial institutions no longer send out canceled checks. The banks copy them on microfilm, record them in chronological order on your statement, and store them in gigantic central shoeboxes rather than go to the time and expense to mail old checks back to you. And guess what? You very rarely need that canceled check anyway, and when you do, the statement they recorded it on will usually stand as proof of payment.

Start Your Garbage Cans Now!

Remember, it is your mailbox, and you can control how you let the mail you receive affect your life. Yes, some of your mail needs your attention. Yes, some of your mail has statements and information that needs to be saved. Most of your mail underwrites the cost of the stamps you buy, but you do not need to give it your time! Learn to tear it in half and throw it away. Learn to file the important mail so you can find it when you need it. If you can't find a record you think is really important, don't panic. Someone out there has a copy and will provide it to you; you only need to ask.

The Least You Need to Know

➤ Develop a daily system to read and deal with important mail.

➤ Toss junk mail and catalogs without even opening them.

➤ Check all statements, and report errors immediately.

➤ File only important records; don't clutter up your life by hanging on to every bill.

➤ Keep tax records and back-up paperwork for 7 years.

➤ Don't panic if you lose a bill; someone will have a copy.

Can I Get Some Help With This?

In This Chapter

➤ Should I go stag, or take a date to the prom?

➤ Taxes and other ugly thoughts

➤ Bean counters and what they do

➤ "Sign here, please"—hiring a tax preparer

➤ Calling in the big guns—lawyers

➤ Stockbrokers—full service or self-serve?

➤ Alphabet advisors—CFCs, CFPs, and FCs

Here we are, only in Chapter 5, and already you are worn out by the thought of all of the paperwork and decision-making! Admit it—you'd hoped that mastering all of this investment and financial stuff would take only a few extra minutes a day, leaving you with plenty of time to enjoy your ever-improving financial status. But will you ever get to that point?

In fact, once you get the hang of all of this it really won't take much time. You'll have plenty of time left over to water-ski or play the piano. A word to the wise, though; we know some women who plunge into the world of investing and adopt it as a new hobby—abandoning water-skiing and Brahms études and letting the weeds grow in the garden while they study yet another annual report.

Shall I Go Stag, or Take a Date to the Prom?

But perhaps you don't anticipate ever embracing your finances as a hobby. Are there folks out there who will be able to help you ease the burden on your time and attention?

You bet! In this chapter, we examine a handful of the advisors, consultants, and professionals who would love to help you manage your money. Take this inexpensive opportunity to familiarize yourself with their

➤ Expertise

➤ Credentials

➤ Fee structures and commissions

After evaluating this info, you just might decide to include one or two of these folks in your life. Or you may further your resolve to go it alone.

Taxes and Other Ugly Facts of Life

We'll start here with two different types of professionals who are standing by, ready and willing to help you deal with your yearly headache—taxes.

Why do we want to start with something as unpleasant to contemplate as taxes?

Cash Cautions

Never sign a tax return that you don't understand. Whether it has been prepared by your husband, your best friend, or a professional tax person, mistakes can happen. And if your signature is on the bottom line, you are ultimately responsible for it.

➤ Because it makes a difference in your annual income and, therefore, in the money that you have available to invest.

➤ Because it is never too early in the fiscal year to start thinking about and planning your tax strategy.

➤ Because as you enjoy watching your investments grow, sadly, your taxes will grow more and more complex.

Face it, if you can file your taxes on an EZ form, you haven't got much to show for yourself financially. And as it is your goal to improve your financial picture through investing, a side effect of your riches will be a bigger stack of tax forms to wade through. And they all have that teeny, tiny print.

The Bean Counters

Hiring a certified public accountant (CPA) sounds so posh. The term conjures up folks with pots of money and complicated finances. So if you are just starting out, why might you want to use a CPA? For any one of the following reasons:

➤ If you are self-employed.

A CPA will stay abreast of the byzantine changes that occur every year regarding deductions. And that means that you don't have to!

➤ If you own rental properties or a second home.

Once again, a CPA can better sort out just which of your expenses related to rental homes or vacation homes are deductible, and which ones will cause the IRS to raise an eyebrow.

➤ If you anticipate the arrival of a financial windfall.

Do you expect to receive a lump sum divorce settlement, an insurance settlement, a large bonus, or any other large sum of money that will change your tax status overnight? CPAs can help you create a long-range tax planning strategy to make the most of what you will receive.

Cash Cautions

Hmmm...is it safe to pay the IRS? Not long ago, an IRS employee named Jack Regan Stevens plead guilty to embezzling a total of $77,218 from money taxpayers sent in. How did he do it? He altered checks made out to "I.R.S." so that they read J.R. Stevens. This little con is not likely to happen again, but just in case, be sure to write your checks out to the Internal Revenue Service.

And should the IRS tap you on the shoulder and select you as the lucky winner of an audit, you won't have to go alone. Your CPA will be there by your side, advising you every step of the way. Too scared to even walk though the doors of the IRS office? You can even grant your CPA power of attorney and he or she can go talk to the IRS without you (but please remember that you must be able to trust someone you give power of attorney to).

What makes CPAs so darned special? These folks have great educations and training. In addition to having a college degree, a CPA must work under the supervision of another CPA for a full 2 years and pass a stringent national exam in accounting, taxes, and business law. Once she or he passes the exam, a CPA receives an actual license from the state.

Wealth Words

Certified Public Accountant—A CPA is an accountant who has earned a license from the state by fulfilling stringent requirements and passing a rigorous test.

"Sign Here, Please"

A step below using a CPA to help you with taxes is doing what most Americans do—hire a "tax preparer." Actually, not only do most Americans use a tax preparer, they seem to use H&R Block tax preparers! In 1996 a whopping 18.2 million folks filed their tax returns through one of H&R Block's 9,700 offices. The company brags that nearly 80% of Americans live within 10 miles of an H&R Block office. Long thought of as catering to the middle classes, Block has recently been targeting higher income tax-payers who currently do their own taxes or use independent accountants. Could Block be looking for you?

Just Walk Through the Door and...

Hand 'em your stuff. When you work with H&R Block, or any other paid tax preparer, the person you hire prepares your taxes for you—for a fee. But don't expect to find the same familiar face year after year. Chances are you will work with a different tax preparer every tax season.

Wise Women Know

You really are better off hiring a professional to help you with your taxes. At the very least, the professional will find enough extra money for you to cover the cost of his or her fee. The fact is that tax laws are complicated. One waggish taxpayer in Philadelphia had a great idea—require all members of Congress and the president to prepare their own returns without professional help. Wouldn't that force them to simplify the system!

Call in the Big Guns

Just like using a CPA, having a lawyer involved in your financial affairs sounds so toney. Either you are rich, or you must be in big trouble, right? Wrong!

Anyhow, lawyers have become a part of ordinary daily life. And why should you get a lawyer involved in your financial life? Perhaps because you are contemplating (or are in the messy midst of) one of the following scenarios:

➤ a divorce

➤ a prenuptial agreement

➤ a real estate transaction

➤ estate planning

But do lawyers actually get involved in your investing? Generally speaking, no. If in the years to come you find yourself contemplating investments like buying part of a business, or loaning a large sum of money to someone, then lawyers should be part of your investment life. But for basic stock market investing, mutual fund investing, or some of the other strategies we will soon discuss, you do not need a lawyer.

So you might not need a lawyer in your financial life for years and years to come. But when you become so successful that you have a pot of money that needs to be divided, protected, defended, or given away, call a lawyer to do the job right.

Wall Street Warriors

"Do-it-yourself" investing gets a great deal of ink nowadays. Story after story about folks handling their own investment transactions fill newspapers and magazines. But are these folks not actually using a broker? No. Unless you own your own seat on the New York Stock Exchange, you must use a broker to handle your transaction.

But what kind of broker do you want? Later in the book we will give you tons of information about discount brokers and online brokers. Right now we'd like to talk about the old-fashioned kind—a full-service broker. What is the difference between a full-service broker and any other sort of broker? A full-service broker is the only kind of broker who will:

➤ develop a personal relationship with you

➤ try to learn about your own financial goals, investment needs, and risk level

➤ recommend stocks to buy (and sell)

➤ calm you in the midst of market turmoil

In short, a full-service broker is someone who will actually *give you investment advice*. Someone who will spend hour after hour discussing your financial hopes and dreams, and help you make the investment decisions that can take you there. And in today's fast-paced world, personal guidance and advice is something we all yearn for. Particularly when we are beginner investors.

Full-service brokers sound great, so why do all of those folks use discount brokers? The bottom line is—price. Full-service brokers can give you a wide range of services and help you with a vast array of investment decisions, but they charge full commission for what they do.

Commissions are how most workers in the investment world make money—by charging you a fee to handle the *purchase* of an investment vehicle like a stock, bond, or mutual fund, and by charging you a fee to handle the *sale* of that same investment vehicle when you cash it out. So the question you need to ask a full-service broker is: "What is the commission for a transaction?"

45

The size of the commission will vary depending on how much stock you buy. The commission you'll pay to buy 100 shares of Stock X will probably be lower than the commission you'll be charged to buy 1,000 shares of Stock Y. Make sure that you have a thorough understanding of how commissions work.

How Do You Choose?

How do you find a stockbroker? Ask your friends. As with most types of service, asking around for recommendations is better than just picking someone from a Yellow Pages ad. "It was easy to choose a broker. We just called up the woman that my husband's family had been using happily for years," said Lindsay Arfsten of Granite Bay, California. "We've had a great relationship ever since."

Wealth Words

Discount broker—Unlike a full-service broker, a discount broker such as Charles Schwab won't give you any investment advice. It is up to you to do the research, make your decisions, and call the broker when you are ready to buy or sell.

There are also hardworking brokers who give free investment seminars—hoping, of course, to pick up a few new clients. You can attend a seminar and decide if this seems like a person you can trust, a person that you would enjoy working closely with for the years to come.

Developing that closeness is key. Full-service stockbrokers are required to "Know Thy Customer." Actually, they are supposed to know you so darn well that should you call up and ask them to place a buy for 10,000 shares of a gold-mining company in Indonesia (or some other wacky-sounding scheme), your full-service stockbroker will actually put the brakes on your plan.

Wise Women Know

In the past, some stockbrokers have developed crummy reputations for pushing stocks on clients not because it was a great investment, but because they could win a free trip to Hawaii if they sold enough of the stock! Those days are long gone; the SEC now requires full disclosure by the broker if he or she is participating in a sales contest of any sort.

The Alphabet Crew

The choice is not just between using a full-service stockbroker or doing it all on your own. You can also use the services of a wide range of advisors who can help you assess needs and plan your investments.

We will warn you, though, your eyes might begin to swim at the wide variety of letters that follow the names of some professional financial people. We call them the "alphabet crew"—CFPs, CFCs, LUTCFs. Who are these people, and what do they do? And just how did they get those initials, anyway? Here's a quick look at some of the most common credentials.

CFC—Chartered Financial Consultant

A Chartered Financial Consultant, or CFC, is a professional designation granted by the American College in Bryn Mawr, Pennsylvania. In order to receive that designation, CFCs must pass 10 courses on a variety of topics. Among the topics CFCs study are:

➤ wealth accumulation planning

➤ accounting and finance

➤ business insurance

➤ estate planning

➤ pension planning

It usually takes a few years to complete the course, and CFCs are required to take continuing education courses in order to keep up with the ever-changing world of investments, insurance, and tax laws.

Cash Cautions

Bob Driezler, CFC, likes to tell his clients that they should "imagine building a castle with a moat around it. The castle represents your home and your investments, and the moat is the insurance that must be in place to protect your assets. It's a real dilemma trying to decide whether to spend money making a bigger castle or increasing the size of your moat.

CFP—Certified Financial Planner

Certified Financial Planners (CFPs) are certified by the College for Financial Planning in Denver, Colorado. The CFP designation requires not only a 2-year program and a 10-hour exam, but also 3 years of work experience in the investment field. CFPs are also required to take continuing education courses to keep up with changes in the law.

LUTCF—Life Underwriter Training Council Fellow

This credential requires classes in personal and business life insurance, disability insurance, retirement vehicles, and annuities (both how they work and when they are appropriate). Applicants are tested on their knowledge and must pass the courses before receiving their credential. Here's how Rita Gibson, LUTCF, of Sacramento, California, describes what she does:

Cash Cautions

How do stockbrokers make money if they don't charge a fee? Simple, they charge a commission to handle your trades. You pay a commission when you buy stock, and then you pay commission again when you sell it, so brokers make money even when you don't!

I help people decide what their goals are, what they hope to achieve financially. We look at the most tax-efficient way of accomplishing that. We examine their budgeting to make sure that they are setting aside enough money to reach their goals. And then I help them decide—based on their age, income, and experience—which financial vehicles are best suited to help them meet their goals. I also help them make sure that their bases are covered with regard to insurance needs.

Sound familiar? Most of these folks do pretty much the same thing. Some may be slightly more biased toward insurance-based investment vehicles, some might steer you toward annuities, but all of them can sit down with you and help you get a good handle on where you are financially.

Wise Women Know

Feeling overwhelmed by all of these different professionals? Follow your instincts about who you can trust and who you would like to work closely with over the years. Don't choose a fancy degree over a sincere person. Make sure that you choose someone who is willing to answer all your questions.

How to Choose?

So how do you choose which professional to use? Pretty much the same way you'd choose a full-service stockbroker: Start asking around among your friends and family. And like stockbrokers, these financial consultants and financial planners hold free seminars for the public. Venture out and attend a few. Not only will you learn more about investing, but you can see for yourself what that person is like and whether you'd want them messing around with your money.

An important question to ask any investment advisor is: "What securities licenses do you have, and what kinds of fees do they allow you to charge?" For instance, a Series 6 license allows the holder to sell mutual funds, and a Series 7 license allows the holder to sell individual stocks. If the planner that you are considering can only sell insurance, it is a safe bet that they will limit their investment advice and strategy to buying...insurance.

Still not certain if you need to hire a financial professional? The next chapter, in which you determine your current net worth, might help. The number you ultimately arrive at might determine whether you need a professional advisor. A net worth that's too small or one that's too large (is there such a thing?) might require advice from the pros.

The Least You Need to Know

➤ There are a number of professionals who can guide you through your financial decisions.

➤ As your investments grow more complex, so too will your taxes.

➤ CPAs can accompany you to your IRS audit, or even go on your behalf.

➤ Full-service brokers will get to know your investment needs and offer actual investing advice, but also charge a higher commission.

➤ Several categories of financial planner exist. Talk to several and choose one that you feel most comfortable working with.

Part 2
I Owe, I Owe, It's Off to Work I Go

Ah, the brass tacks section! Here we help you figure out just how much you are worth at this exact moment in time (gulp!) and how you can work to improve that net worth over time. Cast an eagle eye on just how much you owe for houses, student loans, cars, and the ugliest of all debts—credit cards!

Does it seem like an easy way to get sidetracked when what you really want is to invest for the future? Once you have a clear idea of your financial situation, you will be in a much better position to set reachable goals and work toward cleaning up high-priced debts that might drain your investment power.

Chapter 6

Evaluating Your Net Worth

In This Chapter

➤ Just what is net worth?

➤ Determining the value of what you own

➤ Being honest about your liabilities

➤ Doing the math, facing the music

➤ Become determined to increase your net worth

➤ Goal setting for the future

Most people spend more time planning their family vacation than planning the financial future of the family. As Mr. Scarecrow says in the *Wizard of Oz,* "To know where you want to go, it is best to figure out where it is you are now." Let's add the advice of Glenda, the good witch of the north, as well: You must start at the beginning. Only then can you follow the yellow (gold!) brick road.

Tuning in the Big Picture

And if you start at the beginning, the first must-do is to determine your current net worth. This project might seem like a chore, but it is relatively easy:

➤ You put a value on everything you own.

➤ You subtract everything you owe.

➤ What is left is your net worth.

Wealth Words

Net worth—Total assets minus total liabilities.

This process sounds easy. The problem is that most folks do not have any idea how much they owe. Sit down with all those statements you now save and file carefully. Take a snapshot in time of your bills. Create a list of all your debts. In the coming chapters, we will examine the different types of debt in depth, but for now just write it all down.

Start with your mortgage. It is the American dream to own a home, therefore most of us are owned by a mortgage. Your mortgage should constitute the largest share of your debt. Add up any other loans outstanding, like education loans, car loans, second mortgages or lines of credit on your home, credit card balances, and installment loans. Younger readers will probably have a larger debt number. (The older we grow, the more debt we get rid of.)

Another American dream is to be debt free just as we retire, with lots of savings in the bank to support us. Now be brutally honest in the next part, which is adding up the value of all that we own. Most people have a difficult time putting a solid number on the value of their home. Remember that it is only worth what someone will pay to buy it from you.

Home, Sweet Major Asset

But if you bought your home years ago, how can you really figure out what it is worth now? Here are a few helpful pointers:

➤ Check to see what others have paid recently for their homes of similar size and structure in your general neighborhood.

➤ Study the Sunday real-estate section of the local paper to see what similar homes are listed for.

➤ Call a local real-estate broker and ask him or her to provide an estimate over the phone. The broker should be able to respond quickly, using computerized records.

Take Your Statement

The next step is to consult all those statements you have filed away so carefully. Retirement account values, investment account values, bank savings account values— they all add into the total value of your assets. Some folks are confused in this process because your retirement accounts have rules about when you can spend that money. Don't forget that even though the IRS or your employer has rules about that money, it is still *your money,* and as such, it counts as an asset for the calculation of your net worth.

The Rest of the Story

You then need to place a value on the other things you own, such as cars, furniture, and toys. For those of you with car loans, do not be confused by the loan value as that is written on the debt side of this computation.

To arrive at the value of your car, check your Sunday paper for the asking price on other cars of your style and year. Do not be startled if the loan size is close to the resale value. Cars are notoriously a poor investment and, whenever possible, should be purchased with cash, not borrowed money. Then they should be driven and maintained until they drop! It is very costly to your net worth to add new cars to your wardrobe as if they were winter coats. But you learn more in Chapter 9, "Welcome to Big Al's Friendly Car Lot!," about the actual cost of cars. Keep in mind that a new car loses a significant portion of its value the moment you drive it out of the lot.

The value of your furniture and the contents of your home are easy to estimate; replacement cost is a good guide here. Do not forget the value of jewelry, artwork, collectibles, and toys.

Toys include items such as bicycles, motorcycles, boats, trailers, and recreation equipment. These are difficult to value for net worth purposes, as they invariably mean more to us in their usefulness than they hold in true monetary value. Have you been to a garage or rummage sale lately?

Okay, let's take a look at what you've come up with. Now, the next step is to

➤ Add up your column of assets.

➤ Add up your column of debts.

➤ Subtract the debts from the assets.

➤ And *voilà*—your net worth appears!

Building Toward the Big Numbers

The goal is to grow the net worth number ever larger as you add another year to your life. There are many ways to accomplish this goal. All of them are really quite simple.

The simplest way to grow your net worth is to pay off your debts. And the fastest way to do this is to stop incurring new debts or to stop adding to the amount of money you owe. In other words, stop spending money. Or you can spend it very carefully and in a very measured manner.

You can make debt repayment a real game if you like. Most folks do not realize how much it helps to just add another $50 per month toward principal repayment with your mortgage payment.

The Java Savings Plan

Our baby-boomer preoccupation with designer coffee easily sets us back $50 in 1 month. Imagine the savings from drinking home-brewed coffee versus the two dollars you pay each morning at the Starbucks drive-through window. But how can you get through the day at work without that designer cup of coffee? Buy coffee beans and a thermos. (Incidentally, Starbucks is a common stock that has performed quite well for investors. More about companies like Starbucks later in the book!)

Here is an example of the savings you will experience with the sacrifice of a mere $50.00 per month.

You have a $100,000 mortgage, with a 7% interest rate, fixed for 30 years. The payment is $665.30 per month. This pay-off plan means you will pay $139,508 in interest on the $100,000 loan over the 30-year period.

If you add $50 to each monthly payment toward the principal of the loan, you are *paid off* in 24 years! You will pay a total of $104,742 in interest on that loan over the 24-year period, saving almost $35,000 *and* getting rid of the debt faster! What an amazing reward for making your own cup of designer coffee! Think about it!

Are There Holes in Your Net?

Now that you have determined your net worth, let's take a hard look at those liabilities. This is an area where most Americans have hard truths to face.

Wealth Words

Liabilities—Debts and obligations.

We are a society addicted to debt. Many baby boomers came of age in a high-inflation environment, and our government endorsed debt with generous tax advantages during the 1970s. In the 1980s as those tax advantages dried up, a curious thing happened. Americans did not pay off their credit cards. Another curious thing happened. Even as inflation and interest rates dropped over the past 15 years, many banks and credit companies maintained their high interest rates. Are you wondering why? The answer is simple. We allowed them to.

Most of us benignly allowed banks to gouge us by continuing to pay only the monthly minimum. If you learn nothing else in reading this book, the lesson to take home is *pay off those credit cards*. We continue this lecture on credit card spending in Chapter 8, "Credit Card Bondage—Modern-Day Slavery."

Negative net worth occurs when what you owe is a larger number than what you own. Credit card debt is the largest contributor to this problem. Stop and examine exactly what you acquire with credit cards. Try life without these items and services for a while. Get yourself out of bondage by ceasing to spend on the cards and learning to enjoy life within your budget. You will learn more about this in Chapter 8.

Another Net

Let's delve into the nomenclature of net worth for a moment and put your minds at ease. Anyone can do financial speak, so do not be intimidated. You've learned that the textbook definition of net worth is a number calculated by subtracting total liabilities from total assets. For individuals, total assets are recorded at current market value. The measure is different for companies, but this aspect of accounting is not important right now. *Liability* is an obligation to pay an amount in money, goods, or services to another party. *Liability* is another word for *debt*. Credit cards are another word for *debt* in many people's lives.

Now let's get back to definitions. An *asset* is something of monetary value that is owned by a firm or an individual. In our consumer-driven society, most of us like to own toys and things, but we do not often think of them as assets. Most of us own a home because we like to live there, but we do not necessarily revere it as an asset. Most of us regard our other things as objects of pleasure, not as assets.

Wealth Words

Negative net worth—When you owe more money (liabilities) than you are worth (assets).

The Real Bottom Line

When you think of something as an asset, a curious transformation occurs. You become more sensitive to the cost of acquisition!

There are two approaches to improving your net worth. One is to focus on keeping your debt as simple as possible. If all that you owed was your mortgage, life would be simple, correct? Understanding the value of what you own makes the acquisition of other necessities, such as cars, furniture, computers, stereos, and appliances, individual events for which you plan, save money, and pay cash.

Since minimizing debt requires unlimited patience and an ability to delay gratification, many of us will find it difficult. Try! Try! Try!

Give yourself a 2-month period during which you do not buy anything on credit. Just pay cash. You might learn that leaving the credit cards at home, hidden under the mattress, rids you of impulse purchases.

The second approach to improving net worth is to make your saved dollars produce good growth of their own. This approach is called *investing*. An investment is also an asset. Typically, we invest when we put our retirement savings into mutual funds or money markets. Savings dollars outside of retirement accounts are an asset. They can be invested in stocks, bonds, or mutual funds to produce growth on the asset as well.

Consider the following: We trade time and knowledge everyday in exchange for a paycheck. We spend some of that paycheck to pay for the way we like to live. Whatever is left over can become an asset. We can have the money we save start to *make* money for us.

This scheme is the essence of the retirement dream. We all seek to have enough money in assets so the earnings on our assets support us and we do not have to barter our time and knowledge for money forever. We can have our retirement years free to do all those other things we really like to do.

So the process of planning to grow your net worth can be attacked in each or both the following ways:

➤ Stop spending money unless absolutely necessary.

➤ Start saving. Invest your assets so they can grow safely to a large enough number to sustain you.

➤ Do a combination of both: Moderate your spending (buy only things you need!) and learn to pay cash for everything. Be more deliberate in your investment choices for your savings dollars.

Every so often you'll read in the newspaper about a little old lady who lived and eventually died in humble surroundings. Everyone assumed she was poor—until her will was read. Then it was revealed that she was secretly a millionaire and had left all her money to a hospital, church, or some fine educational institution.

Sound impossible? Not at all—these gals have taken the stop-spending advice to the extreme. Furthermore, they almost always have their assets invested in something more than a savings account. This is how they achieved the high net worth that allowed them to be remembered for their generosity.

Our point here is that anyone, regardless of means, can grow a positive net worth. The most important ingredient is the desire to do so.

Wise Women Know

The best-selling book *The Millionaire Next Door* has opened our eyes to how rich people really live. Flying first class? Nope. Wearing expensive suits? Nope. Driving flashy cars? Couldn't be further from the truth! So what do these folks do? They slowly and quietly build up their total net worth by living below their means, shopping wisely, and investing all they can.

Of course, one way to increase your net worth is to increase your income. Many people pursue this route before they try to learn to spend less money. It is a common belief: "If only I earned more, then I could put more aside." Sadly, for too many of us, more money earned means more money to play with! Just take a look at some of the bumper stickers that flash past on the freeway:

➤ She who dies with the most toys wins.

➤ I wish I was Barbie; that _____ (rhymes with witch) has everything.

➤ I owe, I owe, it's off to work I go.

Try not to be drawn into this point of view. Instead, make life a game of living within 80% of your means. Make the saying "Pay yourself first" your new motto.

Gaining Ground

Once you accumulate enough money, you will see that as your assets make money, you start to gain ground more quickly.

Now that we have focused on how to measure your net worth and how to begin increasing your net worth, you might be wondering just why net worth is relevant. At the very least, when life is said and done, most people do not want their heirs to inherit debt. The uncertainty of what life will cost us in the future is what motivates us to save for that rainy day.

The whole concept of saving for a rainy day is seeking to have a net worth that is positive and growing each year.

Status Seekers

Typically, men in our society measure their status against other men by comparing income and net worth. Women often measure their status against other women more by comparing physical appearance.

Fortunately, we have moved away from the time when women were not allowed to own property. In fact, a woman used to be part of a man's property. Imagine trying to measure the value of a woman as an asset toward her husband's net worth. Or were we considered liabilities, thus the concept of dowry?

Here You Goal Again

In any case, we women have come a long way and can now focus our efforts on creating our own net worth. We are free to build our own shield against the unknown cost of living in the future. A positive net worth, healthy and growing, allows us to decide how to spend each day. If we teach our young children the concept that money begets money, then a family fortune can be built over time. Ben Franklin said it quite eloquently: "A penny saved is a penny earned."

Now that you are determined to grow your net worth, what is a realistic goal? Plan on 20% per year. Not a 20% return, mind you, but a 20% increase in your total net worth.

To reach this goal, you must save 10% of your income and invest that money to grow at a rate of 10%. Let this plan simmer on the back burner for 30 years, and you have a solid, sustaining net worth. In fact, you'll have two incomes: the money you earn from work and the money you earn from your investments.

Check up on your net worth at least twice a year—once at tax time and once in the fall—to see whether your annual savings are on track and whether your investments are growing at the correct rate. Make modifications as necessary.

You'll find that as the asset side accumulates, you no longer want to spend as much as you have in the past. You might be surprised to see how good it feels to have a growing shield against the unknown. You might learn that the shield feels better than the new car or the extravagant travel. Who knows, you might really be drawn into the game of growing your net worth.

Cash Cautions

Credit card debt is the most expensive debt you can have. Pay this off *before* you do anything else. Credit card debt is so expensive that investing is never worthwhile as long as you owe money to a credit card company.

The Least You Need to Know

➤ To determine your actual net worth, add up your liabilities and subtract that number from your assets.

➤ Items like cars, furniture, and collectibles can be included in determining your net worth.

➤ Making extra payments to your mortgage can drastically reduce the time it takes to pay it off and dramatically decrease the interest you pay.

➤ Most Americans with a substantial net worth do not live the lavish lifestyle portrayed on television and in the movies. In fact, many rich people live well below their means.

➤ By keeping debt to a minimum, saving 10% of your income, and investing it at a 10% return, you will build a substantial net worth in the years to come.

Chapter 7

The American Dream— Long-Term Debt

In This Chapter

➤ To dream the American dream

➤ How much house can you really afford?

➤ To refinance or not to refinance—that is the question

➤ Congratulations! You qualify for a home equity loan!

➤ Lock up your house at all times

➤ The sheepskin in wolf's clothing

Every red-blooded American wants to own a home. From the day the Pilgrims arrived here, we have been staking our claim, so to speak. Throughout the centuries, the dream of owning one's own home has prevailed through all kinds of economic ups and downs. Recognizing the importance of encouraging home ownership, the U.S. government has further endorsed this dream with the primary-home mortgage-interest deduction. This critical deduction has weathered all manner of tax reform.

To Dream the American Dream

We are raised with the notion that owning one's own home is virtually a provision of the Bill of Rights. The post–World War II economic good times and the explosive growth in population commonly referred to as the baby boom created a severe need for housing. Combine this need with the general flight from the cities to the suburbs that occurred in the 1960s, and you have the crystallization of the American dream as we know it. Both Hollywood and television have helped clarify our vision by adding the film fantasy that the perfect home has a white picket fence and green window shutters.

Wealth Words

Mortgage—To give a bank or lending institution a claim on property as security for the payment of debt on this property.

Wealth Words

Equity—The part of the home that you actually own free and clear; the current value of your house less the amount that you owe on your mortgage.

Wealth Words

Default—To fail to fulfill one's financial obligations; to fail to make payments on a mortgage, credit card, or loan.

One of the best movies of all times, *It's a Wonderful Life*, is based on the growing pains of the fictional Community Savings and Loan. The climax of the movie was Jimmy Stewart's great speech—when he reminded all the bank customers, as they were trying to withdraw their funds from the bank, that their money was in each other's homes in the form of mortgages. It is a great explanation of how the whole banking and lending system works.

This story brings us to a most important aspect of home ownership: the mortgage most of us need to complete such a large financial commitment. The largest single debt most of us accept in our lifetime is a mortgage, a debt we incur so we can own our home.

Although it would be lovely to advise you to save the cash and buy your home once you have enough money, accumulating this tidy sum could take a lifetime and you would need a place to live while you were saving the money. You would need to pay rent to someone who owns the building you are renting anyway, so it makes good sense to have that monthly flow of money go toward building equity in your own home.

Equity is the part of your home you actually own. Your mortgage is the part the bank owns. The bank does not really want to own real estate. It wants to make money on the interest you pay for your loan, which is why most home purchases require a down payment. The goal is to have you invest enough money so that you will be financially damaged if you default on the payments on your mortgage.

Taking a mortgage can be a large and unsettling commitment. You make a promise to pay, and if you decide to sell the home and no one appears to buy it, you still must pay. We don't mean to frighten you. This is merely a statement of fact. When deciding on the purchase of a home, the first consideration is and should be that your home is the place you live. The next consideration is you must choose a home you can afford.

How Much House Can You Really Afford?

Deciding how much home you can afford is both simple and quick. Here is the formula: Your mortgage should not cost more than approximately 30% of your monthly income.

Banks use special debt formulas to determine whether you can perform on your payments (in other words, send them the money). Banks also have equity requirements, usually a minimum of 10% down—and preferably 20% down if you want to avoid private mortgage insurance (the wasteful and dreaded PMI!).

PMI is insurance you are required to buy. It guarantees the bank that other 10% in equity, should you default on the payments of your mortgage. PMI is very expensive relative to the amount of insurance benefit being provided, and it is of no benefit to you—you buy insurance for your bank! You pay so the bank is not at risk. If you come upon hard times, the bank receives the money, not you! Avoid PMI at all costs. If the only way you can get into the home is to pay PMI, pray for fast appreciation in the value of your home and invest in a refinance to be rid of the necessity for PMI.

For example, if your mortgage is a $90,000 loan for a $100,000 house, that means you own $10,000 of the house, or 10% of it. If the house increases in value to $150,000, your loan is still $90,000, but when you refinance you don't need PMI because you own the rest of the house, now worth $60,000, or one-third the value of the house!

To Refinance or Not to Refinance—That Is the Question

Refinancing your home loan is simply stated: reviewing your loan, reviewing the value of your home, and selecting a mortgage that better suits your needs.

The money folk invite you to refinance for many reasons. And you might decide you want to invest in a new mortgage. But buyers beware! When considering a re-fi, proceed with extreme caution.

Is it free to refinance? Nope. You just can't reorganize that much money without some cost for doing so. Be mindful that many banks that come looking for you, either in your mailbox with an advertisement or in the Sunday paper, mostly want to collect the handsome fees up front to refinance your mortgage. They might also help you by providing the same loan (mortgage) you have now but with a lower interest rate.

Cash Cautions

USA Today recently reported a chilling tale about a woman with a $37,000 mortgage financed in 1988. Six years later she had refinanced five times, and her loan balance had increased to $112,000. According to the newspaper, she'd been a victim of predatory lenders who target equity-rich but cash-poor consumers with high-cost loans. So be sure to read—and understand—the fine print.

Lenders are required by law to adhere to full disclosure of all the costs involved in the refinance (they must tell all). Typically, they add these costs into the size of the loan, but do not be fooled by the wording. Whether you pay out of pocket now or add the refinance costs into the size of the loan, you pay. Either you pay fees up-front or you pay interest on the fees.

So, Why Would You Do This?

Other reasons you might want to refinance are to capture some of the appreciation you have experienced in the price of your home or to make extensive repairs or improvements to your home. Upgrading your home makes sense when the improvements add to the value of your home while causing you to incur more debt. This is not a tricky situation. The bank might suggest a whole new mortgage or perhaps a line of credit against this increase in the value of your home. This type of loan is commonly called "equity access line of credit."

A good rule of thumb is to consider what you plan to do with the money you capture in the process. Pay attention to these two rules:

➤ Finance permanent changes with permanent loans.

➤ Finance temporary uses for the money with a temporary, or partial, loan.

What are possible temporary uses for the money? Your child is about to start college. You haven't saved enough to pay for Harvard, but low and behold, your daughter got in. To make up the difference, you tap the equity you have in your home. Hmmm…was that the right thing to do?

A better example is that you are planning to move soon, and friends have told you that a new roof and paint job would make the house easier to sell. So you borrow short term against the line of credit, invest in the home improvements, sell the house (making enough to pay off the loan immediately), and move your money into the next home.

Any other good reasons to refinance? Sure. One other use of this line of credit might be to consolidate other loans you have let build up. Perhaps you can pay off the last remnants of a car loan, some credit card debts, and some old student loans with the proceeds from equity access in your home. This financial reorganization improves your life because you now have one loan payment a month, the interest on the loan is deductible on your taxes, and the interest rate should be lower (but do check before you decide about the loan). Therefore, equity access, if used properly, is a good idea.

Watch Your Step!

As with all other borrowing, proceed with caution. Too many people are tapping into the equity in their home to bail themselves out of consumer debt they have built up over the years. Using your home to pay off consumer debt does not truly help you build your net worth. Remember our chapter on building your net worth. Remember also, our comments that your home is, first and foremost, the place you live. It is next, and still importantly, an investment. This basic belief should govern all your decisions regarding financing of your home.

Ignore all mail you get about home equity loans or refinancing. Think of these solicitations as the bad guys trying to invade the value of your home. If and when you feel it is time to review the value of your home, and how much equity you have in your home, you can easily find a fair value in the home loan market on your own!

As we have mentioned many times in this book, you govern what you will respond to in your mailbox. Ignore all the offers to refinance your home. They will lure you into eroding one of your most important symbols of security. When the time comes for you to tap the equity of your home, you will be creative enough to find the best deal. More important, do not be seduced into using your hard-earned equity to pay off an over-active appetite for instant gratification in consumer goods.

A Thin White Line

As a homeowner, you will also hear about a "line of credit." Lines of credit vary significantly from fixed-term loans. Lines of credit require you to make up your own payment schedule. And think about this: they require enormous discipline to make them ever actually go away.

A fixed-term loan is established to pay a portion of the principal each payment period until the loan balance disappears. Lines of credit are convenient as emergency funds; they allow you to keep your other savings (that you might otherwise "underinvest" for the sake of liquidity) in a maximum return investment. Any use of a line of credit should be short term.

Fixed-term loans, on the other hand, are for longer-term improvements or other longer term uses of the money. These terms refer to the time commitment for the borrowed funds. Lines of credit have undefined time frames for principal repayment. Fixed-term loans have a "freedom from bondage" day, or independence day as we call it—the day the loan principal is fully paid.

Another important term defines the method used to determine the interest rate on the loan. *Fixed rate* means that the rate does not vary over the course of the loan. It won't surprise you to learn that *variable rate* means that the rate on the loan can vary over the life of the loan. The rate at which your interest can vary is clearly stated and laid out with a variable, but don't be naive. Count on that number changing over the course of your borrowing term.

As interest rates were dropping over the past decade, many homebuyers were advised to invest in variable mortgages, since their payments might go down next year with lower interest rates. Beware of this strategy now, as we are in the lowest interest-rate environment the baby-boomer generation has ever seen; it rivals any rates our parents can recall. Therefore, why, oh why, would anyone currently sign up for a variable rate?

Lock Up Your House at All Times

Variable rates charge between 1% and 3% less than their fixed-rate counterparts. Anne always tells her investment clients to lock in the rate. Put the risk of an interest rate rise on the banks, not on your pocketbook—banks are willing to pay you to take the risk, but they won't pay you enough.

This advice is particularly crucial in that most people who use the variable rate need the lower payment that comes with it to make the deal work. You do not want to put yourself in the dangerous position of having your payments go up next year, as interest rates rise.

What happens if the rates rise, your payment goes up, and you can handle it. This possibility makes the variable attractive, but you still risk not having the income to handle a further rate increase. Why take the risk? Lock in a fixed rate and be secure and happy.

Remember that a home is primarily the place you live. Would you want the unpleasant experience of losing your home, the place you live, while trying to save 2% on the interest rate? When in doubt, it is always best to consider the risk and make a decision that eliminates stress.

The Sheepskin in Wolf's Clothing

Other than a mortgage, many Americans own another type of long term debt—our old friend, the student loan. Sure, you remember, that was the money you absolutely needed to finish college. And without your college degree, you would not have your current job. And without your current job, you would not be able to pay back your college loan, and so on, and so forth. It is the circle of life that most Americans dream of completing, both for themselves and their children.

College loans are very important. Frankly, for many of us, they are essential. The loan is also one of the first entries on your credit history. You must respect the source of the money, and if there was ever a loan that needed to be repaid, it is your education loan. Like every other debt in life, you must evaluate the reward you receive for the discomfort and risk you are entering with a student loan.

Risky Business

Risk? What risk? The risk is that the degree will not translate into a job and the ability to repay the loan. You still have the debt even if you do not get a job. If your parents took the loan, then they still have to repay it even if you do not secure gainful employment.

This predicament leads one to wonder how far out on a limb you should go for the loan to make sense. There are no published formulas, but let's see if we can put this emotional decision in context. Undergraduate education can cost *a lot* of money. Some schools, like community colleges, cost only $500 a year. At the other end of the spectrum, we find the Ivy League universities, which cost more—like $30,000 plus per year.

Like finding an affordable house, which education can you afford? In the worst-case scenario, the most expensive universities, if financed with loans, could put many families into bankruptcy pretty quickly. You and your children should shop for colleges and universities in the same way you shop for other very expensive items—very carefully.

The Graduate

For those who aspire to secure a graduate degree, like medicine or law, this is where you really start looking at a mountain of debt. Many young doctors, for example, are more than $100,000 in debt when they graduate from medical school. This financial burden means starting your work life with a negative net worth. Even if those newly minted doctors, lawyers, and financial chiefs start their work life with a handsome salary of $100,000, they need years and years to pay off the principal.

Wise Women Know

More than a decade after Anne's husband John graduated from medical school, they have friends from his class who have not yet completely paid off the medical school loans.

Does the threat of debt mean you shouldn't strive to become a doctor, lawyer, or biz school graduate? Or that you shouldn't encourage your children or grandchildren to pursue those dreams? Of course not. But be clear-eyed about the size of the long-term debt you are signing up for. It will give you all the more reason to learn to handle other types of credit responsibly.

Now that we've lectured you for page after page about long-term debt, are we gonna let you go? Sorry. Time to settle in for our next big talk—credit card debt!

The Least You Need to Know

➤ A mortgage is the single largest debt most of us take on in a lifetime.

➤ You should commit no more than 30% of your monthly take-home pay to a mortgage.

➤ Refinancing can have many hidden costs.

➤ Long-term debt should be used to finance permanent things, like a house.

➤ Temporary loans should be used to finance temporary cash needs like college or loan consolidation.

➤ Lines of credit should be used only for the short term.

➤ Because of college loans, many graduates start their careers with a negative net worth.

Chapter 8

Credit Card Bondage— Modern-Day Slavery

In This Chapter

➤ Credit card debt—why it's so terrible

➤ Replacing credit card debt with other debt

➤ More from the bully pulpit

➤ Other credit headaches

➤ Surfing the rates

This chapter could be an entire book. In fact, we think it is already an entire book. Credit card debt is the bottomless well we all read about as children in scary stories. Trouble is, no one really warns us, as we approach legal age, that the misuse of credit cards is a very serious problem in our society. So many of us suffer from "spenditus," and credit cards on the surface do not seem harmful. The problem occurs when we spend more than we have available at the end of the month to pay our bills.

Do you make a habit of paying your bill in full each month? Then feel free to skip our upcoming lecture. Or read it and feel smugly superior to those of us who do not pay in full. Skip ahead to the section on securing your credit history and report. But for those of you who do not get to pass go and collect $200, read on!

The Credit Lure

Credit cards lull us into the comfortable feeling that we can buy what we want now and pay for it later (like when we finally get that raise we expect but don't have yet). This situation is very dangerous. Just like the robot says on the '60s television show *Lost in Space*, "Danger, Urgent, Warning, Will Robinson, Warning!" Credit cards can dig a hole so deep for you that you might never climb out.

Best to be mindful of a few ground rules on the best use of credit cards:

First, you should minimize your credit limit to a modest amount, the equivalent of 1 month's salary, for example. This way you can never get in too deep. Setting your own limit is difficult to do. Credit card companies increase your credit limit without even asking you first. You can, however, insist that it be less than they want to provide. Incidentally, in the unlikely event of your card being stolen or lost without your detection, a lower limit also lowers the damage that can be done.

Second, always pay your credit card bills *in full* by the payment date each month. This advice is very easy to give and very hard to take. If you learn nothing else in this guide, paying off your credit cards is a *great* investment.

When Anne is meeting with an investment client for the first time, the question of credit card debt always comes up. And the best advice from us or any financial professional you speak with is

Pay off your credit cards now.

Cash Cautions

Credit card use can be the source of serious conflict in many relationships. According to *USA Today,* 17% of couples disagree on the proper use of credit.

Wealth Words

Credit—An arrangement whereby you can buy something now and pay for it later. What you ultimately pay, however, includes interest for loaning you the money to make the purchase.

The reason this payoff is such a superb investment is that you immediately save lots of money in interest you won't have to pay if you continue to carry those balances.

And the second best piece of advice you can ever get is

Once those cards are paid off, don't rack up charges again!

Oh Yeah Sure, That's Easy...

Let's focus carefully on this enormous task and break it down into smaller hurdles. Most of us constantly fail to live free of credit card debt. Give yourself a break and stop to realize it is not all your fault. It is all your responsibility, but you did not get addicted to credit on your own.

Who Thought These Up, Anyway?

Credit cards swept across the landscape in the early 1960s, quite an ingenious invention at the time. They enable you to carry far less cash than people used to need. Hence that naturally limited the harm that could be done if you were to lose your purse. Think about it. Before credit cards, you essentially had to plan or anticipate all of your spending. In today's world, with overly generous credit lines in our purses, *impulse purchases* are commonplace. You do not have to plan for the acquisition of large-ticket items like a stereo, appliance, or a piece of furniture. The convenience of credit cards seduces people into making the acquisition today, rather than anticipating the need, shopping for the best price, and saving for the purchase.

Wealth Words

Credit limit—The maximum amount that you can charge on a credit card, or the maximum amount that you can owe at any one time.

The Credit Bully Pulpit

We really plan to beat this into you. Here's how it used to work: Before credit cards, people planned for a new washing machine. They would decide on the style and price they could pay. If they did not have this large sum in savings, they would budget for months to save the necessary money. When they accumulated enough money, they would march down to the store, plunk down the cash, and triumphantly return home with this valuable prize in their possession. If an emergency made immediate purchase essential, the money could still be borrowed, usually from the bank, the appliance store, or even a relative. At least you had to *ask* for permission to borrow in that era. The mere exercise of asking made people cautious—made them think and plan carefully.

The innovator of credit cards, Bank of America, changed the entire borrowing and spending process. Basically, the line of credit on your card serves as a chronic reminder that you don't really have to wait to have what you want today. We all sit in a constant state of "pre-approval"—loans that are always available to sink ourselves in debt. The first credit cards, you might recall, we called Bank Americards. Incidentally, an entire industry has grown from this once unique approach to moving money from your account to the store or company's account. Some "banks" nowadays do nothing in banking except issue credit cards.

Your government even helped create our society of credit card junkies. How can this be? For a long period of time, mostly the 1970s and 1980s, the interest you were charged on your cards, or any other loans for that matter, was entirely deductible for income tax purposes. This deduction was phased out in the middle to late 1980s. But did that inspire us to change our credit behavior?

Cash Cautions

Gold and platinum cards have all sorts of perks built into them, but they can also pack a hidden wallop. Gold and platinum cardholders who make late payments or miss payments can get slammed by a hefty interest rate increase *without* being notified. You could end up paying as much as 22.99%! So watch out.

Well, a funny thing happened. Americans did not, we repeat, *did not,* pay off their cards.

You might also have noticed that interest rates dropped significantly, from double digits to 5% and under from the early 1980s through the mid-1990s. Once again, Americans did not, we repeat, *did not,* pay off their credit cards.

But the biggest slap is that credit card companies did not, we repeat, *did not,* lower the interest rates they charged for credit cards.

Recently some issuers are leaving the 20% range and settling into the mid-teens in the rate they charge. When you stop to realize how much the bank makes on your uncontrolled impulse—more than you can make on any investment—you ought to find your blood boiling.

Back to Our Bully Pulpit

Are we making any progress here in persuading you to pay off your credit cards? It is impossible to be specific, but most credit card issuers are making at least 12% on you when you do not pay them immediately. Imagine then, as you walk into the store next time, that the CD player is priced at $150. The price tag has a special footnote for you though. You can buy it now with a credit card and really pay $180 over the next year. This is exactly what you are doing when you purchase the CD player with your already nearly maxed credit card! Some bargain, eh?

This is a great way to make you stop and think before using a credit card for anything. Imagine that the extra line we described really is on the price tag: the selling price of the item and, underneath, the actual cost to you if you buy it with credit and take many months to pay it all off.

Credit card abuse is modern-day bondage. Worse yet, we all accept and condone this problem. We feel helpless to stop it. We are not. Remember the television commercial where the swimming pool was tiled with American Express credit cards. A little super glue, a wooden chopping block, and your credit cards will make a wonderful and unique serving tray. If the cards are not in your wallet, they are not so easy to abuse.

Spoiled Food

So far we've talked about charging big-ticket items like CD players. But what about those small charges that we all rack up regularly at the end of a restaurant meal? Have a nice dinner with friends on a Friday night, charge it, and (if you don't pay your credit card bill in full each month) pay that meal off for *months* to come.

Break the Bonds!

After you have resolved to rid yourself of credit card bondage, it's easy to implement your plan. Take out all of your cards, compare them, and keep one and only one. Anne still uses the card she got when she went away to college (used to have the number memorized, too, but the company finally changed it on her).

This card is like an old friend. Many of you might also have a card like this. The credit limit used to be $500, and now it's $5,000. So keep your old friend, if you choose, and tile the pool with the rest.

When the monthly bills arrive, focus on the biggest payments going toward the highest interest rate cards. Make it a game to pay them off, one by one. Celebrate (inexpensively!) each time you complete payments on a card and ceremoniously cut the card in two and tile the pool.

How Do You Rate?

Now that you are on your road to freedom from credit card bondage, let's investigate your credit rating. Everyone has a credit history: Even people who have never accepted a credit card have a credit history. Various credit agencies might try to sell you an update service that will send you your record annually, plus a notice each time someone makes an inquiry about your credit history. These services range in cost from $25 to $50 per year and are a complete waste of money. Credit agencies are required by law to provide a free copy of your credit report once a year, upon your request.

If you find anything on the report that is incorrect or even suspicious, call the service immediately and inquire about their dispute process. It is crucial to check your report every few years to be certain no mistakes have been made. Do not be surprised if your first Sears charge account still appears on the report. Some credit relationships, though dormant for a decade or more, will still appear on your report.

Do not be alarmed when you add up the column of numbers that totals your credit limits. In many cases, it's tens of thousands that you could charge if you took it all to the maximum. Try not to faint at the total amount in the column that details the outstanding balance! You were prepared for this number, since you already added these balances from your monthly statements.

Finally, try not to grimace when any late payment history is recorded. Ah, you remember now, there was one time right after you graduated from college and had to skip a couple of months of payments on your card. Read about those lapses now and weep.

They not only cost you a stinging $25 late fee, but they blemished your credit rating to boot. Curses.

After you have reviewed your credit history, it is time to go about making any corrections. If you object to any of the records, we urge you to put in the time to appeal and clean up the records. You cannot be too cautious about guarding your good credit standing.

Giving Credit Where Credit Is Due

Anne once knew a man named Jim. In his early 30s, Jim settled down to buy his first home. He was a strictly cash guy who had *never* applied for or accepted credit before he took out his first mortgage. Jim's unblemished history could have been a problem, as banks prefer to see a clean, prompt payment credit history before they embark on a large home loan. In Jim's case, however, the bank approved the mortgage with the following praise: By virtue of the fact Jim had absolutely no credit history, the lenders decided that he must be an excellent credit risk. It is not easy in our society to reach 30 years old and have absolutely no entries on your credit report.

But on the Other Hand

This story brings us to all the problems a poor credit history can cause you. Even when you are not the reason your credit falters, repairing your credit history can be a nightmare.

Credit card fraud is an unfortunate and uncommon occurrence. Should you become a victim, however, you need immediate help and attention. Depending on how clever the credit thief is, the credit card companies cannot always give you a remedy. This is an area where prevention, attention, and detection are imperative.

Your credit report is your clearinghouse authority. The monthly statement you receive is sometimes your first warning signal that something is amiss. The best way to defend against the misuse of your credit card number is to follow a few common sense rules:

➤ Keep a copy of the contents of your wallet in a file at home. Yes, once per year visit a copy machine, take everything out of your wallet, and copy both sides. Also, immediately copy any new cards you receive through the course of the year.

➤ Never give your credit card number to someone who calls you on the phone. If you want to buy the item that person is selling, get his or her name and phone number, hang up, and call back. This should protect you from people who call, sell you something, charge the item to your credit card, and never deliver the merchandise. When you place the call, you avoid possible fraud.

➤ Any callers from charitable organizations should be willing to send you a brochure about their organization before you contribute.

➤ Retain any carbon paper or extra copies of your credit and receipts. Tear any of them in half twice before you dispose of them.

➤ Notify the credit card company the moment your card is lost or stolen. Security numbers are available 24 hours a day and can usually be found on the copy you made of the back of the cards in instruction 1.

If you are the victim of fraud, call the company and plead for help. Unfortunately, many people who seek to default on their bills falsely cry fraud. You need to document in any way possible that your problem is real. You need to enlist the help of the credit card company to resolve the problem.

Surf's Up!

So you've resolved to pay off your debts and do spring cleaning on your credit history. How about learning to lower rates as you pay off your debts? Nowadays it is pretty simple; just get yourself a new card!

So after all these pages of finger wagging, are we now telling you to go out and get *more* credit cards? Yep. You need to start surfing for a better rate.

Here's why—if you're willing to learn to surf to lower interest rates, you can significantly reduce the cost of borrowing. And this tactic, in turn, will significantly decrease the time it takes you to get these cards paid off!

The surf is up in your mailbox everyday. As those low interest rates printed right on the envelope arrive, evaluate how long the offer lasts. A good rule of thumb is to bother only with offers that promise at least 6 months at the low introductory rate.

And here is where you can really save—the application usually invites you to transfer balances as you submit the application. You can also shop for rates with credit card companies that advertise in *Money* and similar financial magazines. Surfing from a 15% card to an 8% card can mean a significant interest rate savings as you pay off your cards.

Wise Women Know

Balance transfers on new cards are great, but the low interest only lasts for 6 months or so. Alas, then it goes back up. Pay attention, though, and you can play the balance-transfer game. By moving your big credit card debt back and forth between new cards with special introductory rates, you can keep paying 5.9% instead of 18% for the foreseeable future!

How Low Can You Go?

You can negotiate with your existing credit card companies as well. All it takes is a phone call. Call the company, prepared to transfer your balance, and ask the representative to negotiate your rate in exchange for keeping your business. What do you mean, negotiate? Don't I owe the money? Yes, but other companies will compete for your business. Let them. This plan works only if you are really prepared to move to a specific other company.

Annual fees are also negotiable. If you decide to leave your current credit card company for another, you can call and ask the old issuer to prorate the annual fee it charged you, usually in advance, to reclaim the portion of the fee for the portion of the year you are not using the card. This project may seem like a lot of work for little reward, but there is no harm in a pleasant request. Push your point and, if the first person denies your request, ask to speak to a customer service manager or quality assurance manager. Always be pleasant and firm. Reinforce your request by asking for an explanation in writing about the annual fee and the criteria for changing your account.

In many people's lives, how you manage your credit is as important as how you manage your assets. Be mindful of how hopelessly in debt you can become if you are not cautious with your credit cards. Consolidate your credit into one good card. Make it your mission to pay off and cut in half all of your others.

Livin' the Good Life

Imagine how good it would feel to actually save money in advance for a wonderful vacation. As you save the money, you research where you want to go and where you will stay when you arrive. You study the life of the people who live there. You learn the history of the people who once lived there! Wouldn't it feel better if, when you arrived home, you did not have a huge credit card bill looming? Think about it!

Surprise—a New Card!

What about these banks that keep sending you cards you did not ask for? Is this legal? Not in the spirit of the law, as it is written in 1998, but in the letter of the law, several very aggressive credit card dealers (not unlike pushers of other addictive substances!) are finding a way to send you a card you did not request.

Here is the deal: The card you get in your mailbox is thinly veiled as a "stored value" phone card. This card looks like a credit card, and it smells like a credit card. When you read the card-member agreement that discloses all the necessary terms and fees, you will see that you can use it like a phone card, or ever so easily convert it to a credit card. The banks that issue such cards plead not guilty with the following excuse: The consumer (that is you) doesn't have to activate the credit card feature.

Whatever name they give it, whatever purpose they use to send it, even though it is sent "inactive," this beast is still a credit card. Worse yet, it is a card you did not ask for, and in all cases, you do not know it is on it's way to you until you receive it. This scenario opens the door to abuse and fraud. What if a ne'er-do-well family member or less-than-trusted roommate intercepts the card and goes on to use it? The issuing banks insist that the 800 number must be called, and the caller must provide details like his or her Social Security number to activate the card. There is still the $50 limit on liability to the consumer if the card is activated under false pretenses, *and* there is the huge nuisance to having your life in turmoil while discovering and correcting the problem.

Not to worry, this method of marketing credit cards is under serious scrutiny and will be prevented at some point in the future. The letter of the law will be rewritten to clarify the spirit of the law, which is to prevent the potential harm to the consumer!

Before We Move On

So, have we nagged you enough about credit card use? Sure, we use 'em, too. But like you, we have made it a serious goal to increase our net worths, and getting credit card debt under control is one giant step in that direction. In the next chapter, we move on to another area in everyday life that can make a tremendous difference in your bottom line—cars.

The Least You Need to Know

➤ Misuse of credit cards can set you back financially for many years.

➤ The best way to handle credit cards is to pay the bill in full at the end of each month.

➤ Easy credit makes for impulsive and frivolous spending.

➤ Keep a careful eye on your credit rating and credit history. Contact the credit-reporting agency to dispute any false or outdated information.

➤ Take advantage of special low interest rate card offers whenever possible, but remember that the low interest rate is short-lived.

➤ Transfer old balances to low interest rate cards to save and pay off the balance sooner.

Welcome to Big Al's Friendly Car Lot!

In This Chapter

➤ Why we drive what we drive

➤ Separate your ego from your car keys

➤ Achieving the old-money look

➤ Today's special—an auto loan!

➤ To decrease, just lease!

So here we are, Chapter 9 in a book on investing...and we have yet to really talk much about investing! Credit, junk mail, net worth—can we just buy some stock here and get it over with? Patience, patience, please. One last chapter on you and your money, and then we will plunge into the investment world. But in the meantime, let's talk about cars.

Cadillac, Mercedes, Lexus, BMW

Cars? We're gonna talk about cars? Yes. Other than buying a house, buying a car is the single biggest investment most of us will ever make. But is it really an investment? No, far from it. As a matter of fact, a car is almost always a depreciating asset. Another, and even more descriptive, way to define it is as an investment with a negative return. Unlike a house, condo, or piece of property that may someday be more valuable than when you bought it, a car begins to lose value the minute you shift into drive and pull out from the dealer's lot. Look closely in your rear view mirror; perhaps you can see your money fluttering in the breeze behind you as you take that first drive....

Make no mistake, the money you spend on your car may well affect how much money you can invest, how soon you can invest it, and how much money you end up with years from now.

Look out the window at the car parked in your driveway. Does it announce that you are a young, up-and-coming executive? a well-heeled society matron? a hardworking single mom with active children? Truthfully, it shouldn't say any of these things about you. In a perfect world, you should be able to understand that the car you drive doesn't say anything at all about who you are—you should be able to separate your public image from your self-esteem.

Wealth Words

Depreciating asset—A possession that loses value with age and use.

All too often we purchase cars with our emotions—we swoon at the sight of a shiny new car and instantly crave the joy of ownership (not to mention the envy of our friends!). And casting all common sense to the winds, we sign up for a large debt that will drain our income month after month after month. Wouldn't it be better to simply acknowledge that a car is really just a handy way to get from point A to point B, and as long as it runs it ought to do the trick? The closer you can come to adopting that kind of an attitude, the sooner you will have more money to invest. Allow us to share a little story to illustrate this point.

"Your Lights Are On"

A few years ago, Jennifer attended a garden club luncheon and sat at a table filled mostly with...well, the polite term is *old money*. Not long into the lunch an announcement was made—there was a car in the parking lot with its lights on. The car wasn't described, only the long license number was given. Most of the table sat calmly, unconcerned by this announcement. One young woman giggled nervously and said, "I wish they would just say what kind of a car it is. I can never remember my license plate, too many numbers and letters." She turned to the old gentleman next to her, "Do you know yours?" she asked. "Of course, my dear," he said, and recited a six-digit number. The other guests at the table joined in—Jennifer included—and recited their simple six-digit plates.

Old Money, Seldom Used

What is our point here? In California, where the luncheon occurred, licenses went to seven digits in 1979. Every last one of those well-heeled folks at the table was driving a car nearly 20 years old! Hmmm...could it be that some old-money families got that way by never buying anything new?

Do rich, successful people always drive new, expensive foreign cars? Movies, television, and magazine ads would certainly have us believe that. But the real story is different, according to the authors of *The Millionaire Next Door*. They discovered that most millionaires drive American-made cars, and few drive this year's car. Also, they buy their cars—only a small fraction ever lease automobiles.

The sooner you move away from the idea that a shiny, brand-new, expensive car will change your life for the better and improve your public image, the sooner you will see how much more quickly your money can grow. Hey, you'll be old money in no time!

Wealth Words

Status symbol—An item that the owner hopes will help him or her project an aura of wealth and success.

I Just Love That New Car Smell!

All right, so maybe we can't quite talk you out of the urge to someday buy a brand-new car. But let's examine how to do it in a way that will cause the least amount of damage to your future wealth. Let's look at a few of the factors that can make a difference here:

➤ Cost of vehicle

➤ Cost and length of loan

➤ Cost to insure

➤ Cost to maintain

Note how all of these four points start with the word *cost*. The car itself, the money you use to buy it, the insurance, and the maintenance it will need to keep it running all *cost*. And before you take the plunge and sign your name on a contract for that shiny new convertible, you need to realistically examine just how much all four of these things are liable to *cost* you over the life of the car.

Zero Percent Financing Available!

On just one day in the fall of 1998, the following interest rates on auto loans were being advertised:

➤ From a major bank—10.11%

➤ From a competing major bank—9.95%

➤ From the credit union for a large high-tech company—7.25%

➤ From a large auto dealer—0.9%

Gee, looks like we should all rush down and buy a new car for 0.9% interest, such a deal! But is it really? When evaluating a car loan you must examine it from all angles. To get 0.9% interest from that dealer, you will have to buy the car at pretty much full

Wealth Words

APR—Annual percentage rate on a loan, includes the total of all of the financing costs such as interest and loan origination costs. A low interest rate charged every month adds up to a higher APR. Use the APR number to compare loan offers.

Wealth Words

Dealer markup—The amount that the car dealer adds over and above the manufacturer's suggested retail price.

markup. The minute you start negotiating for a better deal, that 0.9% is liable to fall by the wayside. If you are in the market for a new car, spend several days acquainting yourself with the different rates—and their special requirements such as car price and length of loan—available in your area. It is time well spent.

Even More Costly

So, you find a loan that you like and a car that you just must have. Is there anything else to consider? One more major bugaboo to come is sales tax. If you buy a $30,000 car in California, for example, the sales tax is a whopping $2,400 more! And that expense is not deductible at the end of the year. With many auto loans, your first-year's payments won't even cover the transaction costs like the sales tax and the new car registration.

Gee, for $2,400, couldn't you get a nice new paint job for the car you already own?

Well, you bought the car. And let's say you'll have to make car payments every month of $350 for the next couple of years. Seems manageable. But is that all your new car will cost you? What about insurance on that brand-new baby? Depending on where you live and what you drive, add another $50 to $100 a month to your car payment figure. And what if that pretty new auto breaks down? The first few things that go wrong will probably be covered by warranty, but soon enough it will be you writing the check out to the repair shop. More money out the window.

Wise Women Know

"Although I work in a bank, I chose to go the dealer financing route. I ended up with a 3-year (36-month) loan at 5.9%," a bank employee confided. "Banks can't bend, but dealers sure can! They started out by offering me 9% but I just kept at them until it was such a good rate I couldn't say no."

Stop and Consider This

Let's say that you decided not to buy a new car, but instead invested that $400 a month for the next 3 years. At the end of 3 years, instead of owning a car that would be worth far less than what you paid for it (a depreciating asset), you would have a nice little nest egg worth approximately $15,500. That's $400 a month for 36 months invested at a fairly reasonable 10% return. If you've chosen an investment that is making better than 10%, the number would be even higher! You decide—which would you prefer: a 3-year-old car that you've grown tired of or $15,500? And don't overlook the fact that the car will just get older, but the nest egg will continue to grow. Better think about it again; do you really need to buy a new car?

Leasing Your Image

Can you skip any of this cost by leasing a car instead of buying it? Allow us to speak harshly here—leasing a car (particularly a big, flashy, expensive car) is hardly ever the right thing to do. It looks so good—for only a small up-front deposit and the promise of monthly payments, you can drive out of the lot with a car much more expensive than you can really afford to own. On the other hand, you *don't* own it. The car isn't really yours (but make no mistake, you are very much responsible for it!), and unlike loan payments, lease payments never stop.

If you buy a car, eventually the loan is paid off and the car is yours—free and clear. And then you can do what you want with the car. If you someday need to raise quick cash, you can sell it. Or if you want to achieve that old-money-I-don't care-what-folks-think air about you, you can drive it for the next 20 years, paying only for gas, insurance, and repairs.

Is It Big Enough to Live In?

But if you lease a car, you pay lease payment after lease payment and never build any equity. And if you really get attached to the car, at the end of the lease contract the dealer will offer to sell it to you—sell you the car you've been driving and paying for for years!

Leasing contracts, once signed, can also be pretty tough to get out of. If you lose your job, if you give birth to twins and suddenly need a van instead of a sports car, or if you decide to cut back and not spend so much of your income on a car—too bad. "When I hear that someone is planning to lease a car I always give the same advice," says consumer advocate Kit Dillon Givas. "You might as well make sure that it is big enough to live in if you lose your job!"

Cash Cautions

"Is the car big enough to live in if you someday need to?" consumer advocate Kit Dillon Givas asks those who intend to lease a big fancy car. Because leases are very hard to get out of, even if you lose your job and suddenly have no income, you will still have to pay the lease every month. So there goes the house—get comfortable inside your car!

Have we scared you away from leasing yet? Well now, just hold on, because sometimes it really does make better sense to lease. When? When you are looking for business tax breaks. Check this out with your tax advisor to make sure it applies to you, but because of tax-law quirks, lessees can write off more of the cost of the car they use for business than owners can.

The Smart Woman's Choice

You might have guessed by now that we don't really approve of anyone spending tons of cash on a brand-new car. Some years ago, the Honda Motor Company had a great advertising slogan: Show Your Wisdom, Not Your Wealth. And we strongly agree; the car you drive should show your wisdom—that you are more interested in growing your money than in tossing it away on a public statement of some sort. But does that mean that you are forever doomed to drive around in shabby, old beaters that belch smoke at stoplights? Of course not; we have a much better idea. Buy yourself a used car.

Used car—sounds sort of sleazy, doesn't it? The latest marketing term is *pre-owned*. And pre-owned cars can be terrific deals and terrific fun to drive. Here's why—as we mentioned a few pages ago, the minute you put a new car in gear and pull out of the dealer's lot, that car is no longer worth anything near what you just paid for it. So why not let someone else take that big hit to the value of a car, and then you can come along and buy it? Check out the cars that sit in the used section of a dealer's lot. You'll see row after row of practically brand-new cars that have been traded in for even newer cars. These cars are only 1 or 2 years old and still have that great-looking new car look and feel to them. They might also come with a warranty of sorts from the dealer. But what they don't have is that big, new-car sticker price!

Great used cars aren't just on dealer's car lots; large rental car companies or large corporations that have fleet cars are also sources of well-maintained late-model used cars. The classified ads are also full of cars for sale privately. If you decide to go this route, take the added precaution of having the mechanic of your choice (not the seller's choice) check out the car.

Let's get back to the concept of depreciating assets or investments with negative returns. If you buy a fairly new used car, the original owner is the one who took the major hit in depreciation. The price you pay should accurately reflect the current value of the used car. And depending on the type of car, the value will drop pretty slowly. You will pay a fair price for a car that still has some significant value as an asset. And the asset should depreciate much more slowly from then on. If you decide to sell in a few years (and if the car has been well kept and is still in good working condition), you will be able to sell it for just a few thousand dollars less than what you paid for it. What a great way to show your wisdom instead of your wealth!

Practicing What I Preach

Jennifer enjoys the looks she gets when she drives down the road in her gleaming green Mercedes 280 SEL. A Mercedes? Sounds like she spent too much money on her car! No, it is a 25-year-old classic sedan. And despite the fact that it looks like a million bucks, it cost only $5,700. (Surprise, she paid cash!) To insure it, she pays just a few hundred dollars a year for a low-mileage policy.

The result is an inexpensive way for her to imagine that she is being trailed by photographers from *Town & Country* magazine. Lots of fun, little money.

Call 'Em Up and Have 'Em Haul It Away!

But what if your car is such an old clunker that you will have to replace it with something, new or used? And you don't think a car dealer will give you much value for it as a trade-in on another car. Should you just turn it into a decorative planter in your driveway (no doubt Martha Stewart would!)?

You can donate it to a charitable organization and take a tidy tax write-off, that's what you can do. Many charities are eager to receive cars as donations. If you believe the radio and newspaper ads, every town has two or three charities that are vying for this privilege.

If you don't want to go through the hassle of selling the car yourself through a used car ad, if you think an auto dealer will sneer at it while you try to negotiate a better deal, or if the darn thing won't start when you climb into it and turn the key, call a charity. Someone will come and haul it away for you.

Let's Go Through This Again

Much of what we have said in this chapter seems to steer women away from buying new cars. We really do not mean to condemn you to a life of driving the same crummy old car you had in college, we just want you to stop and think before you plunk money down on a new or used car.

Cash Cautions

"Just because a charity tells you it can give you top value for your write-off doesn't mean that the IRS will go for it, too!" warns consumer advocate Kit Dillon Givas. "An old clunker that you couldn't get $500 for through a classified ad is still only an old clunker to the IRS. Even if the charity gives you a slip of paper saying it was worth $2,000, the IRS won't be fooled."

Cash Cautions

Don't be dazzled by the prospect of a large charitable write-off unless you qualify to itemize your deductions. If you file with a 1040EZ form, you do not itemize. If you file a regular 1040, you *might* itemize. For instance, in 1997 a single person got $4,150 as their standard deduction. Therefore, the car you're giving away would need to be worth at least $4,000 to make the deduction worthwhile.

Investment professionals hear this complaint all the time from hardworking women with decent salaries: "But I don't have an extra few hundred dollars to invest!" Is that because you have obligated yourself financially to a big hunk of shiny metal? Have you lessened your chances to invest and build up a healthy financial reserve simply because you drive a cute new car? Which will aid you more in the years to come—your fond memories of driving a metallic blue BMW or an ever-increasing investment portfolio?

Chances are you do have the money to invest several hundred dollars a month—which adds up to several thousand dollars a year. If you can just postpone buying a new car for a few more years and invest the money that you would spend, you can have a healthy start on your financial future.

So cast a gimlet eye toward what you drive. Learn to think like the old-money folks—who gives a damn what anyone thinks about the car you are driving? Put that cash in the stock market instead so that a few generations from now your family really is old money!

The Least You Need to Know

➤ The more you spend on the car you drive now, the less you will have to invest for the future.

➤ Few real millionaires drive brand new cars.

➤ Car loans vary tremendously; shop around to find the best deal.

➤ Leasing a car is seldom a smart financial move.

➤ Buying a late-model used car can be a terrific deal.

➤ Used cars depreciate much more slowly than brand-new cars.

➤ Charity car donations can be a good idea, but are not always what they seem.

Part 3

Get Rich Like
Bill Gates Did!

Here we go—let's take the big plunge into the world of investing. Get rich like Bill Gates did? Yep, by buying stocks that increase in value. Here you learn just how the stock market works, all about bonds and mutual funds, and even a bit about collectibles! You learn about several different styles of investing so that you can decide which one best suits you and your future financial needs. Take this new knowledge and start creating your own Gates-sized portfolio!

Chapter 10

The World Is Your Rolex Oyster

In This Chapter

➤ Owning a piece of the action

➤ Create wealth with style

➤ Get rich slowly

➤ Bargains in the basement

➤ Many happy returns

➤ Jump in, jump out

Just suppose for a moment that you could travel back in time to 1956. Your next-door neighbor in Omaha, Nebraska, is Warren Buffett. You engage in a friendly chat across your common backyard fence, and he shares a few of his stock market picks with you. Everything Warren does seems to work out, so you call your broker the next morning and buy a portfolio to match. And if you'd done that—you wouldn't need to read this book! You'd be worth somewhere in the neighborhood of $80 million. Ah, but we can dream, can't we?

Yes, Mr. Buffett is clearly in a class of his own. You really shouldn't count on being as successful as the man from Omaha. However, the average stock market investor over the long haul achieved an average annual return of 12.8% since 1950, far exceeding the 6.9% returned by cash investments and 6.2% by bonds.

You've been patient with us so far in this book, reading through page after page of basic financial information. Now at last, we think your finances are in the proper shape to tackle the next big investment hurdle—let's get into the stock market!

Owning a Piece of the Action

What is the stock market, anyway? A gambling casino? A bunch of half-crazed young guys in suits and sneakers running around like an old fast-motion movie shouting and dropping little pieces of paper on the floor? An auction house? A leading indicator of economic things to come? A place where the greatest companies in the world can be bought and sold piecemeal with a single phone call or mouse click? A supermarket where you can pick up the financial staples you need for a secure future?

Wealth Words

Stock market—The method, and the venue, in which shares of stock are traded.

All of these definitions are accurate. But like any other kind of market, there are good things for sale and bad things for sale. There are good ways to shop and bad ways to shop. There are good deals to be had and bad deals to fall prey to. You can shop daily or once a year. Planning usually produces better results. And (just like on other shopping trips) you will occasionally be tempted to make impulse purchases.

Sure, you've heard that the stock market is a gambling casino. Success or failure depends on the whim of people and forces you know nothing about, or on just pure luck. Well, that is true if that is how *you* approach the market. But the choice is yours.

Going to Market

A stock market is nothing more than a place and a system where people congregate (sometimes in person, sometimes electronically) to buy and sell stocks. No, you don't have to travel to Wall Street to buy your 100 shares of IBM. You can do it through a broker; he or she does the traveling, either electronically or through their own folks on the exchange floor.

The most common image of the stock market is the big, open room crowded with suited floor brokers, hundreds of computer monitors, paper scattered everywhere, and someone banging away on a bell signifying the opening or closing of trading on any day. That's the usual news image flashed to us all on big "up" days (when the market is way, way up) and especially on big "down" days (when the market is way, way down). This stock market is the New York Stock Exchange, or NYSE. Founded in the 1790s on the Lower Manhattan street corner where it still resides, the NYSE is still the granddaddy of them all.

Wise Women Know

The roots of the New York Stock Exchange lie in...a tree. An apple tree at the corner of Wall and Broad Streets marked the spot where colonial stock traders would meet.

But close behind in size and actually exceeding the NYSE in both issues (companies) traded and occasionally daily trading volume (number of stocks bought and sold) is the NASDAQ. The NASDAQ (which stands for National Association of Securities Dealers Automated Quotations) exchange actually has no trading floor at all—no building! It has none of the colorful and noisy features we associate with the NYSE. The NASDAQ is a virtual market. It is a network of individual securities dealers (brokers) who buy and sell shares from their own facilities, dealing through phone and computer network connections. It is the "over the counter" market, that term going back to early days when you literally walked up to a counter, put down your money, and walked away owning shares. Many companies start out on the NASDAQ and move to the NYSE as they grow and mature, although lately that switch occurs less often than it did in the past (Microsoft, now the #1 company in total market capitalization, trades on the NASDAQ). The NASDAQ touts itself as the "stock market for the next hundred years" and is particularly heavy in leading-edge technology stocks.

The United States also has other smaller but important stock markets. The American Stock Exchange (AMEX), physically located across the street from the NYSE and hence sometimes whimsically referred to as the "annex," has many stocks of smaller U.S. companies. Recently the AMEX has been working on an agreement to merge with the NASDAQ. The AMEX also has an equity options exchange...but more on that later.

There are also regional exchanges: Philadelphia, Pacific, and Midwest to name a few. Communications technology has reduced the importance of these exchanges, and you won't need to worry about them in your everyday investing life.

The Global Marketplace

Finally, and not to be overlooked in today's global marketplace, are the many stock exchanges located around the world. Today virtually every major country has a stock exchange, even those who just until recently defied capitalism altogether. It's doubtful

Wealth Words

ADRs—American Depository Receipts are a method by which American investors can buy shares in foreign companies.

that you will ever trade stocks on these exchanges but foreign markets can have a major effect on those here at home (witness the spread of the Asian flu starting in summer 1997). You can, through a device known as American Depository Receipts, or ADRs, buy and sell entrusted shares of foreign companies. So if you really want to own Singapore Airlines, Mitsubishi, or Volkswagen, you may do so without running up your international long-distance phone bill or worrying about your lousy foreign language skills or how to convert your savings to German Marks.

Taking Stock

So, what is "stock"? *Stock* is the collective body of ownership capital, or "equity," in a corporation. In real terms, a *share* of a company's stock is a share of ownership in that company. If you own 1 share of a company that has a total of 100 shares *outstanding* (in existence) then you own 1/100, or 1%, of that company. In the strictest financial sense, you own 1% of that company's assets, less, or net of, its liabilities. In other words, you own 1% of that company's net worth.

The numbers in the real world are larger. Most major companies have between 10 million and 1 billion shares outstanding; some like Microsoft and Coca-Cola have more than 2 billion shares. So where does just owning a few shares get you?

Does Owning Part of a Company Mean You're the Boss?

In a sense, yes. Along with owning a piece of the corporate pie, stock ownership usually also entitles you to vote for corporate directors and on certain corporate issues. You get one vote per share owned.

What Do You Get From Owning a Share of Stock?

As you own a "share" of the company's net assets, you also own a share of the company's income, or profits, or *earnings*. Does your ownership stake show up in your mailbox? Sometimes yes; sometimes no. If a company decides to pay it to you in the form of a *dividend,* yes, you do get a check—sometimes for an amount equal to, or even exceeding, the amount of the company's income in a given time period. Most of the time, however, the company decides that it is in your best interest not to send you a cash payout, but rather to reinvest the earnings in the business, to add to what are known as *retained earnings*. A company that retains its earnings, rather than paying them out, is saying that it can invest the money more productively than you can. (If you don't agree, it is time to sell that stock!) Increasingly, companies, especially in high-growth fields, are retaining earnings in the business. If you want to find a check in your mailbox, check out utility stocks, which frequently pay out some or all of their earnings.

What Is a Stock Worth?

The *theoretical* value of a share of stock is today's financial value of all future cash flows from the company. These future cash flows can be in the form of cash dividends but more esoterically (and over a much longer period of time) are dictated more by the future breakup value or takeover value of the company. These values are in turn dictated by the future earnings growth and retained earnings of the company.

So much for theory. You knew this book wasn't intended for classroom use in an MBA program. What is a stock worth? Simply what someone will pay for it. Supply and demand, it's that simple. Millions of investors have their own idea of what a stock is worth. In theory, a stock price means that half of the investing public think it will go down from there and half think it will go up.

Wealth Words

Dividend—A share of the company profits paid out to the company's shareholders.

Wise Women Know

The stern-voiced radio announcer tells you where the Dow Jones Industrial Average closed today. Sometimes it is way up, sometimes way down. Some days it hardly moves at all. And what exactly is the Dow? Does it affect your own personal portfolio? The Dow reflects the closing price of 30 large companies only. Stocks you own may not have moved at all that day, or they may have moved in an entirely different direction.

So, How Does the Price Get Set?

If everybody agreed on the future value of a company, what it is worth, and this information could be readily reflected in the stock price, we wouldn't need markets as such. Shares of stock would be bought and sold as in a store, with some marketing guy or computer program calculating prices and a stock clerk updating the shelves. But because no one agrees on a company's value, we essentially put it up for grabs. That's where the stock *market* comes into play.

Simply stated, the stock market is a collection of actions from buyers and sellers that all work together to set a price. The goal is to complete transactions, to find buyers for shares that are for sale and to find sellers for shares that buyers want to buy.

The collective buying and selling activity sets the price. If more people want to sell than buy, the price goes down. If more want to buy than sell, it goes up. It's like an auction.

Who Are You Buying From?

Your Aunt Martha left you 13 shares of General Gymshoe, and now you want to sell. Now do you (or your broker) have to go to the market to find someone else like you with exactly the opposite interest, that is, to buy 13 shares? Not 10, not 15, but 13? You might wait a long time if you had no help. Fortunately, brokers handle most exchange trades. Brokers carry inventory and, in this case, would just add your 13 shares to inventory to eventually combine with others to sell.

How Does It Really Work?

Floor exchanges, such as the NYSE, have "specialists" who make a market in a particular stock. A *specialist* is an auctioneer of sorts. Virtual exchanges like NASDAQ do the same but at an unseen trading desk (but NASDAQ may change as lawmakers investigate the process).

The trading specialist keeps a very real-time order book of buy and sell orders as well as up-to-the-minute information on news events and especially news events affecting the company being traded. The trading specialist moves the price to match as many buy and sell orders as possible.

The Movers and the Shakers

Obviously, the larger the share order, the more influence it has on the price. That's why you, as an individual investor, won't have much impact on a stock's price. The big financial institutions, which move 10,000; 100,000; and even millions of shares at a time, are largely responsible for price movements. You're just along for the ride.

How Many Shares Should I Buy?

Once you've decided which company you want to "own," that is, own a piece of, you need to decide how many shares to buy. There is no precise rule to determine this, but a few principles apply.

Round lots and odd lots

A *round lot* is simply a multiple of 100 shares, a convenient trading multiple for all parties involved. Shares grouped in multiples of 100 are also called *blocks*. An *odd lot* is something other than 100 shares. Your 13 shares of General Gymshoe is an odd lot. Nothing wrong with that, but the specialist on the trading floor, already busy enough with round lots, will send your odd-lot order back to a special trading floor, sometimes known as the "garage," where odd lots are traded and often grouped into round lots by inventory accumulation. Still, you may freely buy or sell odd lots. There is a minor penalty: Odd-lot trades are assessed a charge equal to one-eighth of a point, or 12.5 cents, per share. Brokerage commission rates might be slightly higher, especially on a per share basis.

Diversification

Entire books have been written on this topic, but sufficient for now is the advice that you shouldn't put all your eggs in one basket; in other words, don't invest entirely in one or two companies. The common school of thought is that you should invest no more than 5% of your portfolio in a single company. Of course, diversification is impractical if you are investing only $5,000—each of your investments would be only $250! This plan is impractical from two viewpoints: (1) too much spent on transaction costs (commissions) and (2) time spent to research and follow all 20 companies would outweigh the benefit. The 5% rule is broken all the time, particularly by employees engaged in company stock and 401(k) plans, but it is good to keep in mind.

Okay, So How Big a "Nest Egg" to Start?

To buy individual stocks, it probably makes sense for you to have at least $1,000 to invest, and better yet $2,000; $3,000; or $5,000. You achieve "economies of scale" by buying round lots, and the time you spend researching and following a company becomes more worthwhile. For small investments, mutual funds may make more financial sense. Keep in mind, though, you won't learn as much about the market by buying mutual funds!

Being the Boss of Your Portfolio

Some investors buy a stock on a rumor and then sock it away, sometimes never to be found until heirs uncover a dusty stock certificate in a shoebox. Although we do advocate long-term investing, we don't advise the buy-it-and-forget-about-it approach. Remember, you own this piece of the company, and you should manage it!

Cash Cautions

When Jennifer's husband was in seventh grade, he made his first investment. He invested his birthday check into five shares of an $8 stock. With a $29 minimum commission, this may have not been a wise move, but it got him started, and it was fun to watch the paper every morning, receive annual reports, vote for directors, and so on. But the stock would have had to more than double for him to make any money!

How to Manage "Your" Company

The traditional way to "keep up" has been to read the paper each morning to watch price movements. Most newspapers also include yearly highs and lows and key data such as "price-earnings" ratios. As a shareholder you will also receive company-produced annual reports and quarterly statements. These reports are required by law and are often used as a marketing tool to current and prospective investors.

Although this approach is still recommended, technology now provides new ways to keep up almost to the minute and access an ever-widening plethora of electronic investment information. The amazing thing is that it is almost all free! Just to characterize some of what's available:

Real-time quotes

Internet search engines such as Yahoo! and America Online, as well as the expanding group of electronic stock brokers, offer up-to-the-minute (actually, sometimes 15- to 20-minute delayed) quotes during the trading day.

News services

The same sites also collect newswire stories from hundreds of sources, index them by the companies involved, and make them available to you at a simple click of your mouse.

Market analysis

Several investment industry experts have started news and commentary services, again all accessible through Internet gateways. Some of these, such as The Motley Fool, are free (these services actually charge the Internet gateway, which in turn collects advertising revenue). Others, such as TheStreet.com, may charge subscribers small fees. What you get is up-to-the-minute information and "inside scoops" from people close to the trading action.

Chat rooms

Again, the Internet gateways provide a unique opportunity for you access information, this time the opinions of individual investors like yourself. Although the quality of chat-room information may understandably vary, you get interesting insight, sometimes even from employees (not from executives, though, and not proprietary information—that's illegal) of the companies you follow.

In Chapter 16, "Info World," we discuss online financial information in greater detail. An astounding amount of information is available, but some sites are more valuable than others.

A Game Plan for Creating Wealth

Now that you've learned some of the rules of the game, it's time to venture forth and play a hand or two. But like any game involving anything other than pure chance, you need to think a little bit about strategy.

Don't worry, your investment strategy doesn't have to be a 10-page detailed business plan that you deliver to your broker before the execution of your first trade. Rather, a better word for "strategy" is *style*. We recommend that you understand the different investment styles and choose one that best fits you. Some styles are complementary and may work together; others clearly wouldn't make sense to use simultaneously.

Style 1: Get Rich Slowly

This maxim is pervasive in the industry and should normally be pervasive in your investment style. After all, your objective is to get rich, and (hopefully) you've planned far enough ahead that you don't have to do it immediately. Good thing, because getting rich quick, while appealing, is not likely to happen to most of us. The investment world is chaotic, subject to zillions of events beyond anyone's control. No one can figure out just how the investment planets will align on a given day. History has proven that the vast majority of successful investors invest for the long term and ignore short-term perturbations of the market and all of its influencers. Remember how well that guy from Omaha, Warren Buffett, has done by holding long term?

Witness those who sold in the "crash" of October, 1987. The market as measured by most indicators lost 25% of its value in one day. Many sold that day or in the aftermath. Yet those who hung on recouped most of their money during the next 9 months and went on to quadruple it in the next 10 years. Woe unto those who bailed!

Likewise, those who chased the Internet stock boomlet of June/July 1998 may have made some short-term profits, but many, and probably most others took a hit as some of these stocks slid 50% or more in August. True, there was, and still is, money to be made. But is this wild ride for you?

Chances are, probably not. You want to sleep at night and go about your daily chores without worrying about your losses and muttering "if I only had…" in front of your family, neighbors, and coworkers.

Indeed, studies have shown that patience in investing is a virtue, translating to returns that average at least 20% higher for buy-and-hold investors over the long run compared to those who

Cash Cautions

Recent research reveals that frequent traders don't do nearly as well in the long run as folks who buy and then leave their portfolios alone. UC Davis professors Terrance Odean and Brad M. Barber found in a study of 60,000 investors that, during the period studied, active traders made returns of only 10%, whereas in the same time period, buy-and-hold folks made an average of 15.3%. Quite a big difference!

"churn" their portfolios. "Buy and hold" has proven to be a winning investment style, a good, disciplined investment strategy.

However, you still have to manage your investment and your company. Things change. "Buy and hold" was a poor strategy for Penn Central (a large rail company) shareholders, who watched their investments sink into oblivion as the world changed and their company only changed for the worse. You have to stay on top of these things.

Style 2: Bargains in the Basement

This style gets to the *bottom-line* true value of a company, compares it to market (share) value, and if the shares look like a bargain, *voilà!* Sometimes called "asset play" or "balance sheet" investing, stocks with enormous asset bases can often come cheap if asset values are ignored or investor focus shifts to more glamorous pursuits. Witness the Internet stocks. Look at oil companies and other asset-rich companies. If the *price-to-book ratio* is favorable (usually 1.0 or less), you may have a bargain.

Wealth Words

Goodwill—Intangible company assets like brand name recognition, intellectual property, market leadership, or company reputation.

What is the *price-to-book ratio*? Simply the ratio of the stock's price to its net asset value (total assets less liabilities) divided by the number of shares outstanding.

Asset-play investing is a very basic form of investing that works, especially over time. Of course you need to pay attention to other factors—if the company is losing money despite its asset base, that is a warning sign. Likewise, if the value of the assets is declining (gold, for example, or if the assets are out-of-date factories or computers), that also is a warning sign. Also, if the company has been caught playing accounting games in the past or has booked a high level of intangible assets (such as goodwill), watch out.

Style 3: Many Happy Returns

At the core in a capitalistic society, the value of a company is its ability to generate income, or profit. As an investor, you want to find the companies that generate the most profit, or more importantly, have the potential to generate the most profit *in the future*.

The central indicator of profitability is *earnings per share*—total profits after taxes divided by the number of shares outstanding. Although earnings per share is meaningful, especially in comparison to earlier performance and to expectations, alone it doesn't tell you whether the stock is a good buy. So another ratio is born: the price-earnings, or P/E, ratio.

P/E is the ratio of a stock's price to the earnings per share. A stock selling for $50 and earning $2.50 per share in the previous 12 months has a P/E of 20. Is this good? At the risk of beating an old theme to death, it depends. At a very basic level, a P/E of 20 indicates a return on investment of 5%. An investment in this company would return 5% in a year, which is about the same as many risk-free investments at your corner bank. So why invest in a company with a P/E of 20?

A lot depends on growth. If the P/E is 20 but earnings are growing at 30% per year, looking at the long term, the company might be a good investment. That is, if earnings grow at 30% next year, from $2.50 per share to $3.25, and the P/E stays constant at 20, your stock will someday sell at $65. So your return is not only the nominal 5% earnings basis, it now includes a 30% price appreciation! A good investment, most likely.

Our Favorite Ratio Stations

So now, another ratio, new on the scene but being used increasingly: price-earnings/growth, or PE/G. *PE/G* is simply the price-earnings ratio divided by the earnings percent growth rate. So in the previous example, a P/E of 20 divided by a growth rate of 30 gives you a number less than 1. A PE/G less than 1 is generally considered to be a good investment prospect. Watch out when PE/G exceeds 1 and especially gets into the 2 or 3 range.

P/E is a good indicator and is actually listed in most daily newspaper stock listings. PE/G is better, but you have to do a little homework to find it. Both provide insight to a stock's value but need to be considered among many other investment factors.

Strict adherence to P/E and, especially, to PE/G as value indicators has been a successful investing style over time. One problem is that with ever greater access to real-time information, when a stock surfaces with a favorable PE/G indication, the rest of the world knows about it instantaneously, will bid up the price by buying the stock, and it will no longer appear attractive on PE/G basis! So you have to stay on top of trends, keep up the research, be prepared to act quickly, and be able to predict changes (upcoming new products and so forth) that will make PE/G look more attractive in the future.

So far, you've learned two pretty conservative ways to pick stocks, P/E and PE/G. We will now move on to the, shall we say, less conservative?

The Trend Is Your Friend

The previous three styles are "fundamentals" investing—placing the fundamental value of the company at the center of the investment evaluation. But some investors may choose to look at "technical" investing, investing based on trends and the "big mo," momentum. Put simply, momentum investors buy (or sell) what everyone else is buying or selling. These people think stock prices are based strictly on human behavior and that stock price direction becomes a self-fulfilling prophecy.

This approach to investing can be fabulously successful, but when it's over it's over. A trend reversal can more than erase any gains and *very* quickly. Still, if practiced carefully with discipline and unmitigated watching of the radar screen, it can work.

One key momentum investing indicator is the position of a stock's price vis-à-vis its recent history. *Recent history* is quantified as a "moving average," or average of the last *x* days of a stock's trading history. Most momentum investors use either a 50- or, even better, 200-day moving average. If a stock is languishing at or below its 200-day moving average and suddenly "breaks out," moving above this line, it may be ready for a longer run. Similarly, a stock moving above the 200-day average and suddenly falling below is a good candidate to sell.

Of course, market trends external to your stock's chart will influence prices and position relative to averages. But trend investing is still a valid and often successful investing style.

Even if it isn't *your* style, a quick look at trends might help you decide whether the time is right to buy a stock you've picked based on other criteria. Please also remember that this style requires that you understand a lot about the market in general and also that you have a great deal of information about the price behavior of the particular stocks you have selected.

Jumping In and Out

Often a part of trend-is-your-friend investing is the notion of day trading, or "jumping in and out." Day traders look at microtrends that occur within a day, or even within a few hours, and buy and sell (sometimes several times) during that period, reaping whatever short-term fruits are available. The information age, and especially online trading with its fast action and reduced commission costs, have made day trading possible.

Although it is important to act quickly and be able to carry out your decisions as soon as possible, history has shown that day traders are generally not as successful as patient long-term investors.

The Least You Need to Know

➤ It is possible for the individual investor to build real wealth over time in the stock market.

➤ Studies show that long–term investors make greater returns than investors who trade frequently.

➤ Buying shares in a company allows you to profit from that company's future growth and earnings.

➤ Stocks are really worth only as much as someone else will pay for them.

➤ Choose an investment style that matches your personality and your financial goals.

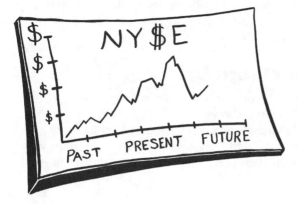

More on the Market

You've learned that there are several different investment styles, from the get-rich-slowly approach to the more frantic day-trading system. Here we introduce a few more types of conservative investing and quite a few more types of, shall we say, non-conservative investing.

Like the Product? Buy It!

Buy the company stock, that is. One of the best-known stock-picking styles to emerge in the last decade is the "buy what you know" philosophy attributed to former Fidelity Magellan Fund chief, Peter Lynch. The basic idea here is that if you pay attention to what is happening in your own neighborhood—gee, look at all of those people shopping at Home Depot and, hmmm, hardly a day goes by that you don't see someone with a Starbucks cup in hand—you can spot a growing company as easily as any Wall Street analyst can.

In a recent *Money* magazine article, however, Lynch now says that the media oversimplified his theory. "You can't buy a stock simply because you see a lot of people buying a product. It's a starting point." But it's a good starting point—a starting point for further research and investigation, Lynch means.

Put Your Money Where Your Mouth Is!

It may well be that your best stock finds will come this way. Look around your house—what do you own and how do you feel about it? Do you believe your Chrysler car is unbeatable? Then check out the stock. Addicted to that afternoon chocolate snack? Hershey's has been steadily paying dividends to its investors since 1929. Perhaps you should put your money where your mouth is and go in search of chocolate chip stocks instead of blue chip stocks!

Time After Time

So you can't put a big chunk of cash into the market tomorrow morning? Not to worry. It might be a good thing. Many investors choose to invest a fixed amount every month as a habit. This program has the obvious benefit of being a good long-term savings plan. But it doesn't stop there.

Suppose you have the big chunk and you pick the right stock to launch your investment program. You buy it tomorrow morning. But did you buy it at the right price? What if it falls the day after? What if you bought on October 15, 1987?

By investing a fixed amount every month (and sticking to it through market ups and downs), you throw the vulnerability to short-term price fluctuations right out the window. If you are investing a fixed amount every month, sure, your monthly investment made tomorrow morning would lose in a market fall the next day. But you have an equal amount ready to be invested the next month, right? That investment would be made at the more favorable price, assuming no recovery before then. You would own more shares and be in position for greater profits once growth resumes.

This approach is known as *dollar-cost averaging*. The concept is simple: Keep investing consistently over a period of time. The ups and downs will cancel, and you will reap the benefits of long-term growth. You will sometimes pay high prices and sometimes pay lower prices. When you pay low prices, you buy more shares, so over the long run, the weighted average cost of your portfolio is lower, as long as the market goes up over the years. Dollar-cost averaging is a good sleep-at-night style, especially if you have a life and aren't inclined to keep track of the daily pulses of your company and the market.

Most dollar-cost averaging is done through mutual funds, sometimes even with automatic payroll deductions. You can also have some or all dividends paid by the company reinvested in its shares. Thus the dividends are actually paid to you in shares. Companies that do this are companies that have "Dividend Reinvestment Plans" or DRIPs. DRIPs are a good way to accumulate wealth over a long period, especially with stocks that pay out significant portions of earnings as dividends. But in recent years, dividend payouts have declined and tax treatment of dividends has become less favorable, so this isn't as useful a style as it once was. Nevertheless, it has merit for the long-term investor.

Optional Direct Purchase Plans

Optional direct purchase plans are often offered in conjunction with DRIPS. Under this program, companies allow you, usually four times a year in synch with dividend payments, to kick in an additional cash sum to be invested in shares at the quarter's closing price. Optional direct purchase plans have all the benefits of dollar-cost averaging and long-term saving, plus you avoid brokerage commissions.

Here's an example: Southern Company, a very large U.S. electric utility holding company traded on the NYSE, allows you to reinvest dividends through the DRIP program and also allows you to make quarterly investments, minimum $50 and maximum $6,000 per quarter.

Of course, every share you purchase is yours and is eligible for future dividends. So direct purchase combined with DRIPs can be a powerful, even though passive, long-term wealth-accumulation tool, especially if the stock continues to rise.

Sounds like a great (and pretty easy) way to invest doesn't it? But how can you find out which companies offer this program to individual investors? There are so many books that we can't list them here.

You can also subscribe to a newsletter called *The Moneypaper*. Run by Vita Nelson, *The Moneypaper* not only keeps you up-to-date on which companies offer DRIPs but also can help you get started buying the shares. For more information, call 1-800-388-9993.

Now it is time to move on to somewhat more sophisticated investing methods: using a margin account, buying and selling options, and some of the futures markets.

Investing at the Margin

Like so many other things in life, you can get yourself in hock by investing. Believe it or not, stockbrokers are willing to lend you money to invest! This is done through a "margin account," an account that is set up for you to make investments partly with borrowed funds.

Unlike credit cards, the rules are strict. You must put up some of your own money, usually $10,000 to $25,000 to get started. Then you can borrow money up to the point where 50% of your portfolio worth is financed by borrowings (in other words, you can borrow another $10,000 to go with the $10,000 you commit in cash). This borrowing is done at fairly favorable interest rates, closer to secured (like mortgage) borrowing rates than the usually outrageous unsecured credit card rates. Each brokerage has its own rate.

Wealth Words

Margin call—A call for more funds in a margin account because the value of the stock in the account has fallen below the minimum required.

But margin investing has its dangers. The 50% rule mentioned above is absolute, and any decline in portfolio value is taken out of your cash position, not the broker's loan position. So if you have the previously mentioned $20,000 portfolio and suddenly your stocks decline 10% to be worth $18,000, your phone will ring and your broker will demand $2,000 to make your account right. This is the feared "margin call." If you don't put up the $2,000 in a day or two, your account will be liquidated, the brokerage will take its $10,000, and you will be stuck with the $2,000 loss on your $10,000 investment, or a 20% loss.

Whoa, What Happened Here?

How did you lose 20% while the stock lost only 10%? This phenomenon is called "leverage." When you borrow, gains and losses alike on your initial investment are magnified. The opportunity for greater gains is, in fact, why you might want to invest on margin—if you have both the stomach and the cash for it. You can greatly increase your gain. However, where there is reward, there is risk.

If you have a high tolerance for risk and have other cash assets that can be put in play in an emergency (to avoid liquidations and the resulting lock-in of loss), margin investing may be for you.

Wise Women Know

Jennifer once wrote a check on her Schwab One account and was astonished to receive a notice that it bounced! She called Charles Schwab and demanded an explanation. "You've sold a call for 100 shares of Amazon.com at 65, and our policy is that you must keep $25,000 in your account if you are writing calls." All the money in her account was frozen until the option contract expired. If you have an account where you also write checks, make sure this doesn't happen to you.

Are You Exercising Your Options?

Also not for everyone, but certainly a fun ride and one way to make the most of your investing, is the use of equity options.

Now, you have no doubt noticed that this book has two authors—Anne and Jennifer—and on this topic the two authors disagree. Anne, the stockbroker, simply doesn't approve of novice investors getting mixed up with options. And Jennifer, the financial writer, enjoys mucking about in the options market. So, while we are giving you this information, Anne really hopes you won't use it....

An *option* is simply a contract to buy or sell shares at a given price at or before a given time in the future. Options are traded on several exchanges in a manner very similar to the equity shares they represent. In the *Wall Street Journal* or similar investment-oriented publications, you will see options listings for the Chicago Board Options Exchange, American, Philadelphia, and Pacific stock exchanges.

How Equity Options Work

Equity options, as stated earlier, are contracts to transfer shares, buy or sell, at a given price at or before a given time in the future. These contracts are sold in lots of 100 shares, so one contract represents 100 shares. (No odd lots in option trading!)

A *call option contract* is an option to buy 100 shares at a fixed price at or before a certain date. So a "General Motors October 50 call" contract is an option to buy 100 shares of GM at $50 between now and the established expiration date (always the third Friday of the month) in October. The $50 is referred to as the strike price.

A *put option* is the right to sell 100 shares at a fixed price at or before a certain date. "General Motors October 40 puts" give the owner the right to sell 100 shares at $40 each at or before the October expiration.

Options Represent a Transfer of Risk for a Price

From the outside, options trading looks to most like pure gambling (which, of course, is one of the reasons why Anne disapproves). Betting "on the come" that GM will exceed 50 by mid-October does seem like rolling dice. Maybe the number comes up, maybe not, and if it doesn't by the third week in October, you lose.

Depending on what side of the trade you are on, options may indeed be a gamble. If GM stock is at 45 and you buy a call at 50, you lose if the stock closes at or below 50. But you may only pay $1 per share for the option. If GM goes to $55, your option is worth $5, a 400% return on your investment in often less than a month! You are taking a great risk in hopes of achieving a great reward.

But suppose you own the stock, and you sell that same option? Whatever happens, you keep that $1 per share. But if the stock goes to $55, you are obliged to sell it at $50.

Cash Cautions

Options trading doesn't make for an easy night's sleep. During the Internet stock madness of 1998, Jennifer spent many a nervous day over her options positions. With one particularly nerve-wracking contract, she chose to close out early at a loss simply because she could no longer take the tension!

That's the risk—you might forfeit high potential returns, but you are getting a certain return of $1, plus the $5 difference between $45 and $50 if the stock sells. In the meantime, if the stock drops to $44, you're still even on the game, because you collected the $1 and you still own the stock.

What you have done is transfer a certain amount of investment risk to the buyer. The buyer is looking for greater leverage and the possibility of a quick 400% gain. You, the seller, are looking to generate a more certain return on your existing investment, opting yourself to forgo the possible rewards above $50.

Puts work the other way. Buying puts is like buying insurance. If you buy $40 puts, you have the right to sell at $40 even if the stock "tanks"—falls to $30. The option is like an insurance premium. Like buying insurance, you're reducing your risk. In contrast, the person who sold the put is making a contract to buy your shares at $40 come what may, thus taking on greater risk and hoping only that the stock closes at or above $40 so that he or she can walk away with your buck.

Advanced Options Strategies

There are lots of options strategies, and we think that for starters you should understand at least two. Selling "covered call options" (contracts against shares that you own at strike prices higher than market) or buying "out-of-the-money puts" (at prices lower than your current holdings) actually reduces your risk. Covered calls have the added benefit of providing short-term income (that buck). It's like writing yourself a small dividend check.

Do straddles, strangles, naked calls, naked puts, bull spreads, bear spreads, or butterfly spreads pique your curiosity? Doubtless. But these option strategies are well beyond the scope of this book (and Anne won't let Jennifer talk about them anyway). Here is a book that can tell you more:

> *Getting Started in Options* (3rd Edition), by Michael C. Thomsett (John Wiley & Sons, 1997).

Pull Out the Crystal Ball

In addition to buying and selling options on individual stocks, you can also place a bet on the entire market! If you think you have a hunch as to where the S&P 500 stock index will end up next month, this is how to make that bet.

How do index options work? Well, this investing style really is pure gambling. Unlike buying and selling options on individual stocks (where at some point you might actually own the stock), with stock index options you are buying a theoretical "basket" of stocks but not the stocks themselves.

These options involve puts and calls, just like the options trading you've already learned about. If you buy a call, you are betting that the stock market index will be going up by a certain percentage. If you sell a put, you are placing your bet on the market going down.

What Else Can You Invest In?

Investment opportunities are plentiful. In the next two chapters, we take a look at investing in bonds and in mutual funds. But as long as we are talking about long-shot investment strategies, let's have a little more fun here.

Not every investment has to be in a stock or a bond. Many people enjoy investing in what are known as collectibles. There seem to be large groups of people nowadays who believe that their Beanie Baby collections will send their kids to college or ensure a comfy retirement. For their sakes, we hope the values and interest hold.

Wise Women Know

Some kinds of antiques and collectibles also have great value as tax deductions. As a young college girl, Jennifer splurged on a Chanel lace dress dating from the 1920s. She paid $250, a huge sum to her back then! She wore it to parties for 15 years, until the curator of the costume collection at the Cincinnati Art Museum caught sight of it. Jennifer had it appraised and then donated it to the museum. Had it increased in value? Goodness yes, that tax deduction was a stunning $3,200. But who could have predicted that back in 1980?

Most investment professionals suggest that folks collect for enjoyment first and investment second. You will know right away whether you enjoy something, but you will seldom know for years whether a collectible will increase in value.

What kinds of things do people collect? Various kinds of art and artists, pottery like Rookwood or Roseville, Arts and Crafts furniture, classic cars, first-edition books, comic books, jewelry, antiques of all kinds, vintage clothing, the list is endless. And the value of many of these items just might increase with time.

But will investing in collectibles ever rival the kinds of returns that you can get for other kinds of investments? Seldom, and it is even more of a gamble. So, collect what you enjoy and keep your real cash invested in other things.

The Least You Need to Know

➤ Some stock-picking experts suggest taking a close look at your life or your neighborhood to spot growing companies to invest in.

➤ Investing a set amount of money in the same stock every month achieves dollar-cost averaging, which is a good way to buy stock over the long term.

➤ DRIPs, or dividend reinvestment plans, allow you to buy a small number of shares and to reinvest the dividends directly in company shares, without a broker.

➤ Direct purchase plans allow you to make larger periodic investments in shares directly from the company, also without a broker.

➤ Once you have a larger investment base, a brokerage house will let you buy more stock on borrowed money.

➤ Buying and selling stock options is another way to generate income from (or protect) your stock portfolio.

➤ Owning collectibles can be fun but is seldom a sure investment with the same rate of return as the stock market. (But it can be fun....)

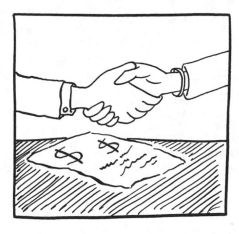

Chapter 12

Never a Borrower, But a Lender Be

In This Chapter

➤ T-bills (not T-bones) and other ways to grow your stake

➤ Where does the money come from?

➤ Become a CD player

➤ Corporate raiders

➤ Who deserves your bond money?

➤ Beware the bond fund

The word *bond* can conjure many images in our minds. There are the immortal words "Bond, James Bond." To hear these words (and to see that face!), we all dutifully make at least a $5 investment at the local movie theater. There is also *bail bond,* which means someone will lend you money, at a very high rate of interest, to make your bail so that you can get out of jail. We hope that you never need to understand this type of bond.

In its purest form, a *bond* is an exchange of money for a promise to repay that principal and interest to the lender in a stated period of time. When you are the lender, you are also the buyer of a bond. Many financial organizations would like to "borrow" from you. Exactly who wants your money?

➤ Banks

The bank where you keep your savings account, certificates of deposit (CDs), or money market fund is borrowing from you. Banks promise to return any or all of your principal on request and pay you interest during the time your money is with them.

➤ The feds

The federal government would like to borrow your money; therefore, it sells U.S. Treasury bonds. Various U.S. government mortgage agencies such as Fannie Mae and Ginnie Mae would also like to borrow from you; hence they will sell you Fannie Mae and Ginnie Mae bonds.

➤ State governments

The state you live in (you can buy any state's bonds, but the interest won't be tax-deductible unless it is your state) would like to borrow your money, so tax-free municipal bonds are available for you to purchase.

➤ Local governments

Even your county, city, water district, school district, and any other entity that provides municipal services to you would like to borrow your money.

➤ Big business

Corporations of various sizes and levels of name recognition want to borrow your money, too. Examples of these borrowers include AT&T, General Electric, and General Motors. When you are a bond owner, you are lending money to the company. As a stockholder, you are an owner of the company. This distinction is important.

With so many choices, how do you find the borrowers who will give you the most for your money? Each borrower puts its own unique qualifications on its bonds. We will explore the relative advantages and disadvantages in this chapter.

T-Bills (Not T-Bones) and Other Ways to Grow Your Stake

The U.S. Treasury issues bonds on a regular basis. It holds an auction, and everyone is invited. The interest rate the Treasury assigns to the bond issue is determined by how much it has to offer to get anyone to go to the auction.

You don't actually get in your car and drive to this event. But you do or don't decide to participate based on the rate the Treasury posts on the bond. If the government needs more money than the bonds can raise, it increases the rate on its bonds to make them more attractive to investors. The variety of maturities is as follows:

➤ T-bills: 13 weeks, 26 weeks, or 52 weeks

➤ T-notes: 1 to 10 years

➤ T-bonds: 5 to 30 years

Wise Women Know

A recent policy change at the Treasury Department has made it easier for the average Jane to buy T–bills and notes. It used to be that the minimum investment for direct purchases was $10,000, but that has dropped to $1,000. However, the new policy applies only to purchases made directly from the treasury through its Treasury Direct program. Soon you'll be able to buy over the Internet, too. Check out the site at www.publicdept.treas.gov for more information.

The Treasury has never repaid a bond early and never will. A few other little-known truths about treasuries: They are the most widely traded bonds in the world. Many people from other countries buy our treasuries. Purchasers often do not own their bonds for the entire period, but instead sell them in a secondary market before they mature. Someone else owns them for a little while or until they mature.

Most of us would methodically buy treasuries with the plan to hold to maturity. But more investors than you can imagine buy and sell large amounts of treasuries every day. The Treasury bond is regarded as one of the safest investments in the world, based on the popular belief that the "full faith and credit" of the United States government will repay the bond.

And Where Does This Money Come From?

"We the people," of course, and the taxes we pay generate the money to repay these bonds. If you add up all the treasury bills, notes, and bonds, you have a number that represents the national debt. The *national debt,* therefore, is the money your government borrowed and then spent. Imagine balancing the government's budget they way you balance your checkbook. Our presidents and congress have been spending more money than they've collected in taxes for more than 25 years. Meanwhile, they have borrowed more in the past 25 years than any of us can ever hope to see repaid.

This amount of borrowing means that we should all care more about the national debt and encourage our government to stop spending money it doesn't collect from taxes. By the way, occasionally you hear the mention of a budget surplus. In this context, *surplus* means that the government expects to collect more taxes than it plans to spend. Do you ever hear officials say they will apply the surplus toward the national debt? Just as we are emphatic that you get a hold of your finances and pay off those credit cards, we are emphatic that your government should pay down its debts whenever possible.

Become a CD Player

On a happier note, let's move into music to your ears—the certificate of deposit. Commonly known as a CD, this financial product is your bank's way of borrowing money from you. Banks want you to lend your money to them for a stated period of time, usually 1 month to 10 years. The bank will let you break your CD early, before the stated maturity, but will charge you a 6-month interest penalty to do so.

When banks are bought, sold, or "reorganized" as many were in the 1980s, they sometimes break the CD early, too. You usually do not lose any principal, but the banks do not pay you an extra 6 months' interest!

Where does this money go? The bank takes the money it borrowed from you and lends the funds out to others—of course, at a higher rate than it paid you. The difference is usually at least 2% or 3% and frequently more. This differential enables the bank to make a profit.

Over the years, Anne has had many investment clients who truly believed that their money was in the vault at their friendly corner bank branch and that they could visit their savings at any time. Not true! Sure, some of your money is "in the bank," but just enough to keep bank robbers interested. Most of what you have deposited in the bank has been loaned to other people.

Is this a potential problem? Not to worry, the federal government supports insurance corporations that insure you against the loss of your money in the bank, up to $100,000. Even if that other person the bank loaned to did not repay the bank, the bank would still pay you. The Federal Deposit Insurance Corporation (FDIC) ensures this.

While many might wonder if this system is truly a safe way to save money, let's remember the savings and loan crisis of the '80s. Gross (and in some case criminal) mismanagement of the lending/borrowing function in the banks led to their inability to pay CD holders. So many of the banks and savings and loans were calling on the FDIC and the Federal Savings and Loan Insurance Corporation (FSLIC) that the government had to find extra money to make good on the depositors' investments. Not to worry, no one lost any principal. Your CDs are safe.

Corporate Raiders

If you want to pick up a little more interest than a CD will pay, remember, everybody wants your money. You can call your local investment advisor and arrange to buy a corporate bond. These range in maturity from 1 month to 20 years.

At first glance, corporate bonds may seem less safe than treasuries or CDs. In technical terms, they are less safe. The key difference is that a corporation cannot tax you to pay you back! Federal insurance and safety is based on the government's ability to tax you and pay you back! Because corporations have to successfully produce a product or service and then sell it to someone (sometimes you!) to secure the money to repay you, their bonds are considered less safe than government-guaranteed bonds.

Therefore, corporations usually offer a slightly higher rate of interest to attract your attention. While corporations are just as legally bound to pay you back, they vary in their credit worthiness to do so (if they go bankrupt, you may not get your money back).

To help you determine which corporation to lend to, several rating services provide third-party opinions about a corporation's ability to repay its debts. This opinion is called a "credit rating." Standard and Poor's and Moody's are the leaders in this service. Triple A (AAA) is the best score. Then you proceed down a scale as follows: AA, A, BAA, B, BB, BBB, and so on. BAA is the cut off for what's considered investment grade. In other words, it's understood that you might lose some or all of your money if you buy a bond with a rating lower than BAA.

Wealth Words

Bond rating—A way of assigning grades to bonds based on the issuer's ability to pay. Bond ratings are issued by three organizations: Standard & Poor's, Moody's, and Fitch.

Who Deserves Your Money?

An all-purpose rule of thumb to use when deciding which bonds to buy is to compare any long-term corporate bond to the 30-year treasury. The difference in interest rate promised gives you some idea of the additional risk (that is, that your principal might not be repaid). Ask yourself or your advisor to justify that difference and proceed accordingly.

One of the most popular ways for people to invest in bonds is to buy a mutual fund that buys only bonds. But can you trust your Uncle Sam? Please make note of the important truth that follows: Your principal is not, we repeat, *not*, guaranteed in

Cash Cautions

Mutual funds that buy only bonds are riskier than they appear. You stand a real chance that your principal will decrease, rather than increase.

a mutual fund that buys bonds. This is true, even when every single penny in the fund is invested in government-guaranteed bonds.

How can this be? This is a disturbing fact. A mutual fund that pools your money with money from other investors and then buys the bonds on your behalf is providing both a service and a danger to you. First, it is managing your risk for you by diversifying your dollars into several hundred (if not thousand) different bonds. Where's the rub? You own shares of a mutual fund, not the actual bond. Mutual funds, by definition, take away a precious privilege of the bondholder: the right to hold it to maturity when your entire principal amount must be repaid to you. Without the ability to hold the bond to maturity yourself, your principal is *not* guaranteed. Financial professionals refer to this situation as the "bond fund sham."

You have to understand how the bond price can and will fluctuate from the day it's issued to the day it matures. Only then will you understand how your principal is at risk. An inverse relationship exists between the interest rate of the bond and the resale price because you can get your money back at maturity.

Wealth Words

Maturity—The date on which the issuer must retire the bond and repay the bondholder.

If you own a mutual fund that owns a lot of bonds for you, the price you pay per share of the fund on the day you buy is determined by this "resale price" of all the bonds in the fund. A mutual fund is a big basket of investments. The fund calculates the total resale value of all the bonds and then divides that large number by the number of shares in the fund to determine the price you pay for the fund and the price you can get when you sell your shares of the fund some day. Incidentally, this value is the price per share you see quoted in the newspaper each night.

Immature Money

Fund managers do not always hold a bond to maturity. For many different reasons, they might buy and sell a lot of bonds. They trade in both new and used bonds, those that have already been owned by someone else. As funds buy and sell these bonds, that inverse relationship matters to you and your principal. Fund managers can't always sell a bond for as much as they paid for the bond.

How does this inverse relationship make me lose money, you might ask? When interest rates go up, the resale price of a bond goes down. The reason is that a new, never-been-owned bond can be purchased with a higher interest rate on it. If the fund manager needs to sell a bond before maturity and all the new bonds have a better rate of interest, the only way someone would buy a lower interest rate bond is to put it "on sale" for a discount rate. The interesting point is that the amount of the sale mark-down is just enough that, when combined with the remaining interest payments of the bond, the new owner's yield (return) is the same as the yield of a brand new bond! A coincidence? Not at all. It's the result of a very efficient market. It also means that you can't beat interest rates, and you never get something for nothing.

For example, if you have a $100 bond that pays $100 (face value) plus $5 (interest) after 1 year, that's a 5% annual interest rate. If rates rise to 6% and you want to sell your bond, you have to pay the purchaser so that he or she will earn as much with your bond as with a new 1-year bond, which would pay $106 instead of your $105. As the owner of the 5% annual interest bond, you could entice a buyer by selling your bond to them for $99. At maturity they will get $100 plus $5 for their $99 investment.

We Wouldn't Want That Job!

The bond fund manager is not in an enviable position. If guarantees on your principal were required, no one would take this job. Most people chase a higher yield. Therefore, as interest rates drop, people pour money into bond funds that are advertising their higher yield. As all this cash pours into the fund, the manager is forced to find more bonds to sustain an attractive yield. As interest rates rise, bond prices drop, and the value of the fund goes down, so you see your principal shrinking. Money investors want out in a hurry to protect their principal. The fund manager has to sell bonds at permanent losses to create cash to give to these departing owners.

The shareholders that leave, or those who stay for that matter, never recover this loss. The fund manager is, unfortunately, not in a position to hold the bonds to maturity when your full principal is guaranteed. You don't have that choice because you're a shareholder, not a fund manager.

Wise Women Know

After all is said and done, if guaranteed principal is your goal, do not buy bond funds! If you own a bond fund, sometimes you'll wish that you'd just bought bonds and held them to maturity. The only risk would be the risk that the bond issuer would default—not repay it's debts. Instead, bond funds turn bonds from investments that pay a specific rate into investments that have the risks and rewards of stocks.

The name U.S. Government Bond Fund does not mean that your principal is guaranteed. Billions of dollars are held in these bond funds. Take yours out and buy the bond itself. If you have no other choice in a retirement account, at least understand that your principal can fluctuate.

Yippee—It's Tax-Free!

The previous comments about bonds are true of tax-free municipal bonds, too. The only difference is the interest you can earn is free of federal (and usually state) taxes. What makes this interest tax-free? The U.S. Constitution prevents government entities from taxing each other. Therefore, the interest you earn on a bond from the U.S. government is free from state income tax. The interest you earn on a state-sponsored bond or municipal bond is free from federal tax. States take it one step further and let you off without paying them a state tax on the bond as well. Your federal government is not so generous. While you avoid state income tax on a treasury bond, you still pay federal income tax on that interest.

Corporate bonds do not have any special tax considerations. They are often held in tax-favored accounts, such as retirement accounts, which are thoroughly discussed in Part 5, "When I Am an Old Woman, I Shall Wear Purple Cashmere." CDs are not granted any special tax consideration, either. Therefore, both federal and state governments tax the interest on these bonds, which is one reason why these types of investments generally offer higher interest rates. The need to compare the relative value of apples and oranges is the reason that a bond's yield is often quoted to you, the potential buyer, as both a taxable-equivalent yield and a tax-free yield.

Most of us should consider the merits of taxable investments first and then compare the tax-free yields to make our decision. A final comment on which is better: taxable or tax-free? Whichever leaves more money in your pocket is better for you. If you are making the investment in a tax-sheltered account, like an individual retirement account or an annuity, taxes are not a consideration, because movement of money out of the account determines those taxes. All kinds of dividend or interest payments in the account are treated the same way; that is, taxable events do not occur within the account (so the higher interest from corporate bonds is as tax-free as the interest from government bonds).

And there you have it, your first lesson in bonds. Bonds generally offer higher current income with less volatility than stocks do, but bonds also have limited potential for increasing returns (stocks can—but do not always—rise and fall farther and faster than bonds). Bonds are often recommended by investment advisors as a critical part of asset allocation. Now that you know what the world of bonds is all about, you will be able to determine if they belong in your portfolio.

The Least You Need to Know

➤ A bond is an exchange of money for a promise to repay that principal and interest to the lender in a stated period of time.

➤ Many entities issue and sell bonds: the federal government, state governments, local governments, and large corporations.

➤ Compared to stock, bonds offer a higher current income with less volatility, but they have limited potential for increasing returns.

➤ Certificates of deposit (CDs) are insured by the FDIC.

➤ Bonds are given ratings from AAA to BBB according to their issuer's ability to repay them.

➤ Mutual funds that invest solely in bonds are actually quite risky for individual investors.

➤ Bonds are frequently recommended as a low-risk way to balance a portfolio.

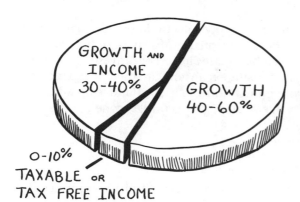

Chapter 13

GROWTH AND
INCOME
30-40%

GROWTH
40-60%

0-10%
TAXABLE OR
TAX FREE INCOME

Is the Feeling Mutual?

In This Chapter

➤ An investment soup pot

➤ Let someone else do the cooking

➤ How do I order?

➤ Recipes for success

➤ Examining the ingredients

➤ Is that a fly in my soup?

You know you need to invest for the future. Everyone from your grandmother to your neighbor's kids is telling you to diversify, diversify, diversify. So far in this book, you've learned about stocks, bonds, and the markets, and you're still not sure this is for you. Numbers, numbers, numbers. Bull markets, bear markets, indexes, futures, options, brokers, NASDAQ, and so on. Annual reports, proxies, prospectuses. Read the paper every morning, hope for the best when you travel. A big responsibility, a lot of work, sounds overwhelming? Not to mention risky?

If this sounds like you, you're not alone. In the not-too-distant past, sharp marketers in the investment world created a product just for you and your peers.

No, it's not microwaveable, but it will add convenience and value to your life just the same—it's a *mutual fund*.

An Investment Soup Pot

What exactly is a mutual fund? A mutual fund is simply a portfolio of securities owned and managed by a professional company. The professional company is, in turn, owned by the public; that is, the public (like you) can buy shares in it. Your investment dollars, instead of funding a single company's plant expansion, are used to expand the mutual fund's securities portfolio. And your mutual fund shares will move up and down in value according to the *aggregate* value of all of the securities owned in the portfolio.

Soup or Salad?

Is this a good idea? Well, let's check the menu. Buying a mutual fund accomplishes at least four things:

➤ Mixing it up

Can't afford to buy and own companies in the 25 industry groups that you feel are destined for success?

Want to own foreign stocks, but can't pick the right country, much less the right stock? Diversify. Mutual funds provide an answer.

➤ The professional edge

You're a reluctant investor, or you may just not have the time and energy to mess with it every day. Answer: Turn it over to a professional. In a sense, that's what you're doing by buying a mutual fund. These guys and gals are *paid* to watch the soup.

And because it's their full-time job, they have the resources (and the time) to find those special companies that would easily escape your looking glass.

➤ Big menu and a bigger wine list

More than 5,000 funds are available for you to invest in—and more funds are being created every day! These funds run the gamut from very specific category investments to broad-brush "market baskets" of securities from all over the world. And, of course, everything in between.

➤ Portion control

You have only a few thousand dollars to invest? A mutual fund gives you access to a complete portfolio of stocks without paying megabucks in commissions. Mutual funds are a favorite for small investors or investors who invest small amounts regularly in a savings plan. They are ideal for retirement or 401(k) plans.

Wealth Words

Mutual fund—A portfolio of securities managed by professional managers. Investors buy shares in the fund, and when the value of the stocks the company owns goes up, so does the value of the shares in the mutual fund.

Wise Women Know

Owning shares in a mutual fund is a great way to invest in a broad basket of stocks—without having to buy all of those stocks yourself and pay the commissions on each trade. Warning: Although this system may be good for your nightly sleep, it does *not* mean you are free to go about your business, never to look until your 65th birthday. Mutual funds are an investment and, as such, need to be watched even if just out of the corner of your eye. Things *do* change!

Gumbo Is Gumbo—or Is It?

No two gumbos taste the same; each depends on the ingredients used and the style of the chef. Similarly, no two funds are alike; each will have a different mix of securities, that is, different companies constituting different percentages of the portfolio. You can find a mutual fund "product" to fit every investment goal, style, and interest. Funds can be categorized by:

➤ *What* they buy

A very broad categorization, and the place to start:

Stock funds buy equities, or stocks. No surprises here, but the real "flavor" comes in when we start discussing what kinds of stocks they buy and what their investment objective or *style* really is.

Bond funds buy bonds, corporate and sometimes tax-free government and municipal bonds. Bond funds are a good way to invest in bonds and achieve relatively high interest returns at relatively low risk. But as you learned in the chapter on bonds, these funds are far from risk-free!

Money market funds buy short-term "commercial paper," debt instruments that do not fluctuate in value, but pay market short-term interest rates. Money market funds are a good safe place to park cash while getting a relatively high return versus the risk.

➤ What they buy *for*

Now we talk about the investment *style,* the goals and objectives and risk/reward tradeoff to which the fund management is dedicated. These styles are so established that they actually appear in the daily mutual fund tables in major financial publications, such as the *Wall Street Journal*. Literature published by mutual fund companies is also quite clear about the objectives of a given fund.

Aggressive growth funds are looking for maximum capital gains and typically invest in growth stocks, often in emerging, technology-oriented companies. Highest risk; high potential return.

Growth funds are similar but are a bit more conservative and long-term oriented. They, too, mostly invest in growth stocks but in bigger, more established companies. They may also invest in a few bonds to diversify or "round out" their portfolios. Higher risk; more modest but predictable returns.

Growth and income funds invest in more conservative stocks and some bonds also. As the name suggests, they look for some growth in capital appreciation but also want to use dividends and interest from their portfolios to provide their investors with a steady, more or less predictable, return. Lower risk; lower but steady return.

Income funds look for income in the form of high dividend and bond yields. These funds can and do grow, but growth is clearly a secondary objective. They might buy a lot of utility stocks, for example. Lowest risk, with higher, more predictable returns.

Fixed-income funds do not invest in stocks at all. They invest in bonds, often largely or maybe even *only* government bonds. Prices vary little if at all. As the name implies, the return is fixed, and the risk is minimal.

Money market funds as mentioned earlier invest only in short-term money market instruments and provide a modest return. Major objectives from an investment point of view are *liquidity* (immediate convertibility to cash) and capital preservation (there is almost zero risk). Money market funds are usually used as the cash instrument in a stock portfolio—money is "parked" here until put to work somewhere else. Think of these funds as "almost cash" funds. Many women with money market funds like the fact that a checkbook comes along with the account. You can treat it like a checking account that pays higher interest than the account you can get at your local bank.

Special Items on the Menu

In addition to the "entrees" just listed, the mutual fund menu includes the following specialties:

➤ Minestrone

A little of everything but in a carefully crafted mix: *Index funds* buy stocks in exact proportion to the major market indexes—the Dow Jones Industrials, Standard and Poor's 100 or 500, the Russell 2000, for example. If you buy into one of these mutual funds, you are buying into the performance of that index.

➤ Liver and onions

Might not be what you want or what others at the table want you to have, but it could turn out to be good for you! *Contrarian funds* invest in what people don't want—out-of-favor investments. These funds can provide a useful "hedge" against unforeseen events and can be a good idea if you think normal stocks or stock funds are overvalued.

➤ Chicken Vindaloo

Option funds buy or sell options to spice up, or sometimes to hedge, a portfolio's performance. Both stock and bond funds may do this.

➤ Smorgasbord

Can't pronounce the name of the company, let alone understand what it does or how well they do it? *International funds* provide a key vehicle, too, for overseas investments that would otherwise be difficult to make. International funds can be presented as country-specific, regional, or global funds. We'll cover this topic in greater detail in just a moment.

Wise Women Know

Jennifer first heard about mutual funds in the early '70s, when her father inherited one from his father. Even to a 14-year-old, it sounded like a pretty good idea, and throughout her teens she pestered her parents not for a cute car, but for a mutual fund in her name! P.S. They never gave her one; she had to buy it herself. Parents are *so* unreasonable!

Let Someone Else Do the Cooking

So the idea of eating out sounds attractive. Now, what restaurant is best? How can I order if I don't speak the language?

Like so much business today, you will find few of what you would call "mom and pop" mutual funds. Most are very large investment companies, with large staffs and highly sophisticated information and analysis tools.

Wise Women Know

Some mutual fund companies are so large that you can buy shares not just in the fund, but in the company itself. In this case, you are buying shares of the company stock in the hope that the fund will be so successful that the value of the fund company will rise. Good examples of this are Nuveen and T. Rowe Price.

All in the Family

Most mutual funds are presented as *families* of funds. Each mutual fund company creates a series of products to satisfy the diverse interests and needs of its investors. Most companies offer at least 5 to 10 funds categorized by style—aggressive growth, growth and income, income, and so on. But some, such as Fidelity, offer an extensive series of "select" portfolios, where you can invest solely in biotech, domestic energy, gold, entertainment, or whatever you please.

There are dozens of fund families. You will see their names in the newspaper, usually the bold headings above the individual listings. Fidelity, T. Rowe Price, Franklin-Templeton, Lord Abbott, and Kemper are a few of the many big names.

Open Sunday, Closed Monday

What's this I read about "open"-ended funds and "closed"-ended funds? Do I need to take off work to buy shares when the fund offices are open? Do I have to take an admission test to be admitted to "closed" funds?

In a word, no. *Open* and *closed* refer to the way a fund gets money. Put as simply as possible, open-ended funds take your money and invest it directly, and the price, or net asset value (NAV), of a fund is simply the value of the portfolio divided by the number of shares. These are the funds you see listed on the mutual fund pages of the *Journal*.

Closed-end funds are slightly different. They are normal stock corporations with shares that trade on the various exchanges, mostly the New York Stock Exchange. Your invested funds may or may not be invested directly in the portfolio. Stock price is determined by floor trading and may be as much based on future expectations of the portfolio as the portfolio itself.

Many "country" funds are closed. You can invest in the Singapore Fund, the Spain Fund, the Brazil Fund. These shares often trade at a premium or discount to the portfolio value, so often a country fund will appear to be "on sale." The comparison of closed-end fund share price to actual value is published every Monday in the *Wall Street Journal*.

Do I Know the Chef?

Each mutual fund portfolio usually has its own manager. Usually these fund managers are highly trained to carefully analyze and track investments. Lots of Ivy Leaguers go into this business. No, you won't get to meet or talk to the manager personally, but the fund's literature often describes his or her track record. Many of these folks move around, and many investors follow the portfolio manager instead of the fund itself.

Many funds or fund families have a top strategist, or *guru,* looking above the portfolios and into the crystal ball of general investment trends. Some of these gurus have become quite famous—Peter Lynch, for example. He's that guy with the white hair and glasses you see in television ads and magazine mastheads; he probably has his own record label by now!

Most of the time, you will order from the menu without knowing the chef or her or his credentials. Occasionally you might know the chef, but you should be more interested in the results.

How Do I Order?

There are two basic ways to buy mutual funds: (1) from the fund itself and (2) through your stockbroker.

With most funds, you simply set up an account, send a check, tell the fund company which fund you want to invest in, and you're in. Your investments will be tracked in monthly or quarterly statements.

Most brokers also sell mutual funds, adding (usually!) diminished commissions for executing the trade. The advantages of buying mutual funds through your broker are that the funds are presorted for you, and, yes, all your investments show up on one statement (it's nice to be organized). The disadvantages are that the funds are presorted for you (yes, you might miss out on some good ones) and—watch out—brokers may push their own product, which might not really be the right match for you.

Do I Tip the Waiter?

Tipping is a very important question in this case. Now that you are tired of categories, here's two more: *load* and *no-load* funds. *Load* refers to a fee charged to purchase (and sometimes also sell) the fund.

Start with the simpler of the two: no-load funds. You probably already figured this out—no-load funds charge no transaction fees to buy or sell. Sounds like an obvious choice. Well, there's a little more involved. Load funds collect fees to pay those Ivy League guys and gals and their staffs. What do the no-load funds do? No, they don't employ summer interns at next to nothing. Instead, they pay these folks out of the investment pool.

Wealth Words

Load and no-load funds—Load funds charge either to buy into the fund or to leave it (but not both). No-load funds charge no transaction to buy in, but do charge an annual fee to own. *All* funds do charge some sort of annual management fee.

If annual expenses are 1.5% of a fund's total value and the fund earns 10% in a year, then only 8.5% is available to distribute to the fund's shareholders—you.

Load funds, on the other hand, break out this cost and leave the portfolio returns intact. The problem is that loads can be very heavy, sometimes 5% or more on the front end and another 1% to 5% on the sale. Load funds are prohibitive for short-term investing or if you change your mind about the fund. They're expensive any way you look at it because 5% deducted from your nest egg *up front* is more expensive than 5% deducted later.

Most investment advisors recommend no-load funds, the exception being very long-term investments where you are *sure* you will stay with the fund.

How Big a Tip, Anyway?

This subject is a bit controversial in the industry, but annual expense norms are about 1% of asset value for a typical large cap stock fund. For small cap funds, this amount goes up to 1.5% (because more time is spent on company research), and for bond funds the percentage should drop to 0.5% to 0.75%. If the figures in your prospectus are significantly higher, write and ask for a picture of the company's corporate jet(s)!

Maybe I'd Rather Have the White Wine

Most mutual fund families offer customers a privilege unique in the investment world: the ability to *switch* funds *within the family* at no cost. This can be done with a simple phone call or (sometimes) mouse click. So if you decide biotechs are out and a broader growth and income portfolio is in, you can switch all or part of your assets to another portfolio. These switches won't have a transaction cost (even if the fund family is a load family), but they are a taxable event. Unless, of course, you own it in a tax-free account like an IRA.

Mints After Dinner?

Okay, so now I've invested in a mutual fund. What do I get in return? The (usual) answer: It depends.

Most open-end mutual fund earnings are paid out annually either as income or capital gains distributions. Most funds pay a mix unless they are invested in strictly fixed-price securities. Income payouts reflect dividends and interest received by the fund from its investments.

Capital gains distributions are a bit more complex: They are the realized gain from securities sold during the year. Gains on securities held but not sold are reflected in the fund's price or NAV (Net Asset Value), but are not distributed to shareholders.

These earnings can be turned into a check in your mailbox, or, better for longer-term investment objectives, reinvested into the fund.

Recipes for Success

The choices can be daunting, and the advertising can be confusing or even misleading. Entire magazines are funded by investment companies crowing about their "phenomenal" 1-year, 5-year, and 10-year track records. These numbers look great—until you take a closer look at market performance during these time periods. You should look at performance relative to the markets and relative to the fund's competitors (other funds operating in the same arena).

It's also nice to look at the recipe—what individual stocks does the fund own. Are they stocks you would buy? You *are* buying them, you know, if you buy the fund. The problem here is that funds are only required to report this information quarterly, so by the time you see it, it is already out of date.

If You'd Rather Switch Than Fight

Remember those large funds companies that allow cost-free switching between funds in their family? Some gutsy investors have made a lot of money timing these switches to swings in the market. Many have also lost! But switching does provide you a convenient means to remix your investments to meet changing investment needs or goals.

All Over the MIP

Most mutual funds offer monthly investment plans, or MIPs. You simply send a check monthly or, better yet, use direct deposit. Your nest egg grows and compounds automatically.

Many people sock a chunk of their investment portfolio away in mutual funds and leave the rest for individual stock investing. The mutual fund portion of the portfolio tends to be stable and low maintenance. You get the benefits of diversification and professional management, and you also get to try your own hand at picking investments that are relatively better than the pack.

Cash Cautions

As we write this book in the fall of 1998, momentous changes are afoot in the economies of several parts of the world: Russia, Southeast Asia, and Japan among them. International events can all too quickly affect the value of your mutual fund, so pay attention to what is happening on the international scene and act accordingly.

A Trip Overseas

Most pros recommend that you put at least some money to work in foreign stocks. After all, it is a global economy, and if we start to flounder, someone else over there is likely to be doing better.

But these investments have to be watched a little more carefully. Not only are most offshore economies inherently less stable, but there is currency risk as well (if your Brazilian stocks rise 50% in 1 month but the currency falls 50%, you lose—a 100 peso investment rises to 150, but those 150 pesos are now worth only what 75 pesos were worth 1 month ago). If you are investing in a particular country, know it well, keep up by reading *The Economist* or something similar, and have fun watching. You might also want to find a fund that invests in a region—Europe, Latin America, Asia—instead.

Examining the Ingredients

You can get information about mutual fund investing from many sources:

➤ Your daily and weekly fish wrap

   Most daily papers provide mutual fund listings, and the *Wall Street Journal* and *Investor's Business Daily* enhance these listings with historical performance indicators and such. *Barron's* weekly financial paper provides a good weekly summary of mutual fund performance. By its very nature, mutual fund investing doesn't really require daily monitoring, though. It would be a bit like watching ice form.

➤ Prospectus

   Mutual funds are required by law to make a prospectus available, conforming to specific regulatory requirements. A mutual fund prospectus contains a detailed listing of the fund's portfolio, as well as objectives, performance history, management bios, and administrative costs. These documents can be dry and will usually be accompanied by some nice glossy marketing literature in a professional looking package.

➤ Rating services

Seems like there are companies that rate everything. No exception here. Two big ones, Lipper and Morningstar, provide detailed analysis of mutual fund performance.

➤ Newsletters

Seems also like there are newsletters for everything. Yes, here, too. One recently published investment book lists 36 newsletters that track specific mutual fund families. Newsletters recommend funds and fund strategies, and a few (like *Fidelity Monitor*) recommend when to switch funds within a family. You'll see ads for these newsletters in any financial magazine.

➤ The Web

If you go into any of the popular gateways, Yahoo! or America Online, you will find copious mutual fund information: profiles, history and performance, and chat rooms where investors can discuss their fund strategy and performance (or lack thereof). We give you more specific information on how to find these sites in Chapter 16, "Info World."

Is That a Fly in My Soup?

No investment is perfect. If there were a perfect investment, everybody would flock there and it wouldn't be perfect anymore. Mutual funds, of course, are no exception.

The Capital Offense

Many investors, especially in the 1996 and 1997 bull markets, got nasty end-of-year surprises from their growth-oriented mutual funds. Many had good years and sold a lot of their holdings—sometimes several times during the year. Good news, bad news. The good news is that these gains were substantial and, of course, passed directly to investors. The bad news: so was the large, unforeseen tax liability. Investors had no real idea of the size of their gains and how much had been realized until the end of the year. Would it have been better not to sell but let the capital continue to gain (for the investors investing for the long term)? Don't know. In some cases, it seemed that the Ivy League gals and guys never thought about the taxes their customers would have to pay. Watch the portfolio "churn rate," another stat showing up in the prospectus. This rate gives you an idea of how often the fund manager likes to buy and sell stocks (churn) in the fund.

Driving With the Rearview Mirror

Funds get a bit caught up in their past performance and seem to tout it as a guarantee of the future. Check out their ads and read the fine print! We all know better than to be dazzled by a good-looking ad.

129

Too Much Water in the Soup

Sometimes a fund will own (and may have to own according to its charter) several hundred stocks. The very diversification that is supposed to make the fund so good actually starts to work against it. If the fund managers pick 20 or 30 really good stocks, there are 270 other fair-to-middling performers that render the victories pointless! Be on the lookout for funds that seem to have too many holdings.

You Still Have to Pay Attention

Yes, you've hired a gun, and you've diversified. But it is still your money; you have to manage the hired gun, and you have to react to change in the world. Mutual funds are investments, and they need to be managed. Not as closely, perhaps, as individual stocks and bonds, but they need to be managed.

The Least You Need to Know

➤ Investing in mutual funds can be an easier than investing in individual stocks.

➤ Buying into a mutual fund gives you a broad-based portfolio without making you pay commissions on individual stocks.

➤ Funds vary greatly according to the part of the market that they invest in—some funds buy stocks in particular industries; some buy strictly bonds.

➤ Funds also vary according to investment philosophy. Some are committed to aggressive growth; some are fixed income. Investors need to decide the level of risk that they are looking for.

➤ Investing with a large mutual fund family also gives you the chance to switch among the family's funds, sometimes at no charge.

➤ Buying into a mutual fund is easy, and a fund is a low-maintenance investment. But you should still pay attention to what is happening with it.

Part 4
So Much Money, So Little Time

Ever wonder why wealthy folks are always off meeting with their accountants? Because as you begin to invest, your life can get much more complicated. So here you learn a strategy or two to help you stay in control of your increasing net worth and to just keep it simple.

Computer software programs, centralized asset management accounts, and the plethora of online information can all help keep you on top of your money. You also learn about a simple method of group investing—the fascinating world of women's investment clubs.

Do You Still Own Your Money, or Does It Now Own You?

Now that you have cleaned up your debts and commenced the saving and investment programs we have discussed, you will have even more records to keep! Look at it this way: Where once you might have been managing your debt and been buried under a pile of bills, now you are managing your wealth and are buried under a pile of account statements.

Help—I'm Drowning in Paperwork!

For every account you own that has reportable interest, dividend, or capital gain activity, you have to report that information on your tax return. Banks, brokerages, mutual funds, and insurance companies that hold your assets are required by law to send you a notice of all reportable activity each year. This statement is the infamous 1099 tax form.

The 1099 must be postmarked by January 31 of the year following the tax-reporting year. Therefore, you should have all your 1099s in hand by the end of the first week in February. These are crucial to the accuracy of your taxes. The loss or misplacement of even one 1099 is very inconvenient.

An old adage among tax preparers is that the Internal Revenue Service (IRS) can always identify your income, but it has to take your word on itemized deductions. Why is this true? Every financial institution that sends you a 1099 sends a copy to the IRS as well. The IRS has the data before you send it in! By the way, the IRS has a copy of your Wages and Earned Income (W-2) as well!

Headache-free?

Because you spend each January waiting by your mailbox, we wish to make a strong case for consolidating your investments into one, all-purpose account. This is not hard to do. Anne asks her clients to imagine how wonderful life would be if all their tax-related income for the year was reported on one statement? Expanding on that thought for a moment, imagine how wonderful it would be to have your entire financial life summarized each month on one statement, in one envelope? This dream is very nearly impossible, but worth striving for nonetheless.

Filegate II

For all of you who cannot accomplish this level of consolidation, set up a file for each investment and, as the monthly statements arrive, do the same with these as you do with your bills. Review the statement immediately for accuracy. When you find a questionable entry, or simply something you do not understand, call the issuer of the statement immediately and inquire. If the statement has no surprises, file it for future reference.

Wealth Words

Street name—When the stock certificate is held in the name of the brokerage house rather than in the name of the individual client. Holding stocks in street name simplifies trading.

For those of you who can make some changes toward consolidation, please invest the time to do so immediately. You might start by asking each place where you hold an asset about who actually can hold the asset.

For instance, a mutual fund company might say something like this: You can hold a certificate, the mutual fund company can hold your shares, or most investment firms can hold your shares in street name. But which alternative is best?

Financial professionals like Anne are least in favor of you holding your stock certificates. From years of assisting clients replace lost stock certificates, Anne has come to believe the most convenient, reliable, and (in the long run) most affordable way to hold your assets is in a central asset account. Most people opt for the brokerage house to hold the asset, and the investor then receives monthly statements about the value of the asset.

Hold That Asset!

When you hold the asset in certificate form, you run the risk of losing the certificate. Although certificates can be easily replaced from an administrative point of view, replacements cost money. Why? Because if the certificate is lost or stolen, it might find its way into unfriendly and dishonest hands. You will have to post a bond to replace it. This bond is usually 2% of the value of the asset at the time of replacement. For example, $10,000 worth of a mutual fund would cost $200 to replace. The bond you post insures the issuer of the certificate against the loss if someone fraudulently represented himself or herself as you, sold your asset, and collected cash in payment. Obviously, when you someday go to sell your asset, you are essentially selling the same shares, which means that both you and the thief are collecting on the same asset.

Cash Cautions

Lose your certificate? Sure, you can replace it, but it won't be cheap, and it could take longer than you imagine. This is the best reason to let the broker hold your certificates in its street name.

For those of you who say, "Not me, I never lose anything—especially not important things!" stop to consider fires, earthquakes, floods, and bad luck. Now you must be saying, "Not me, I keep it all in the bank safety deposit box." For many reasons, this alternative is not always the best idea. Remember, the bank itself could be destroyed in a fire, earthquake, or flood as well!

When you hold the certificate, the mutual fund company will ask you how you want to handle your dividends and capital gain distributions. It will either mail you a check or automatically reinvest on your behalf each time a dividend occurs. Regardless of who holds the certificate, the mutual fund company sends you a 1099 at the end of the year.

Wise Women Know

Most people opt to have the mutual fund company hold the certificate. This choice is the default option when you buy shares of a mutual fund from the fund directly. Whoever sells you the asset usually holds it unless you ask the seller to do otherwise.

Lump It All Together

The final and best alternative (and Anne's recommendation) is to hold all mutual fund investments in one consolidated brokerage account. What happens when you do this?

➤ Your shares are held in broker's street name for your benefit.

➤ You get only one 1099 per year with the details of your many different investments summarized and totaled for you.

➤ Your investments and dividends can be credited directly to your money market account.

Don't worry, these places won't lose track of your investments. Financial institutions store this vital data in several secure places around the country and are protected against disasters of Mother Nature. A natural disaster would have to occur simultaneously in several distant locations to destroy these records.

Your dividends and income can be reinvested if you choose, or you can accumulate these various sources of dollars into the money market fund within the account and make periodic investments with the built-up balances.

You Own Your Money—and Your Time, Too!

The key benefit of consolidation is that you own your money, rather than letting the record keeping and paperwork associated with your investments own you. Many central asset accounts, or cash management accounts as they are commonly named, are now accessible via the owner's home computer. What a wonderful world! You can turn on your computer and—info ahoy!—your investments are detailed and recorded for you in living color. What is more, the information is updated daily, sometimes even moment by moment for you to watch! We'll talk more about how software and online access can change your financial and record-keeping life in the following chapter.

Top Time-Saver

If you haven't gotten the message in this chapter, we strongly suggest you keep your life as simple as possible by holding as many of your investments as possible in one consolidated account. This system is a major time-saver. Arranging for consolidation is as simple as collecting statements from all your holdings, walking into a financial firm that offers a central asset account, and asking anyone who works there to gather your assets. They are experts at collecting your assets and putting them in one convenient place. The challenge is finding someone you would like to work with at these firms.

Even firms where you do not have a personal advisor provide central asset accounts. You simply appear at the door and ask the service clerk to arrange to consolidate your assets. The hardest part of this project is making the commitment to do it. The project will flow thereafter.

So, More Is Less?

Like many other good ideas, it takes *more* paperwork to make your life end up with *less* paperwork! After your accounts are consolidated, your mailbox will be a little emptier. You will also find that crazy time of year when you fret and frenzy over taxes will be more serene. You can smugly gloat as your friends who have not read this book run search frantically for that one misplaced 1099 tax-reporting statement! All the information you need is on one elegant master statement!

Why do you need to be organized? Can't you just put everything in a shoebox and store it in the garage? The need for financial organization and consolidated 1099 reports is too compelling to cover in one book! Suffice it to say, an ounce of prevention is worth a pound of cure. Ask anyone who has ever suffered a setback of any kind in his or her life. This setback could be a natural disaster, as previously mentioned, a sudden illness that temporarily forces you to get help with your paperwork, a death in the family, the loss of a job, or a serious car accident.

Wealth Words

Central asset account—An account with a large brokerage house that includes checking, debit or credit card, margin loans, all investment accounts, and mutual funds in one numbered account with one monthly statement.

The reasons to have your life organized on all fronts, *especially* the financial front, are too numerous to list. The reasons *not* to are very simple to list. Complacency. Fear. Inertia. Dare we say it—laziness.

Just One Short Week

What we all need to do is work into a personal organization week—a time set aside to get ahead of all these issues and focus on doing the things that can truly streamline our lives. Short of that, perhaps setting aside one Saturday a month for the purpose of streamlining would work in your life. Choose your most realistic strategy and go for it!

While we are on the topic of 1099s, it is important to emphasize there are different kinds of 1099s. For example:

➤ 1099 DIV (as in dividend)

➤ 1099 INT (as in interest)

➤ 1099 OID (original issue discount as in zero coupon bond interest)

When they are consolidated on one statement, the different kinds become very obvious because they are sorted for you. Another bonus of consolidation is that the tax-reporting statement usually includes instructions on how to transfer the various numbers to specific lines on your tax-filing form 1040, Schedule D, or Schedule A. For those of you unfamiliar with Schedules D or A, you will be once you have investments that generate significant interest and dividends.

Warning, Warning!

One other 1099 important to mention is the 1099 R (as in a distribution from a retirement account). These strike fear into the hearts of all who receive them. They are very important for tax purposes. When you take a distribution from a retirement plan, the custodian of that plan is required by law to send the tax-reporting statement to you and the IRS. This statement reports the distribution as income. You will owe income taxes on this income. If you remove the money prior to age $59^1/_2$, you must prove a disability or pay a fine to the government of 10% of the money withdrawn. This penalty is a painful slap on the wrist.

Not to worry, though, if you took the distribution and rolled it over into another retirement account; a compensating entry will appear. You have 60 days after the date on the distribution check to redeposit the funds in another retirement account. You can make only one rolled distribution in a calendar year. The IRS gets suspicious when money goes out for several consecutive 60-day periods.

Beware the 1099 R and be sure you have some proof of the compensating deposit for your tax records. Many custodians forget to forewarn you that your distribution triggers this tax-reporting notice, so clients are surprised and concerned to receive one of these required and routine statements. If you rolled over the funds, the receiving custodian is also required by law to report the receipt of your deposit. If the report happens, all is acceptable!

Too Much Time on My Hands

With all this free time you have suddenly captured, you can more thoroughly study the statements when you receive them to ensure their accuracy. It is a rare event indeed when a math error shows up on a statement from a major investment firm or bank. The computer is not really very creative, but it never makes math mistakes, and it always remembers the numbers it put on your statement (until a human changes the numbers). The good thing about computers is that they never forget.

The most important way to check the data on your statements is to verify that data entry was done correctly. The clerk recording your deposit can accidentally transpose a number. Another common problem is that the wrong account number is typed in, so your account (for example, 1234) gets someone else's deposit (1243) by accident. Don't worry if you do not notice or do not report this problem; the rightful owner will certainly ask about it.

Wise Women Know

If you have the time and enjoy the process, you can check the math, too. While addition, subtraction, division, and multiplication functions are very nearly flawless on computers, one can never say never. On the other hand, a spot check and an eyeballing of the figures in question should be 99.99% accurate. Save yourself some time by verifying the data input, like whether the list of checks deposited and withdrawn is correct, *before* you check the math. What good *is* accurate computation when the wrong numbers are being added, subtracted, divided, and multiplied?

Be forewarned, though, that the firm that holds your account will correct the entry "as of" the original date it was meant to happen. If the correction occurs months later than the error, be prepared to lose any and all interest earned on the money that was not truly yours. This settlement method is important for both the beneficiary and the victim of the error. This is why it is usually best to report mistakes that go both for you and against you as soon as you notice them. The computer never forgets and will eventually find you.

Statement Overload

In case we have not yet persuaded you to consolidate, let us remind you one more time of the savings you can enjoy! You'll have only one statement, rather than several. The world of financial statements is far from standardized.

Financial services institutions are very competitive. They want to provide the best investment results and to present their performance on statements that are as client-friendly as possible. In general, the readability of financial statements has improved greatly in recent years, and frankly, if you encounter one that is difficult to comprehend or simply not very informative, you have a reason to find a better service provider.

Over the years, as Anne has met with clients for hours to teach them how to read their statements. If the statement is hard to read, do not be too quick to judge yourself harshly. On the other hand, give the service provider a chance to answer your questions, and put in a little time yourself.

If you do find a mistake, you might not be the only one. As an example, say that the dividend that was credited to you for your General Electric stock was $500, and you know it should have been $50. It is very likely that all GE-owning clients of that investment firm found the same mistake on their statement. Remember that computers are very good at repetition of data. If the wrong data goes in, the wrong data also comes out. These systemwide errors are corrected with one sweeping correcting entry as well.

In most cases like this, the firm will have discovered the problem itself. When you call, the representative will probably tell you to expect the correction to appear on the following month's statement.

Safe and Secure

Security of your account is, understandably, of paramount concern to you and the company that you have selected to use. It actually has more to lose than you do if your assets are not secure. "How can that be, since they have all my assets," you might be asking. "I have *everything* to lose." The company has all of your stuff, the assets of millions of other clients, and its entire reputation and ability to stay in business to lose if it mishandles your investments. This is a stern and powerful motivator. These firms do not take their responsibility lightly.

Security is of grave concern to everyone. This is why you're safest if you do the following:

➤ Always have a copy of last month's correct and accurate statement and a record of all transactions in the account since the statement.

➤ At the first sign of a problem, bring the question to the attention of your trusted advisor. We say *trusted advisor,* purposely, since this will usually be one more person who agrees with you that a problem in your account needs attention.

➤ If your advisor makes light of the problem, or fails to explain the problem to your satisfaction, politely ask for the administrative manager.

For those of you who are do-it-yourselfers and prefer to use an account without an advisor, call the impersonal toll-free number, talk to who knows who, and ask that voice to help you correct the problem.

Once the item in question is corrected, the firm can usually send you a printout that confirms the correction. Or you can wait for the correction to appear on your next monthly statement. As long as you are on record as looking for the correction, you are on your way to a positive result. Be prepared to learn that the mistake was yours as well and, in this case, thank them profusely for his or her time.

The Least Ywou Need to Know

➤ More investments mean more paperwork with monthly statements and tax-preparation work.

➤ A central assets account can lump everything together and send out only one monthly statement.

➤ You will receive one 1099 for every investment account you own. These statements are important for your tax returns. If you have a consolidated account you will receive one 1099.

➤ Replacing lost investment certificates can be a costly matter; it is better to have your broker hold them.

➤ Carefully examine your monthly statements and report any errors right away.

➤ Investment houses never actually lose your investment records.

Chapter 15

Software to the Rescue

In This Chapter

➤ Can a computer help you invest?

➤ Which program do you really need?

➤ Evaluating the majors

➤ Filling in the blocks

➤ You're organized now!

The *Wall Street Journal* recently ran a column in which its technology expert, Walter S. Mossberg, passed judgment on how computer companies are doing with the Big Question: are the products easier, simpler, and more reliable for the average, non-technical user?

And his answer was (drumroll, please): maybe. "The personal computer remains the only common possession that makes smart people feel stupid and requires the constant ministrations of a priesthood of experts." In part, that is why only 45% of American households have a personal computer.

Can a Computer Help You Invest?

Why are we talking about computers? Because in your lifelong quest to build up wealth, a computer can be a true ally. Many a clever software creator has seized on the opportunity to make computers useful to investors, and even better—to help them manage their finances in the most efficient way.

Are you a part of the 45% of the population that already owns a computer? Then skip along to the section where we discuss the different types of financial software available. But if you are in the majority, the 55% of American households that don't have a computer at home, read on.

We start with a basic overview of computers and the difference they can make in your financial life. Next, we sample the software you might acquire to make your computer a useful investment tool.

The computer is a machine that remembers every fact you tell it (unlike our own faulty memories or spotty record keeping). With the right financial software, a computer is a terrific administrative assistant. With the proper software, you can easily turn your PC into an assistant that

➤ Pays bills

➤ Prepares taxes

➤ Finds information

➤ Keeps financial records

Something Might Go Wrong!

If you are like many people, you fear that merely by touching such a powerful machine, you are bound to break it. Lots of people are computer phobics. Do you imagine yourself in that panic situation where one press of the wrong button and all your hard work is gone in an instant? You are not alone. Read on and prepare to learn a whole new way of living.

Step 1: Press the Power Button

Prepare yourself for one important reality. In the long run, computers can save you enormous amounts of time. In the short run, you must invest a lot of time to harness the power of the machine. Be patient, and believe. Computers can perform nearly miraculous timesaving feats. Work through your fear and let's get started.

Hunt and Peck

One skill that is invaluable for the use of a computer is the ability to type: not the hunt-and-peck style typing, but instead the look-away-while-your-fingers-do-the-work typing. Can't really type? Not to worry; for some kinds of programs you need only move a little handheld device around on the table and click the arrow on various pictures to make your computer do terrific tasks for you. And then you punch in the numbers. What could be easier?

Now, if you do not have a computer, you might want to take a course or two, just to get comfortable with a machine before you actually purchase one. Do you use a computer at work? Computer courses are standard for most employers. You can find courses for all levels, beginner to extremely sophisticated, at any local adult education, community college, or technology trade school. You can also take a course offered right in a store that hopes to sell you a computer. Lots of stores do not mind if you play with one of their many display computers.

When you are finally ready to buy a computer, shop around for the best buy. But remember that the box and software you bring home are only the beginning of your relationship with the person who sold you the computer. Instructions and support in case things do not go as planned are also very important considerations. A good way to find a reliable computer dealer is to ask the computer owners you know for their recommendations.

Buying a computer is not a daunting task unless you are worried that you will never master the use of such a powerful and (at first glance) expensive tool. To that end, we remind you that you will never master the use of a computer if you do not get your hands on one! Any time of year is a good time to be a computer buyer. As new machines and software are announced, the soon-to-be-slightly-obsolete models are put on sale. And even a slightly obsolete computer can help you organize your finances.

Got One, Now What?

Once you buy that computer, be prepared for everything to take much longer than you think it should. Once you dive into the computer and later cyberspace world you will not know where all those hours go.

One of Anne's clients recently went out and purchased a very spiffy laptop computer, powerful enough to go on the Internet. This client is in her mid-60s, and surrounded by friends and family who use the computer daily. She calls to report how immersed she has been after a several hour stint trying to get the computer to do what she wants it to do. Anne frequently reassures clients that the computers we all use are far more capable and powerful than we understand. Even the most frequent users of computers find they do not fully utilize these impressive tools.

So you learn to type, if you had not already mastered this life skill. You prepare yourself by sampling computers. You surveyed your friends and associates, then bought one. You identify a course or two you might take to become acquainted with your new miracle tool. You have yourself mentally prepared for the reality that computers, while they ultimately perform numerous repetitive activities for you, take a lot of lead-time from you to be effective.

The worst thing you can do is to ignore your machine. When you get on the machine, and noodle around on it, to use the lingo of the computer community, you slowly become comfortable with all that this precious tool can and will do for you. Be stout of heart and think of this as an adventure. Remember, software makers are on your side and have helped design safeguards to keep you from hurting yourself or the machine!

Software, Software Everywhere and Not a Drop to Drink!

Software is sold just about everywhere these days. Any store with the word *computer* in its name—CompUSA, Computer Universe, Computer City, and so on—is likely to carry the kinds of financial software you need. Other choices include office supply stores, such as Staples, Office Max, Office Depot, and local shops. Bargain hunters can even pick up good deals at Costco and Sam's Club. Bookstores like Barnes and Noble and Borders carry some software and lots of user guides for these various software packages. With so many choices out there, what do you want to start with in financial software?

Which Program Do I Really Need?

Your selection will come down to a matter of personal choice, but let us point you in a solid direction. One rule of thumb about software is that there is safety in numbers. If you see a certain software title on the shelves in every store you walk into, join the masses and give it a try. On the outside chance you get a program with a bug in it, which is computer speak for "it does not work right," most big manufacturers have great customer-support services. You simply call them, usually via a toll-free line, and they help you work through the problem you are experiencing. Among the more popular financial help programs are Anne's favorite, Quicken, and its close cousin, Quicken Deluxe.

Software usually evolves, with companies rolling out new generations of their flagship products on an annual basis. Quicken 96 replaced Quicken 95, and now we are up to Quicken Deluxe 99. If you own last year's version, you can usually purchase an "upgrade" for the newer version. Upgrades, which are slightly less expensive than the complete program, typically write over your existing program to give you all the new goodies, bells, and whistles the software designer dreamed up over the year without requiring you to reenter your data.

And What's in It for Me?

Although this book is not a commercial for Quicken, we are using it to point out the features that financial programs offer. Imagine a screen on your computer with pictures and labels of the following topics:

➤ My Accounts

➤ Bills

➤ Planning

➤ Investments

➤ Home and Car

➤ Online

➤ Reports
➤ Address Book
➤ Calendar
➤ Mutual Fund Advisor
➤ Quicken Lawyer

Click on Something

You start by moving the arrow to the picture over the title "My Accounts." Click once, and a whole world opens up, preset for you to use as your checkbook register. When you click on the picture with the title "Bill" under it, you can pay your bills online. Did we remember to mention that you should buy a printer at the same time you buy a computer? Printers are very affordable, and your computer cannot produce a written copy of your hard work without a printer!

Wise Women Know

"I like the pie charts; they're very pretty," says Jennifer's mother, Mary Alice, about Quicken. Jennifer's parents, who are in their 70s, were "early adopters" of Quicken—they've been using it for financial management since it was released some 15 years ago. They use it primarily for check writing and to quickly categorize expenses at the end of the year. And the pie charts? At the push of a button you can generate a pie chart that shows how you are spending your money—what percentage goes to food, to your mortgage, and so forth. "There are more bells and whistles in the program than we can ever possibly use," her mother admits, "but it is great fun to play with."

Auto Pilot

The beauty of paying bills this way is that you do not have to write the same checks over and over each month. You can handle any recurring bill that is the same amount each month very conveniently this way. You can even schedule future payments and then send them online or print them when they come due.

Click on the picture with the "Planning" title, and Quicken displays a fill-in-the-blanks budget for your spending, a plan for taxes, and a form to create a debt-reduction plan; you can even order your free credit report with this software. The possibilities are endless, and the format is easy: fill in the blanks and answer the questions. What could be easier?

Quicken is the granddaddy of financial software programs. It boasts that it has users in 10.5 million households. But a fierce competitor is gaining ground—and in the world of computers, hmmm, who could that be?

More Products From Microsoft

Quicken is by no means the only personal financial management software available. Surprise—Bill Gates will sell you one, too! His product is called Microsoft Money. For investors, Money has a great feature that links you to a database of more than 16,000 stocks and mutual funds. It also gives you access to recommendations from various Wall Street analysts and "insider" trading information (not real insider trading information, mind you, as that is illegal). This service is free to Money users for the first 6 months, but after that you'll need to pay $9.95 as month. In the next chapter, we examine a number of sites like this, some of which are free.

In addition to the investment help, Microsoft Money offers many of the same financial planning and money management features as rival Quicken does. It also has calculator functions that cover many financial-planning situations. Just type in the numbers for advice on whether you should convert your regular IRA to a Roth IRA or to find out how much you'll need to save for retirement or college.

Wise Women Know

There's that name again—Microsoft. As you learned in the investing chapter, some stock-picking experts suggest that you keep your eyes and ears open in your everyday life to spot up-and-coming stocks. Had you spotted Microsoft years ago, you'd be out sailing, instead of reading this book. A recent *People* magazine article featured all of the ordinary folks who'd made pots of money on Microsoft stock. Lucky folks. This is not a recommendation to buy Microsoft stock, of course, just a friendly nudge to remind you to pay attention to your own daily experience as a source of stock and company info.

Rev It Up!

When you decide to take the next step toward harnessing the power of your computer, online access is the key. Going online is so easy, you will be astonished. You do not even have to buy software to go onto the Internet. America Online (AOL) readily makes available the software you need to sign up with its service. AOL's free disks seem to come in the mail whether you want them or not! In many cases, your new computer comes with certain software already loaded in for your use. Two of these programs are for Internet users. AOL and Netscape Navigator are "standard equipment" on many new computers. You see, these companies are happy to let you get started for free (or minimal start costs, which you do not see wrapped into the purchase price of your new computer). Naturally, they hope to get you hooked. Your ongoing use will become a regular source of monthly income for them.

Once you go online, you will really feel the world has opened up to you. The Internet is where you can find any information you need.

When you are comfortable online, you will find that you can get a lot of services and information for free. It is there, right now, free for the asking and waiting for you to find it. In addition, many programs are legitimately for sale on the Internet. The amount of information available will only increase over time. Not to worry, though, the access providers and search engines will improve their search and sifting abilities as well, so finding the data will also be easier.

The next chapter will steer you toward the wide array of free information available online.

Taxing Topics

Returning to the comfort of software that you actually buy in the store and install yourself, we want to point out that many of them work together. For example, the Quicken program you can use to organize and manage your daily finances has a "companion" program called TurboTax. At tax time, you will see many software programs for tax filing. TurboTax happens to be fully integrated with Quicken. In plain talk, that means the information you have input about your finances over the year is now sorted, and you can move it to your tax forms and schedules with the stroke of several keys. The same company, Intuit, publishes both software programs, which is why they are designed to be used together.

Let's imagine the timesavings you experience because of this convenience. Be honest with yourself about how much time you spend fretting about the nuisance of pulling your tax records together each year. Next consider how much time it actually takes you to go back through your spending over the year to isolate the items you can write off. If you used the Quicken program to manage your finances over the year, your entries were being assigned to the relevant tax consequence right along. Think of it as doing your taxes in tolerable and accurate increments over the year. You are breaking down a huge project into smaller tasks. Some of what you do will be "extra" work over the year, but much of it actually eliminates the duplication of effort involved in the process.

Wise Women Know

Anne uses the high-powered combination of Quicken and TurboTax to handle her family's financial information and generate tax returns. An unbeatable combination, she claims, and she can't imagine life (financial life, anyway) without it.

Who Needs This?

So you're asking yourself, why do I need this information? I file 1040EZ each year. Remember what we've tried to warn you about throughout the book: the more successful you are at saving and investing your money, the more complex your taxes will become. Distressing as this news sounds, do not let it hold you back from becoming more and more involved with your finances and your investments!

Many people who are fully capable of doing their taxes, don't. We addressed some of the reasons for not doing your own taxes in Chapter 5, "Can I Get Some Help With This?" Time conservation is one reason. Stress reduction and anxiety are other contributing factors. Sheer confusion and impatience are most common.

Even if you still opt to visit your local tax preparer or H&R Block, gathering all the information you need to provide the preparer will be easier with Quicken or a similar program.

If you feel adventurous, invest in TurboTax and begin filing your own taxes. Once again, you will find that this software is written for the layperson. You start by answering a series of questions. It may seem quite baffling at first because you are not even looking at a copy of a tax form as these questions are asked. As you proceed through the process, the questions are culling the various tax forms you will need and assigning your answers to the correct lines on the forms. Imagine a tiny assistant in your computer dashing around the room grabbing the forms you need. What a help!

By now, you are becoming so experienced with computers, do we need to remind you that the program automatically does all the addition, multiplication, subtraction, and eventually, the *tax computation*. Turbo Tax even has a little fun with you by keeping a running estimate of your tax liability or refund in the upper-right corner! Try not to allow this number to affect the truthfulness of your answers.

File Online

When you are finished with the process, prepare yourself for the invitation to file electronically. This choice is available at tax-preparation services as well. More and more Americans, especially those with refunds due, are filing electronically. With Turbo Tax, you can file electronically for no charge with WebTurboTax.

Feeling a Little Insecure?

Is my very private tax information secure, sending it into the big World Wide Web in the sky? The answer is yes and no. Many programs and financial institutions use special encryption to secure the data being transmitted.

Encryption, as you readers of spy and mystery novels will know, is the process by which something is translated into a special secret code. In this case, your scrambled tax forms travel through cyberspace, and only the intended recipient (the IRS) has the combination to unscramble the message.

Wealth Words

Encryption—The process by which data is scrambled for security purposes. The legitimate recipient of the data has the key to properly unscramble the information it receives.

Code Breakers

Obviously, codes and combinations exist to be broken. Let's compare the security of electronic filing to the good, old-fashioned method of filing printed forms and mailing them. The same dark forces that might want to steal the envelope can be waiting in cyberspace to take your data. The chances of this actually happening are minimal. What would the villains who might steal the data do with it? It is important to keep your data secure, but the risk of your tax return failing to arrive at the IRS is similar for both filing methods.

Storage Boxes

After you have filed through the mail or electronically, how should you store the information for future reference? Keep the information on the computer and keep the information on a disk. Keep the entire filing in written form, in that filing cabinet we recommended earlier in this book. You need to have access to your tax records for

7 prior years. If you intentionally give the IRS incorrect data, you'll need to keep a lifetime's worth of records.

You always need to be mindful of losing your records in fire, earthquake, flood, or some unimaginable natural disaster. If you were to lose your tax records, you might not think it important at first, but it could turn out to be important 5 or 7 years from now! But please do not take the need to keep your financial records secure too lightly. However, if you do lose them in a disaster, take a wait-and-see attitude about what you might eventually need to reconstruct.

I'm Ready for More!

So, have we built an effective case for just why you need a computer to help you maximize your ability to invest? Not just because you can play Solitaire on it during the slow parts of the day, but because it is a powerful tool to help you get organized and sensitized to what is going on in your own financial world. And in addition to having a place to store your numbers (which will be growing large in no time!), your computer also is the key to a whole universe of online resources. Once you are connected, you will be astonished at the kinds of information that you as an investor can find. So let's move on to Chapter 16, "Info World," in which we share some of our favorite investing sites with you.

The Least You Need to Know

➤ A computer can be a powerful tool for both personal money management and investing.

➤ If you are still intimidated, sign up for a course to learn how to master your computer.

➤ At least two major software programs help users organize their financial information, pay their bills, and even sort their expenses.

➤ Using money management software enables you to prepare your taxes much more quickly because your data is already organized.

➤ With the help of tax software, you can save time and a trip to the post office and file your IRS return electronically.

➤ Adding online access to your computer enhances your ability to use it as a financial management and investment tool.

Info World

If you've slept through the last few years, you might be one of the few earthlings who aren't yet aware of the fast-paced world of online stock trading. It's amazing—turn on your computer and *bam*! The whole financial world is quite literally at your fingertips.

It wasn't so very long ago that trading online was pretty far out there, something only real tech-geeks would do. Nowadays it is pretty mainstream, and you should certainly check it out at your first opportunity. But like everything else in life, you must first learn how to make the most of it. By the end of this chapter, you might decide to never use a broker again! Or you might also decide that, while fascinating to the extreme, the world of online trading is not one you'd like to enter.

Wise Women Know

Online trading has exploded in the last few years. There are now some 80 online brokerage houses moving an average of 192,000 trades a day. That figure is double the number of online trades that were executed online just 1 short year ago!

Wealth Words

Online trading—Buying or selling stocks, bonds, or commodities via your computer connection to an online system. Most online trading is done by individuals without the help of a full-service stockbroker.

And These Guys Want Your Money, Too!

Remember all we told you in Chapter 2, "Gosh, Will They Let Me In? Isn't Investing a Boy's Club?," about how sought after you and your investment dollars are? Watch over your shoulder dear; we women are being pursued online, too! A recent issue of *Working Woman* magazine opened to reveal not the usual cosmetics or perfume advertisement inside the front cover, but a two-page spread for E*Trade, a major online brokerage house. But rather than hand over our money to the broker with the nicest advertising, let's take an online tour and see what's available.

Logging on to Learn

Step 1, turn on your computer. Step 2...oh all right, so you do know how to get yourself online without our help. But then where should you go, and what should you look for? Allow us. We'd like to share with you the Web sites that we believe have the most useful information:

➤ Yahoo! Finance (quote.yahoo.com) is Jennifer's top choice. It loads much faster than her online broker (who shall remain nameless) and is a faster way to get up-to-the-minute real-time quotes. And get a load the other stuff you can find here—charts of daily, weekly, monthly, or yearly price and trading activity; trading volume charts; links to recent news stories that affect the stock you are researching; and insider trading information from the SEC. Bookmark this site; you will use it often. Did we mention that all of this amazing research and information is free?

➤ Quicken.com (www.quicken.com) is a good source for mutual fund investors. For one thing, it's free. For another, it has good mutual fund selection tools to help you decide which fund (or what kind of fund) is right for you. Through the Quicken site, you can also evaluate insurance plans and costs, calculate how much house you can afford, and complete a home loan pre-qualification form.

➤ The Motley Fool (www.fool.com) site is the creation of two brothers who have combined the offbeat with a fresh market perspective. The result is an extremely popular and informative site for investors. Talk about opinionated—these guys and their other "fools" (stock specialists in various fields) have something to say about almost everything. Very active message boards, too.

➤ The money area of Women's Wire (www.womenswire.com) (click on the money icon) has several calculator functions that can help you make financial decisions. By filling in the blanks, you can calculate the future cost of a college education, learn just how long it will take you to reach your financial retirement goals, or examine the bottom-line difference between buying or leasing a $30,000 car. Good stuff. The Women.com 30 Index, created with Bloomberg News Service, is a stock index that tracks the 30 publicly traded companies either headed by women or owned by women.

➤ ivillage (www.ivillage.com) bills itself as "the women's network." After reaching the site, you can ignore the silly stuff like "If you were Oprah, what would you want to ask Monica's mom?" and click on the money channel. Unlike womenswire, ivillage does not maintain its own financial site but links you straight away to The Armchair Millionaire site.

➤ *Smart Money* magazine (www.smartmoney.com) is a visually attractive site (compared to most other money sites, anyway) with several key functions—a complete hourly market update, a good selection of timely and in-depth financial articles, a fund analyzer that lets you see how your current funds is doing, and a mutual fund finder to evaluate others. This site also has a stock quote function, but the quotes are delayed by 20 minutes or so.

➤ Microsoft Investor (investor.msn.com) is not free, it costs $9.95 a month. But it lets you track up to 10 investments and will even automatically email you an alert if the price of any of your selected stocks makes a major move. Kind of cool, don't you think? Useful for tracking gains (and losses, too), the calculator here factors in the commission you paid on the trade.

➤ H&R Block (www.hrblock.com/tax) has a useful calculator for...guess what, tax refunds. You were expecting something else from H&R Block? In addition to up-to-date information on the recent major changes to the tax law, this site also has a good checklist to help you make sure that you haven't overlooked any deductions for which you are eligible.

➤ Microsoft Money Insider (moneyinsider.msn.com) is a separate site from Microsoft Investor. The emphasis here is not so much on investing, but on financial education and information. There is a monthly fee for this site, too.

Investorama!

Want to go straight to a Web site that will link you to just about anyone or anything financial? Type in www.investorama.com and watch the fun begin. This amazing site has links to more than 8,136 sites in 89 categories. In other words, you can get just about anywhere from here.

Among the categories are:

➤ The stock market

➤ Quotes, charts, data, & portfolios

➤ Educational & general sites

➤ Brokerage & investment firms

➤ Tools for investors

➤ Investment talk

➤ Global investing

➤ Personal finance

Wealth Words

Real-time quotes—The most up-to-date information on the current trading price of a particular stock. Not to be confused with delayed quotes, in which the information is sometimes 15 to 20 minutes old and may already be outdated.

Just where will some of these links take you? We clicked on the brokerage and investment firms category and found, among other things, a link to a site that rates and ranks online brokers. Pretty useful stuff. In the same category, click on the listing of discount brokers and find a way to contact at least 46 of them.

Anne also recommends logging on to www.smartquote.com to get links to a great many other financial sites.

Wise Women Know

Who has time to wander around the Web in search of financial sites? Just check out www.investorama.com for a pipeline into more than 8,136 links in 89 categories.

Hot Tips and Hyped Stocks

In the same way that folks used to gather on front porches or talk over back fences, individual investors now have a place to exchange the latest gossip on the stocks they own. Where do they do it? In online investment chat rooms and stock message boards.

➤ The Motley Fool (www.fool.com)

These guys run message boards for a huge number of individual stocks. Fans (and sometimes foes) of the stock post comments, information, and predictions.

➤ Yahoo! Finance (quote.yahoo.com)

Also has a number of message boards for individuals.

Investment chat rooms are fun, particularly if you read them on a regular basis to follow a stock. Talk about devoted—the fervor that some stockholders have for their stocks on these boards is amazing!

There is a downside, though. Message boards and chat rooms have been blamed for artificial run-ups in stock prices in which the early investors make money, and the folks who see the messages and buy in on the tail end get stung. The most famous example is a company called Iomega. The stock ran up to dizzying heights due to online fervor and then sunk just as quickly.

Cash Cautions

Don't believe everything that you read in online chat rooms. Some of the peppy, positive messages have been planted by folks who hope to manipulate the stock price by touting it under several different screen names. Even consultants interviewed in the *Wall Street Journal* sometimes tout stocks they own.

Push Button, Buy Stock

Are you ready to buy stock from home, wearing your robe and slippers? Many broker-age houses would love for you to try! By logging on to any of the sites that we list below, you will learn just what each house requires in the way of financial backing. Some want even more than your money—they want experienced traders only! One company advertises that it only accepts investors with 5 years of investing and trading experience. Harrumph.

Some industry folks are alarmed at the rapid rate with which investors have embraced online trading. They think that it encourages too much quick trading and is danger-ously close to gambling. One interesting theory to emerge from all of this comes from Christos Cotsakos, the head of E*Trade, an online discount broker: "Internet investors do their own research and get emotionally attached to their stocks. That's far better than having some broker call you up and say, 'Hey, there's a company I'd like you to look at...'" Cotsakos believes that online investors are so attached to their stocks that they will hang onto them through thick and thin.

Wise Women Know

Most online discount brokers use fixed commissions for the first 1,000 or so shares traded. In other words, the commission on a 100-share transaction involving $1,000 of stock is the same as a 1,000-share trade involving $50,000 of stock.

According to your computer screen, the stock you want to buy is selling for $12\frac{1}{2}$. Great, you place an order with your online broker and await confirmation. Minutes (or seconds) later you get the confirmation—you just bought your shares for $12\frac{3}{4}$. Huh? Be warned; the price of the stock might well change in the time it takes your trade to go through. You may use "limit" orders (to buy, or "stop" orders to sell) to fix a price. But you may end up not making the trade at all, potentially a high price to pay to save 25 cents a share.

Wise Women Know

Is everyone trading online nowadays? It certainly seems that way. Fully one-fourth of all trades now come in over the net. Five years ago, online trading didn't even exist. But now there are upwards of three million online trading accounts, and the figure is expected to rise dramatically in the next few years.

Here are some (but by no means all) of the online brokerage houses that would love to place your trades for you:

➤ E*Trade (www.etrade.com) offers in-depth charts, company information, and personal portfolio management. Commissions start at $14.95.

➤ Muriel Siebert & Company (www.msiebert.com), owned by the first woman to buy a seat on the NYSE, has moved into online trading, too. Commissions start at $14.95 for the first 1,000 shares.

➤ Charles Schwab (www.cschwab.com) is for Schwab customers only. This discount broker's online site executes trades quickly and gives you in-depth portfolio information.

➤ Waterhouse Securities (www.waterhouse.com) was ranked at the very top of all online brokers by *Smart Money* magazine. Commissions are $12.95 for up to 5,000 shares. Real-time quotes and a fair amount of free research information are available.

➤ Ameritrade (www.ameritrade.com) offers real-time quotes and research. Commissions are as low as $8 per trade.

➤ InternetTrading.com (www.internettrading.com) margin accounts are eligible for free trading; most other trades are $14 per trade.

➤ National Discount Brokers (www.ndb.com) provides up-to-date financial news and other investment tools; most trades are $14.75.

Wealth Words

Day trader—Someone who jumps in and out of a stock on a daily basis, hoping to eke out a profit on the daily movements in price.

What About the Big Guys?

Are the full-service brokers on the verge of closing up shop and going home, unable to make money if folks are executing trades themselves? Not any time soon. A recent *Wall Street Journal* article on the future of online trading included this comment from Randal Langdon of Merrill Lynch: "There is a quantity of clients who are self-reliant. I think there is a significantly larger quantity of clients who recognize the importance of financial planning." P.S. Merrill Lynch does plan to begin offering online trading sometime in 1999.

Cozy Bedtime Reading

Some women don't spend all of their time reading a computer screen, nor should they (say the women who write books for a living...). Nothing beats curling up on a window seat in the morning with a good cup of coffee and a newspaper, or propping yourself up in bed with lots of soft pillows, maybe a little sweet snack, and a stack of magazines to read through. So here are the best of the old-fashioned paper-and-ink sources of business and financial news:

Magazines About Money

These magazines generally cost between $3 and $5 per issue.

➤ *Smart Money*

Published by the folks at the *Wall Street Journal*, *Smart Money* is an interesting read. Filled with articles on financial topics, as well as some general-interest consumer and smart travel pieces.

➤ *Worth*

Worth is a relatively new and fairly upscale magazine for the individual investor. Lots of articles on topics of interest to rich folks.

➤ *Individual Investor*

Founded 10 years ago by a fellow who wanted to educate individual investors, *Individual Investor* is a terrific source of information, analysis, and research.

➤ *Fortune*

Fortune is the magazine of *big* business. Filled with in-depth stories about major publicly traded companies, readers can learn quite a bit from this magazine.

➤ *Working Woman*

Not strictly a business or financial magazine, *Working Woman* is more career oriented. It does, however, run a monthly analysis of a stock index of the major woman-owned/woman-run publicly traded companies (just like womenswire.com does).

➤ *Forbes*

Much like *Fortune*, *Forbes* focuses on big, big business. Unlike *Fortune*, the articles seem to focus more on the personalities behind the companies, rather than on just dry biz info. A handy index in the front of the magazine lets you quickly see whether any articles pertain to companies in which you own stock. Owned by the Forbes family, this magazine is beholden to none and therefore can criticize anyone, no matter how powerful.

➤ *Money*

Among the oldest of the bunch, *Money* has just undergone a major graphic redesign to give it a fresher look. Its very readable articles frequently focus on "real people" and their investments.

➤ *The Economist*

A copy of *The Economist* on your coffee table is sure to impress your friends (assuming they know what it is). An international business and political magazine, the perspective is distinctly global. Frequent reading will broaden your ideas about how the international markets really link together. This British magazine also has sarcastic, amusing insights into U.S. politics.

➤ *Business Week*

True to its name, *Business Week* gives a good overview and in-depth analysis of what is up in the business world. This magazine will help you understand large business markets (like transportation or manufacturing) and how they might affect your own investment portfolio.

➤ *Wired*

Anne finds *Wired* to be a tremendous resource for keeping up with the high-tech business world (also, you can't miss the fluorescent covers on the newsstand).

Financial Newspapers

➤ *Wall Street Journal*

The grand old dame of financial news, the *Wall Street Journal* is still a must-read for everyone either employed or interested in the world of money. Its information and articles range from the global business world to wacky stories of entrepreneurs. Highly recommended for anyone serious about investing.

➤ *Investor's Business Daily*

Investor's Business Daily is heavier on the technical data than the *WSJ* is. Sections include "The New America," which covers rising new businesses, and "Leaders and Success," which traces the careers of well-known businesspeople. Each issue is filled with stock-rating tables and industry rankings.

➤ *Value Line*

Not strictly a newspaper, but not a magazine either (and definitely not a TV show), *Value Line* is a whole system of stock information, analysis, and ratings. Subscribers get an initial dose of very detailed financial information of companies organized by industry, complete with *Value Line*'s own analysis and rating of the industry and each company in the industry group. Monthly updates focus on a new group of industries. Each page of a *Value Line* edition describes one company. It has statistics on company debt, future retirement costs, number of employees, and other accounting statistics as well as a large chart showing past and projected future stock prices. If you're in the public library, take a moment to look at *Value Line*.

A 1-year subscription to *Value Line* will set you back the price of a medium-size TV set, but the company also offers trial periods for less than $100. Many subscribers have stayed loyal for years and have done quite well. An excellent source of detailed information, especially for those reluctant to chase it online.

The Financial Soaps

Television shows about money and finances used to be rare, but now they run all day long! You could, of course, just leave one of the big financial networks like CNBC or CNN on all day long and watch the ticker tape go by, or you could tune in at the end of the day for a daily wrap-up of the financial world. It's up to you.

➤ *Wall Street Week with Louis Rukeyser*

Would our week be complete without Lou to tell us about it every Friday night? A PBS version of *Friends,* Lou gathers expert after expert together to ruminate and pontificate. And please do not miss his pithy monologue at the beginning of the show.

➤ *The Nightly Business Report*

An early-evening show on PBS (check for local times in your area). The two anchors do a fine job of covering the day's stock trading and business news.

➤ CNBC

CNBC has established itself as the place to watch financial news all day long. A continuous loop of ticker tape across the screen shows the latest NYSE trades as well large block trades and prices from the smaller exchanges. CNBC has many shows to choose from—*Squawk Box, Market Watch, Power Lunch, Street Signs,* and *The Edge.*

➤ CNN

CNN does run many financial stories and reports on the market throughout the day but its primary money show is the afternoon and evening *Money Line News Hour with Lou Dobbs*.

➤ *The Wall Street Journal Report*

Produced by the venerable financial newspaper, check listings for the time and channel in your area. Note that it doesn't appear in some areas.

The Least You Need to Know

➤ The World Wide Web is a great place to find investment information and financial advice.

➤ Some sites have blank spreadsheets and financial calculators you can use to help you with investment and financial decisions.

➤ Online stock chat rooms and message boards are fun to read, but be wary of stock touters.

➤ Online broker commissions vary greatly, as do their financial requirements for opening an account.

➤ Financial newspapers and magazines still have much to offer. Serious investors should subscribe to at least two publications.

➤ While many networks offer financial programs, CNBC runs financial news all morning and afternoon.

➤ Never miss an episode of *Wall Street Week with Louis Rukeyser*.

Chapter 17

And the Ladies of the Club...the Investment Club!

In This Chapter

➤ Is there a club I can join?

➤ But will I get in?

➤ How does this all work?

➤ Meet the Sand Dollars

➤ Can I start a club with my friends?

What if there was a way to learn more about investing, rack up some pretty good average profits, and spend the entire time with a glass of wine in your hand enjoying the company of friends? There is such a thing, and it is happening in towns and neighborhoods all across the country. Investment clubs. Remember that big, best-selling book a few years ago with the group of ladies from Beardstown and the solid performers they'd chosen for their portfolios? They had an investment club.

What exactly is an investment club, you ask. Is that anything like the Christmas club that the bank runs? No, it is not just a savings plan. An investment club is a group of ordinary folks who commit to form a club that does the following:

➤ Meets monthly to discuss and examine a few stocks

➤ Invests on a regular basis in stocks that the members decide have good long-term prospects

➤ Is committed to investing for the long term, not simply for quick profits

Where does the money come from for an investment club? From the members. Each member commits to a monthly contribution that ranges from $25 to sums in the hundreds or thousands. The exact workings of an investment club depend on the members and what they have agreed to when they formed the club.

Imagine—if you pool your small monthly investment with the same amount from a group of other people, you all have greater purchasing power and the concepts of dollar-cost averaging and compounding interest will kick in on a higher level. Brilliant! Why didn't you think of that before?

A Short History Lesson

Investment clubs are not a particularly new idea. They have gotten much more press in recent years due to the popularity of the *Beardstown Ladies'* books and countless magazine and newspaper articles, but the very first club is believed to have been formed in Texas in 1898. The modern investment club movement really began in 1940, when a club in Detroit took it upon themselves to try to formalize the process and teach others how to form investment clubs. And in 1951, the National Association of Investment Clubs (NAIC) was formed. Some years later, the official name was changed to National Association of Investors Corporation. This organization's mission is to spread the message that investment clubs can be a great way for folks to participate in the stock market.

Under the aegis of the NAIC, thousands of investment clubs are operating around the country. And the majority of these investment clubs are made up of...women!

Wise Women Know

Small monthly investments certainly can pay off in the long run. The NAIC likes to point to the success of one of its longest running clubs—the Mutual Investment Club of Detroit. If a member joined in 1940 and paid in $20 a month for years for a total investment of $8,120, by average retirement age that sum would have grown to a value of $158,962. Quite a nice return on an investment of 8 grand!

The Ladies Club

Women have really taken to investment clubs as a way to both increase their financial education and increase their investment portfolios. According to the NAIC, 60.5% of NAIC members are women. How are these clubs doing?

The latest figures available show that women's investment clubs had an average return in 1997 of 17.9%. Not too shabby.

Why have women taken to investment clubs in such a big way? Shy and reluctant as some of us are to ask financial questions in mixed company, with a bunch of other women we can really ask anything and not worry about looking foolish. Some clubs—like the Beardstown Ladies—also combine a real social aspect with investing. Members swap recipes, family news, and bits of gossip in between stock reports. Other clubs are 100% business, no time to waste on trivial things when the topic is money!

Of course, not all investment clubs are limited to women members—nor should you just consider joining an all-woman's club. Find a group—or found a group (we'll tell you how in just a minute)—of people that you want to spend time with in the coming years, a group of people whose company you enjoy and whose knowledge you respect.

Wealth Words

NAIC—The National Association of Investors Corporation. Based in Michigan, this governing body helps investment clubs around the country.

You Again?!

And remember, you will be spending lots of time with these folks. The longer the club exists, 5 years, 10 years, 20 years, or more, the greater the odds for dramatically increased portfolio worth. Choose wisely.

Wealth Words

Investment club—A group of private individuals who pool their money and invest on a monthly basis in stocks that they have chosen for their long-term growth potential.

Get Educated

The real emphasis of the NAIC is investor education. The organization firmly believes that individual investors must research each and every stock purchase before making the decision to buy. Does that mean that you, as a member of an investment club, will be learning, too? You betcha. One of the requirements of membership in an investment club is that every member participate in researching and recommending stocks. Later in this chapter, we look closely at the inner workings of a real investment club—the Sand Dollars of Carmel—and you will see this principle in action. You will also see the very real benefits that club members get from all of this research and education.

The NAIC has developed quite a stock-picking program over the years. Revered by investment club members, it is called the Stock Selection Guide. When it is your turn to examine and recommend a stock to your fellow members, this is the method you will use. The Stock Selection Guide has five sections, and by researching and filling in each section, you slowly develop a complete understanding of the particular stock you are studying:

> Section 1: You begin by doing a visual analysis of sales, earnings, and price. To achieve this, you simply research and record sales, earnings, and stock prices for the past 10 years of the company's history. This information gives you a solid trend line that will help you quickly decide whether the stock merits further study.

> Section 2: Management is up next. You learn to determine how good a job the current management of the company is doing by evaluating them on the basis of two factors—(1) the sales and earnings per share trend line and (2) the pre-tax profit margin and return on shareholders equity.

> Section 3: You then record the last 5 years' high and low stock prices, earnings per share, high and low price/earnings ratios, dividend payouts, and yield figures. This information allows you to make estimates for the company's future.

> Section 4: Adjust all the figures you have gathered so far and estimate the future price action of the stock—whether you think it is headed up or down.

> Section 5: Evaluate the stock's potential in light of your investment club's goals. Does this stock fit in? Will you recommend a purchase or a pass?

Hmmm…sound like the math homework you used to try to get out of? Once you learn how, doing the research is not as daunting as it appears. And the research and evaluation skills that you will develop while doing this exercise will make you an extraordinarily well-informed investor. No more buying stock on a hot tip you overheard at lunch!

You also don't have to learn alone. When you join an investment club, ask to be paired with another member for research and recommendations. You two can divide up the research and then work through the evaluations together. You will also find that some clubs rely more heavily on the formula of the Stock Selection Guide than others do.

Goal Setting

Clubs may vary in terms of how much they invest monthly, but do they have different investment goals, too? No. The NAIC recommends that a club's objective should be to double its money within 5 years. This fairly conservative goal requires only an average 14.9% compounded annual growth rate to achieve.

As you read in earlier chapters, this growth rate will not come like clockwork every year. Some years the club's investments will return less than 14.9%, and in some glorious years it will do better than 14.9%. But remember, that is why it is best to invest for the long, long term. You will end up with a healthy average return as the years roll by.

Belonging to an investment club can be a valuable lifelong experience. But as with long-term returns, this approach works only if you stick with it for the long run. To help you decide whether an investment club is for you, take a close look at the four basic principles by which they operate:

➤ Invest regularly, regardless of the market outlook

➤ Reinvest all earnings

➤ Invest in growth companies

➤ Diversify to reduce risk

These good basic beliefs will help you and your fellow club members ignore the daily ups and downs of a fluctuating stock market. These beliefs, when consistently applied, should help you grow your money in the years to come.

But How Can I Find One, and Will I Get In?

Chances are that no matter where you live, you are not far from an active investment club. But is it looking for new members? When investment clubs are formed, they decide on a maximum number of members allowed. Some have up to 25 members; others have limited themselves to a much smaller membership. So, if you would like to join up with an already existing investment club, you will have to find one that is accepting new members.

Your best bet is to call the headquarters of the NAIC at 248-583-6242. You can also visit its Web site at www.better-investing.org. Once you have contacted the national headquarters, ask for the number for the NAIC council in your area. And it is on the local level that you should be able to find out whether any clubs in your area are seeking new members.

Wise Women Know

Although the local representative of the NAIC in your area can tell you how to contact the clubs in your area, he or she cannot recommend one over the other. Linda Johnson, who heads the Sacramento Valley Council for the NAIC, explains: "Investment clubs are considered by the SEC to be 'privately-run mutual funds.' And since they are considered to be mutual funds, that means that I can't recommend any particular fund over another as the SEC would consider that to be recommending funds without a broker's license!"

Check 'Em Out

Once you locate a club or clubs that do need members, arrange to attend a meeting or two as a guest. That way you will get a good sense of what the other members are like, how well their investments have done over the years, and what the club's overall investing philosophy is. Don't join an investment club without first checking it out thoroughly. Treat it just like you would any other major financial decision—do your homework!

If you can't find an investment club in your area that is accepting members, or you don't really feel like joining the clubs you do turn up, are there any other options? Sure, you can start your own investment club! Later in this chapter, we will tell you just how to do it.

What If I Need the Money?

So you join a club, invest on a monthly basis, and take great pride in watching the club's portfolio increase in size. And every month the financial officer of the club tells you just how much of that rising pie is yours. The number gets bigger and bigger and then...what if you actually need some or all of the money? How the heck do you get your money out of an investment club?

The ultimate goal is to leave your money in for as long as you can. But in the meantime, life happens. Your children need braces, private school, or soccer camp. And you need a second honeymoon, a home office, or a faster computer. There are two ways to withdraw money from the investment club:

➤ The club can cash you out. According to the guidelines drawn up by the NAIC and agreed to by all investment club members when they join, the club can either transfer securities to you that equal your share (you can then sell them to get the money) or can sell securities that it owns to raise the cash to buy you out.

➤ You can find someone to take your place. Let's say that your total piece of the club's pie—both through your monthly contributions for the last few years and the increased value of the portfolio—is now $9,000. The quickest and cleanest way for you to get out is to find someone else to buy into the club for $9,000. That way the club doesn't have to sell any stock to cash you out. There may well be a waiting list of folks who want to join your investment club, or you might have someone to recommend.

Now That I Belong, Can I Stop All My Other Trading?

Does being a member of a thriving investment club mean that you can sit back and let the club's investments do all the work for your portfolio? Heavens no! Educational as the clubs are, profitable as they can be, participating in an investment club should not be your only form of investing!

Wise Women Know

"Now that I belong to the Sand Dollar Investment Club, I am even more interested in trading on my own," Elisabeth McPhail told us. According to statistics gathered by the NAIC, when a club is formed, only two of the founding members will already have their own investment accounts. But after belonging to an investment club for 5 years, almost all the members have their own investment accounts.

Move over Beardstown Ladies—Here Come the Sand Dollars!

In the quaint little seaside town of Carmel, California, a group of women meet monthly—not to talk about their golf handicaps, not to organize the annual Carmel Bach Festival, but to talk about money. Serious money. Let's meet a few of the members and learn why they joined an investment club:

➤ Elisabeth McPhail is a married artist who paints both traditional landscapes and wall-size abstracts. For the first time in her life, she is learning something about money and finances. Her husband, as estate attorney, is pleased by her participation. He sees far too many widows who are unschooled in money matters.

➤ Maureen Chodosh is a residential real estate agent on the Monterey Peninsula and a recent widow. She was one of the founders of the Sand Dollars. As a result of her participation, Maureen feels much more confident dealing with the financial matters in her life.

➤ Dorothy Bradbury is now remodeling her house. Dorothy relies on her outside investments as a major source of income. She thought joining the club would be a good way to sort through the onslaught of financial information, and at the same time learn about finance with friends.

➤ Barbara Reding is a full-time watercolorist. She views her membership as an educational process and hopes to use the knowledge she gains to build her own portfolio.

➤ Myrna Brandwein, one of the founders, has been investing in the stock market on her own for many years. She joined because she thought it would be fun to get together with a group of other women and see what kind of investment ideas they might come up with together.

➤ Joan Schaffer, the club president, belonged once before to an investment club in southern California. The two groups are quite different. The first group was very much wedded to the NAIC philosophy of stock selection; the Sand Dollars are less committed. Joan just moved to the Carmel area and helped form the club to meet new friends.

The members of the Sand Dollars meet in the late afternoon once a month at a local golf club. Early on, the members decided that the club's meetings should be focused on the investment business at hand, and not revolve around lunches or dinners. Here is a brief glimpse of a typical meeting:

Their most recent meeting started off with a special presentation on how to read *Investors Business Daily*. Dorothy Bradbury taught herself about the different types of information readers can glean from this specialized publication, and shared her new-found knowledge with the other members. At past meetings there have been special presentations on topics like how to establish investment goals.

The members then gave their stock manager's reports (each member is assigned a stock to research and follow). Here are a few brief examples of the reports that the members gave on some of their holdings:

➤ Elisabeth reported on EMC, and mentioned that it still had a "strong buy" rating from several brokerage houses.

➤ Myrna gave the closing price on Cisco, and informed members that a stock split was coming later in the month. She recommended that the club buy more shares.

➤ Joyce gave her report on Abbot Labs, and said that it should be considered a long-term hold with an A+ rating.

The club members also discussed whether to buy Coca-Cola, and whether to sell Disney and buy more Cisco. This led to a larger discussion on the balance of their portfolio and just what was a good reason to sell a stock. They all agreed that unless the fundamentals had changed within a good company, it would be better to hold the stock. Another member pointed out that the club would be liable for a higher capital gains tax if the stock was not held for at least 18 months.

Sounds Great—I'm Calling All My Friends to Start a Club!

Would you prefer to start your own investment club rather than join up with a group of strangers? New investment clubs are being formed at an astonishing rate. Here is a basic sense of what you must do to start an investment club:

First, get a copy of the NAIC's book, *Starting and Running a Profitable Investment Club,* by Thomas O'Hara and Kenneth S. Janke, Sr., published by Times Business (ISBN 0-8129-9032-3).

This handbook contains all the information about standard membership agreements, the system of accounting you will need to track and record each member's holdings, and the stock evaluation system that the NAIC recommends. You should be able to get a copy through your local bookstore.

Your next step is to identify prospective members.

Just like joining an existing investment club, take the time to make sure that these are people that you wouldn't mind seeing every single month for years to come. Also, make sure that the folks you approach are all of one mind when it comes to the club's investment philosophy: long-term, modest growth. If those conservative concepts aren't sexy enough for some folks, best not to invite them in. The NAIC cautions that a conflict in philosophy has wrecked many an investment club.

You'll need to decide how big the club should be. Most clubs average around 15 members. That gives you a large enough pool from which to draw club officers, yet small enough to run fairly informal meetings. To end up with 15, however, you might have to start with 20! Count on a few dropouts in the beginning.

Call an informal exploratory meeting.

This way you can all get together and check each other out, discuss investment philosophy, and broach the topic of how large the monthly contribution should be. Pass out copies of the sample club agreement form from the book *Starting and Running a Profitable Investment Club*. Try to find an experienced investment club member from another group to attend your meeting and give folks a sense of what it is all really about.

Then form an investment club!

Once the other prospective members familiarize themselves with how this works, if enough of them want to form a new club—go for it! Using the advice in the NAIC book, draw up the partnership agreements, elect your officers, decide the amount of your monthly contributions and where and when your meetings should be held—and you're off!

From Investment Club to Country Club

As we've pointed out before, participating in an investment club is a wonderful move for any individual investor. But it should not be your only investment account. You will learn more than you ever thought possible about investing and stock selection, and you will become more methodical and analytical in your approach to the stock market. Take all of that knowledge and use it to build your own separate investment account.

The sums of money that investment clubs accumulate over time are impressive—but are seldom enough for all the club members to retire on. In your own separate investment account, you might well mimic many of the club's purchases and trades. You might also include stocks that you have studied on your own or stocks that the club decided not to purchase. Over the years you will have the satisfaction of watching two accounts grow—your investment club money and your own private money. Just think—you'll have two baskets of eggs that you can use to steady yourself in the years to come!

Cash Cautions

Be warned—25% of newly formed investment clubs close down within 2 years. The NAIC attributes this phenomenon to "poor member selection," and a "get-rich-quick" mentality. Remember that, to avoid disappointment and frustration, all members need to agree at the outset to common financial goals with a long-term philosophy.

The Least You Need to Know

➤ Investment clubs are groups of people who pool their money to make monthly stock purchases with long-term growth in mind.

➤ Investment clubs are a great way to acquire in-depth stock analysis skills and to enhance your financial education.

➤ You can either start your own club from scratch with the help of the NAIC or find an existing investment club that needs new members.

➤ Most investment clubs in the country are run by and for women. Many women are more comfortable talking stocks in a woman-only environment.

➤ Each member is required to do in-depth research and analysis of a stock from time to time and to follow that stock after the club purchases it.

➤ The goals of an investment club must be for long-term, slow growth. Clubs with unrealistic expectations generally dissolve within 2 years.

➤ Do not rely solely on your investment club participation to secure your financial future—start a second account in which you can invest larger sums and control yourself.

Part 5

When I Am an Old Woman, I Shall Wear Purple Cashmere

At some point, it will be time to retire. And by starting now, you are working to ensure that your retirement will be a comfortable one. Walk through the basics of retirement investing and through the specifics of the different types of retirement accounts. Not all plans are designed to meet everyone's needs, so you'll soon see which is best for your life.

And a bit more about taxes…how to defer them for as long as is legally possible to keep your money working and growing.

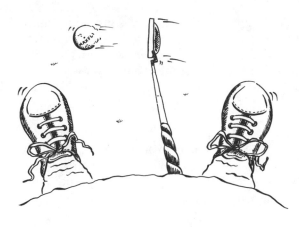

Chapter 18

Basic Retirement Planning

In This Chapter

➤ Women—the stronger sex

➤ Social Security—it's no way to live

➤ But won't my costs go down?

➤ The good life—guaranteed?

➤ No more bills to pay!

➤ The old family home

Gender is a much-discussed issue in our society. When facing the realities of retirement, a woman's gender works both for her and against her. The good news is that we live longer, and generally enjoy healthier lives than our male counterparts. The bad news is that by virtue of our longer existence, it costs more to sustain us in our old age. To complicate this problem, we often make less in income than our male counterparts, and we save a smaller percentage of our smaller income toward our retirement. And where does that get us? Alive and healthy, but widowed and sometimes just scraping by. The statistics support these general comments. Women have to work harder and longer to save an adequate retirement nest egg. To feel the peace of mind that comes from knowing that you will not outlast your resources, read on and remember.

The Stronger Sex

The U.S. Department of Health and Human Resources provides the following estimates for income sources during retirement. (The estimates apply to households where the occupants are age 65 or older, and have an income greater than $29,000 per year.) The category for *other sources of income* applies to government employee pensions, railroad retirement and public assistance, and accounts for 12%. *Earned income* accounts for 27% of a retiree's household. Income from *savings and investments* accounts for 33%. *Pensions* sponsored by private industry—your non-government employer—account for 10%, and finally *Social Security* provides 18% of the retirement income for these households.

What does this tell us?

Take a look at your current plan and resources. Are you a government employee? What does your employer project your retirement benefit to be? We know it's only a guess but go with us for a few paragraphs on this topic. Do you plan to do any work during retirement that would provide you with earned income?

And here is the really critical question—are you accumulating enough in savings and investments to provide you with at least 30% of your required income in retirement?

For example, if you need $40,000 per year to live, you need approximately $120,000 in savings, yielding a 10% return to give you $12,000, or approximately 33% of your required $40,000. Are you on your way to accumulating the $120,000?

Do you work for an employer who offers a retirement plan? If so, do you participate in the plan to the full allowable amount each year? Finally, how big a part of your retirement income depends on your Social Security benefit?

Lighten Up!

Yes, these are profound questions, but we want you to lighten up and enjoy the process of exploring your planning. We want to motivate you to look at the future, make your best guess, and start committing some of your energy and resources to providing for retirement. Let's call this the concept of paying yourself first. After all, most of us live in the present and do not allow ourselves the time or energy to consider our needs in retirement. Then, as we open the cover to the deep dark box called retirement, we shudder at the enormous task ahead of us, slam the door shut, and hide in deep denial. Instead, let's approach this as a serious, but surely not insurmountable, issue. As Anne sometimes must gently remind her clients, we all have the option of *not* ever retiring!

Work Without End

You might scoff at such a notion, but many people who retire actually do other work in retirement. Others continue their career in a semi-retired state. The motivation to do so is not always financial, but even when it is, many people still find working more comfortable than complete retirement. At the other end of the spectrum are people who retire comfortably and cannot imagine how they ever found time to work, since they are so busy in retirement.

Will My Costs Go Down?

Many people also find that life is less expensive in retirement. They are comfortable and happy each day, without spending as much money as they did in their working life. This feeling is easy to understand when you remember you have *time* to shop for better prices. You have *time* to repair or make a broken appliance last longer. You do not need to update your wardrobe as much. Your car usually has less mileage without a work commute. The reasons it can be cheaper to live retired are endless.

We do not mean to imply that you can plan your retirement around "living on less." We only mean to stress that statistically, people tend to spend less to maintain their happy existence in retirement. The exception to this picture is the unknown costs of health care.

Social Security—Save Me!

Many Americans rely too heavily on Social Security as a component of retirement income. Women are statistically more vulnerable here, too. We strongly recommend that you proceed from this point forward in your life with the goal that Social Security account for only 20% or less of your retirement income. If you are starting without other resources, your work is cut out for you.

While many people seem to think it tantamount to treason to believe that the Social Security system might not be there when they retire, the plain truth is that we should all be wary of relying on Social Security. Based on our government's ability to manage money (witness decades of budget deficits and a national debt too big to count, or measure), we strenuously recommend you make other plans for your retirement income. We do not say this to frighten you, just to keep you on track for securing your retirement.

Consider the history of Social Security; it was never intended to be a national pension plan or a primary retirement program. It was intended to act as a safety net for people who did not make adequate plans for themselves. If you turn the clock back 100 years in this country, most folks' retirement program was to rely on the generosity (or guilt) of their grown children. Presumably, your personal wealth grew, and your children had both the means and the heart to care for you. The government did not provide Social Security until early in this century. At that time, the creators of Social Security did not intend to keep you comfortable, but rather to rescue you from unforeseen disaster. This philosophy should be obvious in the meager size of the payments.

Should You Go With the Flow?

If we have not persuaded you to make plans that can secure you against relying on Social Security, please read on. Remember that it is the public faith that ultimately keeps the retirement system afloat. We are not here to break your faith in the public trust, but in the end, do you want to count on your own plans or leave your retirement livelihood in the hands of the government.

Let's remember, "we the people" are the government. Social Security is not a pile of money in the big bank in the sky.

Think of the Social Security system as a kitchen sink that is holding a little water (money). The water going down the drain represents the retired people who are drawing out of Social Security. The working people, who see their paychecks devastated by taxes and Social Security deductions, are the water flowing from the tap into the sink. Once the baby boomers (those born between 1945 and 1965) leave the tap (retire from their work) and descend into the drain (begin drawing their Social Security benefit monthly) a potential problem exists. Will there be enough workers to maintain the flow of the tap water so that it doesn't all disappear down the drain?

Wealth Words

Social Security benefit—The monthly amount you receive upon retirement from your lifelong contribution to the Social Security system.

Do not imagine that Social Security acts like your individual retirement account (IRA), where the dollars the Social Security folks withdraw from your paycheck are put aside with your name on them for the future. Many people erroneously believe that Social Security is a forced savings program. We hate to break it to you, but it is much more like another "entitlement" program, where the dollars you put in now support the people retired now. This system works as long as there are more workers than retired people. It does not work when the baby boomers (who represent a big slice of the population) stop paying in and instead begin drawing out.

More Water Under the Bridge

Let's continue the kitchen sink analogy for other forms of retirement savings and income. Your employer's (both government and private industry) pension plan actually has water (money) flowing into a big sink, accumulating there, for your future use. In some cases, such as a 401(k) plan, the funds are in your very own mini-sink, with your name and only your name on the sink. Even with the other kinds of pension plans, where all the water is in one sink, you are accumulating credit toward using your share of the water in retirement, and it is truly building up in a very large sink! You could, over time, consider this to be like a small lake, or at least as big as a water-storage tower.

Continuing to earn income in retirement is like continuing to spend some of your time in the tap while you start to spend some of your time in the drain! Obviously, it follows that saving money and investing on your own, in retirement plans like IRAs or any other savings accounts for that matter, is our favorite plan. This is because you are selecting your own sink, committing yourself to slowly filling it from this day forward, and rewarding yourself in retirement by allowing yourself to move from tap to drain!

Priming the Pump

In our ongoing effort to keep you from going down the drain, the next several chapters explain in detail about these other special sinks you can create to accumulate your own Atlantic Ocean of water. Regardless of how you choose to do it, the pay yourself first attitude is key. Would 10% of the dollars you earn today, when put aside in this sink, grow to be enough for your retirement? This question is a common one, and there are many computer programs, advisors and methods to extrapolate and predict the correct amount to set aside.

The most important point is not to let the process get clogged up in the effort to determine how much is enough. Any amount you can afford to save is better than not saving at all. If 10% is not a hardship for you, save more. If you simply can't do it, save as much as you possibly can. Once you have committed to filling the sink, regardless of the rate, invest some time exploring opportunities to "lend your sink of water" to someone else (for example, a bank, the U.S. government, or a corporation). The borrower will pay back your water and much more (interest, capital gains, or dividends). This effort to make your water useful to someone else will help you to grow your supply as fast as possible.

Area 51

On a lighter note, we read in a brochure recently that, according to one survey, more people believe in the existence of UFOs (unidentified flying objects) than in the future of Social Security. The government is aware of these fears. The projections show there will be money available when baby boomers start retirement in large numbers around 2010. What changes is our government considering to assure us that this source of income will be there for us in the future? Let's take a look at some of the options:

➤ It could increase the "retirement age" to reflect the increasing life expectancy of Americans.

➤ It could decrease benefits to people who enjoy a higher income in retirement.

➤ It could increase the amount the working population pays in payroll taxes.

➤ It could allow individuals to invest a portion of their Social Security contributions in the private investment vehicle of their choice.

All of these options essentially change the flow into and out of the sink. Unfortunately, even these kinds of "reforms" will be selected and modified in the name of political expedience. This situation reinforces our insistence that you make plans to aggressively fill your very own sink with water.

The Good Life—Is It Guaranteed?

We do not use the word "aggressive" lightly. You must secure enough education to be comfortable with investments that are not strictly guaranteed. At the time this book was published, interest rates on guaranteed investments were at a 20-year low. In a time of low interest rates, your sink of water will accumulate painfully slowly if you can only sleep at night with guaranteed investments. As you commit yourself to saving your hard-earned income for your retirement, you need to make an additional commitment. You must learn about risk, volatility, and reward. You must learn about the relationship between the time you commit to an investment and the reward you garner from the investment.

If you start very young, and get lucky with some rise in interest rates over your lifetime, you might be able to fill your sink as full as necessary, using only guaranteed investments. But the good life might be very far out of reach to those who do not undertake any risk at all.

No More Bills to Pay!

It is not possible to discuss a plan for retirement without deciding where your debts fit into the picture. The American dream has many components. Right there next to the white picket fence is the dream of retiring debt-free. Why do you suppose the 30-year mortgage is standard form? The post–World War II explosion of home building and mass exodus to the suburbs involved people in their mid-20s to early 30s. These people all wanted the house paid off before retirement, which at that time was nearly 30 years off for them.

While 30 years is still the most prevalent mortgage time frame, statistically, mortgages are usually rewritten every 7 years. This number reflects two important trends in our society:

➤ We move around a lot.

➤ We have had such sweeping interest rate declines that refinancing a mortgage often makes sense.

Do most Americans achieve debt-free retirement? No, most retired Americans do not live free of a mortgage.

Is it advisable to be mortgage-free upon retirement? The answer is truly a matter of personal tolerance and preference. The last bastion of tax relief is the interest you pay on your primary mortgage, and even on a second mortgage. If you feel secure about your income stream in retirement, your monthly mortgage payment will not be a big burden and you will continue to enjoy

Cash Cautions

Even if you keep your old house and live there until the end...your children might not be able to afford to inherit it! In Jennifer's family, the house her parents still live in was built by her grandfather and has always been in the family. But it is now worth close to a million dollars. Should she and her three siblings inherit the house and one of them wanted to live there, he or she would need $750,000 to buy out the others!

some tax relief. On the other hand, imagine what you could do with the money if you paid off your mortgage and retired debt free! This is a goal you should consider. One other consideration here is that you might not live in your current home in retirement. It might be more than you want or need at that time in your life, and prove to be an ideal time to move to a cheaper, smaller home.

The Old Family Home

The old family house is a tradition that is waning in our society. There are many reasons for this change in tradition. The prevalence of divorce is a primary reason. With approximately half of all marriages ending in divorce, many families cannot afford to retain the "family house."

Furthermore, many people do not want to grow old alone in the family house. Time was when perhaps a grown child and his or her family would move in as mom or dad got on in years, eventually handing the family house down through the generations. This situation is not as common it used to be. And the fact that we all move around so much in our careers is another reason why the old family house tradition is waning.

Your government will even make the decision to sell the family house easier by granting a tax break to you when you sell your home. At the time of this book's publication, the government allowed you to sell your home and retain up to a $500,000 profit without paying a capital gains tax. Many folks about to retire opt to sell the house. They then pay off the remaining mortgage. This plan allows them to capture some of the cash value of the home for investments that will provide them with retirement income. They take some of the proceeds from the larger home, purchase a smaller home with cash, and invest the remainder for income.

Your home is one of your largest investments. But most of you will not grow old and retire in your current home. Therefore, the quest to be mortgage-free can be accomplished in many ways. You need only decide which is most comfortable for you, and plan accordingly.

Taking the Plunge

As we plunge forth (or wade through, to continue our watery metaphors) into the following chapters, we will explore your employer sponsored retirement plans. We will also examine the kinds of retirement plans available to the self-employed and to small-business owners. Finally, we move into annuities, a type of investment that combines some of the advantages of retirement accounts with some of the advantages of insurance. These are basically all sinks of water you can select for the accumulation of your private ocean. They might not all be

Wealth Words

Tax-deferred—To delay the tax liability on an investment until a later date. Keep in mind that this is a postponement, not a total elimination, of tax liability.

appropriate for you, but at least one of these alternatives is imperative. They all assist you in your quest for retirement security.

One crucial feature they all share is *tax-deferred* accumulation of your money. *Tax-deferred* means that your money is in a sink that receives special consideration from the IRS. "What kind of special consideration," you might ask. In this case, the IRS only monitors the flow of water *into* and *out of* the sink, that is, deposits and withdrawals of money. The growth (income and capital gains) that you achieve within the sink are not of interest to the IRS. The result is that your dollars build faster—significantly faster. This is good news. Growing money tax deferred is an advantage to all of us.

Back to the Sink

In terms of our water-in-the-sink analogy, these retirement accounts and annuities are sinks that do not have an IRS hose dipped into the top—a hose that in other kinds of sinks is constantly siphoning off 20% to 35% of the yield or growth that you have been clever enough to secure. For the sake of this example, think of the IRS as the suction hose the dentist uses. Obviously, your pool of water will grow deeper, faster, without the IRS continuously suctioning off the tax portion of the build-up.

Wealth Words

Tax-free—A type of investment that is not subject to income tax.

Let us be mindful of the fact that *tax-deferred* is not *tax-free*. The IRS is closely watching the water tap and the drain. When you reach retirement age and start to remove money from your tax-deferred investments, you will pay your tax. Your withdrawals will be taxed as ordinary income, at whatever your income tax rate is at the time you are retired.

Taxing Matters

This brings us to an important point. Most people believe their income tax rate will drop at retirement. This is usually not true.

Granted, it is a benefit to grow your funds without taxes constantly eroding your growth. But it is important to make the distinction between tax-deferred, which means you do pay income tax eventually, and tax-free, which means you never pay a tax.

Meet Your New Friends—the Roth Family!

Just when you think you have these various differences squared away in your mind, your government rolls out another alternative. The Roth IRA reverses the tax bite. With the Roth IRA, you put dollars in that have already been taxed, but all the growth of those dollars will come out the other end at retirement tax-free! To use our sink analogy with the Roth IRA, the IRS has its suction hose on the tap, taking its tax out of the dollars (water) that flow into the Roth IRA. They leave the sink alone, and the big reward for the use of a Roth IRA is that the IRS never asks you for a tax when the water leaves the sink through the drain.

You might be very excited and want to run right out to sign up for your Roth IRA. But first read the next chapter because not everyone qualifies for a Roth IRA. At the risk of sounding cynical, the Roth IRA sink is not available to many members of the voting, tax-paying population, but your government has received some swell publicity from creating the new savings vehicle.

Cash Cautions

Despite widespread publicity of its availability and attractiveness, the recently created Roth IRA is not really available to everyone.

The most important part of retirement planning is to do something. Start as soon as you can. Save as much as you can. Learn as much as you can about investments *beyond* the guaranteed choices. Be consistent in paying yourself first. Start to imagine exactly what lifestyle you hope to enjoy in retirement. Imagine what that style will cost. Save, Save, Save.

The Least You Need to Know

➤ Women generally outlive men but have far less money in retirement.

➤ Some retired people find that daily life is much less expensive when they no longer have careers to maintain.

➤ Social Security will probably still be there when you need it, but the actual monthly checks are not large.

➤ Regardless of how much you have paid into Social Security, your benefit is predetermined. But there is no limit on how big your other retirement accounts can grow.

➤ More people believe in the idea of UFOs than in the idea that Social Security will still be there when they need it.

➤ For greater growth potential, you should put some of your retirement money into riskier, more aggressive investments, rather than putting it all into guaranteed investments.

➤ Many folks opt to retire their mortgage (that is, pay it off so they have one less bill to worry about) at the same time as they retire from the workforce.

➤ You may sell your long-time family home and not pay capital gains tax on the first $500,000 of gains.

Chapter 19

All About Employer-Sponsored Plans

In This Chapter

➤ Say goodbye to the traditional pension plan

➤ 401(k)—the better way!

➤ What you contribute

➤ What your company might contribute

➤ How to invest your contribution

➤ Spreading the risk

You've heard us emphasize repeatedly that saving money requires two things: the commitment to save and the right vehicle for saving. Without the proper vehicle, no amount of desire will help you reach your goals. Similarly, unless you're truly committed to saving, no investment vehicle can do the job by itself. One can't work without the other.

That's what makes employer-sponsored retirement plans like 401(k)s ideal vehicles for putting money away. The best part is that you participate automatically through payroll deduction—the money never passes through your hands, so you're never tempted to spend it on something else. Better still, your employer does most of the work while continuing to bear the legal duty (called a *fiduciary* responsibility) to provide you with a sound investment. Investing for retirement doesn't get much simpler than that.

Say Goodbye to the Old Company Pension

It used to be that the only retirement benefit most employers offered came from a traditional pension plan. You qualified for the plan by passing an initial probationary period of employment. Then, over the course of your employment with that employer, money was contributed on your behalf to a pension fund, sort of a giant kitty, which the employer invested (wisely, one hoped). Earnings on those investments funded the benefits paid to retired employees. Social Security works similarly.

Wealth Words

Payroll deduction—Money that is taken from your paycheck before you receive it. The deductions are listed on your pay stub.

When you retired, usually at age 65 or older, you began drawing a monthly pension. The amount you received depended on your salary and how long you had worked for that employer. For this reason, a traditional pension plan is sometimes described as a *defined-benefit plan*: the amount of the benefit is defined by length of employment and earnings.

Designing a Better Way

Traditional pension plans began to disappear in the 1970s when the first baby boomers entered the job market. Employers found they needed new ways to attract the best employees. Attractive benefit packages, including generous retirement plans, became a prime recruitment tool.

But to offer generous retirement benefits, an employer either had to pay more into a retirement fund for each employee, which would simply cost more money, or had to be able to grow a bigger retirement fund by investing it more aggressively, which meant taking on more risk. The solution? Retirement plans that gave employees more control over the size of their retirement benefit.

Here is how they work: Instead of putting money into a retirement plan, the employer would give that money directly to the employee in the form of salary, which the employee could then invest in a tax-deferred retirement account provided by the employer. The employee's incentive to participate included the opportunity to shelter income in a tax-deferred investment, as well as the control the employee had over the potential return on that investment. Risk-taking employees—and the baby boom generation has produced more than a few risk takers—could do very well for themselves with these kinds of plans.

Employers also liked these plans. The potential for greater returns attracted employees, which made the funds bigger. Spreading the investment risk over a greater number of investors made the investment more stable. For although employers were giving employees more say in how their retirement funds were invested, the employer remained legally responsible for the soundness of the investments they offered. Greater participation helped keep things sound.

401(k), the King of Plans

Nowadays these kinds of plans have almost entirely replaced the traditional retirement pension. The most common of these is the 401(k) plan, which is available from large for-profit employers. (Public and not-for-profit employers can offer 403(b) plans. Except for the names, which simply refer to the sections of the federal tax code that govern them, these types of plans are functionally identical. For the sake of discussion, everything we say about 401(k) plans applies to both.) People working for smaller employers and the self-employed have other options discussed in the next chapter.

Such plans are known as *salary-reduction plans*. They allow you to reduce your salary *before* taxes by the amount of your contribution to the tax-deferred retirement plan offered by your employer. These plans are also sometimes called *defined-contribution plans* to distinguish them from traditional pension plans, where the benefit was defined by your salary and length of employment. With a defined-contribution plan, your contribution is fixed, either as a dollar amount or a percentage of monthly earnings up to a maximum each year.

Wealth Words

Tax code—The body of law that covers taxes. The codes are identified by a system of numbers and letters, hence the 401(k).

Who's Putting Up the Money?

With this type of plan, you contribute toward your own retirement, usually by arranging to have your contribution taken directly out of your paycheck. Some employers also match an employee's contribution. This program is known as *profit sharing*, since the money the employer contributes comes out of profits. Some employers even match employee contributions dollar for dollar. Needless to say, the profit-sharing component is quite attractive to employees who have access to 401(k) plans and is yet another way employers encourage participation in a retirement plan.

Wealth Words

Matching contributions—A program whereby some employers will match dollar for dollar the employee's contributions to a retirement plan, up to a certain maximum percentage.

The Power of Your Money

Now listen carefully: If your employer offers this type of retirement plan, you *must* participate. Okay, it's your money, and you always have a choice on how to invest it, but you'd be a fool not to take advantage of a 401(k).

First of all, the payroll-deduction method of contributing makes it extremely easy to save for retirement. Any investment vehicle that lets you save automatically without having to think about it is better than any vehicle that requires you to handle the money you intend to save.

A far more important reason to participate, however, is the fact that you'll be investing with *pre-tax* dollars. The money gets invested *before* you pay taxes on it, so you have more to invest. Instead of saving just 72 cents of every dollar—which is all that you'd have available if you're in the 28% federal income tax bracket and plan to save from your after-tax earnings—you get to use 100 cents of every dollar. That 28-cent difference can become huge over the lifetime of the investment.

Wise Women Know

You can use pretax money for more than 401(k) contributions. Check with your company's human resources department. There may be a program already in place to use pre-tax money for a day care or health care savings account. These plans can greatly reduce your costs.

So you'd be crazy not to participate, particularly if your employer offers profit sharing. Yet not everyone who is eligible to participate in a 401(k) does so. Merrill Lynch's Ninth Annual Retirement and Financial Planning Survey, conducted in 1997, showed that less than 75% of employees who have access to a 401(k) plan actually participate. Even more astonishing, 25% of the employees who didn't participate couldn't give a reason for not doing so! (The remaining non-participants said they couldn't afford to participate, weren't yet eligible, their employers didn't match contributions, or they didn't like the investment options.) Ignorance may be bliss, but we can't recommend it as an investment strategy.

What You Contribute

As a participant in a 401(k) plan, you choose how much to contribute. Usually, it's a specific dollar amount or a percentage of your monthly salary, up to an annual limit set by federal law. For the 1998 tax year, the limit was $10,000 or 20% of compensation, whichever is less.

Max Out!

If you can possibly afford it, you should contribute the maximum amount each year. Remember, your goal is to retire in a manner to which you'd *like* to grow accustomed—the more you put away now, the more you can count on later.

And don't con yourself into believing you can afford to put off contributing the maximum amount until later. If you short yourself now by contributing less than you can really afford, you'll simply have less opportunity to make up for it as you get older. Making up for years of neglect is never easy, whether it involves saving money or working on your abs! Pay yourself (and your future security) first, before buying more toys today.

By contributing the maximum, you'll actually be killing two birds with one stone. Since your contribution reduces the amount of your salary that is subject to federal income tax, you're not only building a retirement nest egg but also reducing your annual income tax burden. Once you retire, your income will be somewhat lower—*that's* when you want to be paying taxes on this money, not now, while your tax liability is high. (And when you retire, you may still want to defer taxes by rolling the distribution into another tax-deferred investment. See Chapter 20 for some options.)

If you're earning enough that you can save still more money even after making the maximum contribution, talk to your investment counselor about investment options for that additional money.

How to Invest Your Contribution

Your employer is required by law to provide you with a selection of at least three widely differing tax-deferred investments, ranging from conservative (relatively modest returns, but with little risk) to aggressive (potentially lucrative, but riskier). The number of options varies with the employer. Larger employers can count on greater participation in their plans, so they typically have the resources to offer more options. These typically include some or all of the following:

➤ Money market fund

➤ Equity (stock) fund

➤ Bonds

➤ Balanced (stock and bond) fund

➤ International (stock and bond) fund

If for some reason you don't indicate where you want to invest your retirement contributions, your employer will choose for you. Typically that choice is a money market fund, the most conservative of the options.

Otherwise, you choose among the options the way you would choose any investment, according to how much risk you can afford to take. This, in turn, depends on how soon you need the money.

When you're younger, you can afford to take a chance on a somewhat riskier investment, since you have plenty of working years to recover from a less-than-ideal result. Since you'll be investing the money for a longer period, the standard advice is to lean toward equities (stocks), which tend to outperform other types of investments over the long haul.

If you're older, you'll need the money that much sooner, so you may not be able to afford the same degree of risk. Bonds are less volatile, though also less potentially lucrative, over the short term. This is why bonds are the preferred choice for older investors.

Cash Cautions

Never have your retirement funds 100% invested in the stock of the company you work for. This strategy is putting all of your eggs in one basket—a risky proposition. Own a mixture of items to lower the risk.

For older employees, other factors to consider when choosing an investment vehicle include the interest rate environment, the amount of money you have to invest, and how soon you'll need it. Losing part of a very large nest egg to a risky investment has very different consequences than losing most of a smaller amount.

Some publicly traded companies also offer employees the option of buying stock in the company, usually at a discount. Before going this route, consider our advice about investing in the stock market. Generous as that may sound, remember that you *never* want to invest all of your money in a single stock, so consider this as just one of your options for investing your contribution.

Spread the Risk

For most employees, the goal in selecting investments should be diversification (variety). It's best to put some of your money in more conservative (safer) investments and some in riskier investments. This approach increases the chance that you'll benefit from growth opportunities while insulating your money from the ups and downs that may occur with any one of these types of investments.

As we've said before, the exact mix of investments depends on factors such as your age and the amount of money in question. You should count on periodically reviewing and adjusting the mix depending on financial conditions and how close you are to retiring. Federal law allows you to adjust the direction of your contributions as often as every quarter. However, if your time horizon is long term, please be certain you don't make adjustments too often. A good plan is meant to be reviewed, but should not need frequent revisions. Stay your course.

This Money Belongs to You

Another important fact to remember about salary-reduction plans is that it's your money. With the old pension fund, an employer added money on your behalf to one big pot. With a 401(k), you make the contribution directly.

Because it's your money, you still have access to it after you stop working for your present employer. However, because this type of investment is tax-deferred, you face penalties for using the money before you reach age 59$\frac{1}{2}$. Therefore, when changing employers (for whatever reason) and withdrawing from your employer's 401(k) plan, you must make provisions to reinvest that money. Receiving a large check from your retirement plan may seem like a windfall, but avoid any temptation to treat yourself by spending this "new" money. You'd be scrambling your own nest egg!

The law allows you to avoid paying taxes and penalties if you reinvest the money within 60 days in another tax-deferred plan, such as a rollover IRA or an annuity. You also are free to roll your assets into your next employer's sponsored plan; however, we do not recommend this alternative. You're always better off taking the opportunity to regain control over your own money. Your best bet is to put the money into a rollover IRA *and* participate in your new employer's retirement plan.

Stiff Penalties Ahead

Fortunately, the penalties for using the money before age 59$\frac{1}{2}$ are stiff enough to make most people think twice. If you don't directly reinvest the money in a tax-deferred investment (by sending your employer instructions with the new account number), your employer will withhold 20% for any income taxes you owe (you'd have to pay the difference if you owed more than 20% in taxes). You would also pay a 10% premature-distribution tax for early withdrawal, although this penalty is waived if the money is withdrawn because you have become disabled, used it for deductible medical expenses that total more than 7.5% of your gross annual income, or died. (But you would still owe taxes.)

Penalty-Free!

Upon reaching age 59$\frac{1}{2}$, so long as you meet your employer's other eligibility criteria for withdrawing retirement funds, you become eligible to use your money without paying the early-withdrawal penalty. Your options at this point include accepting the money in a lump sum, in which case you must pay taxes on it; reinvesting the money in a rollover IRA or an annuity, which allows you to continue sheltering it from taxes; or arranging to receive regular payouts from your former employer, which would also be taxable as they are distributed.

Cash Cautions

Be sure to investigate all tax implications before deciding to cash out at retirement age.

Each option has different tax ramifications, so get your tax advisor's or accountant's advice about which strategy is best for you.

Dealing with Risk

With 401(k) plans, employers shifted some of the risk of investing to their employees, even though employers continue to have a legal duty to ensure that the investment vehicles they offer are sound—a sound investment vehicle can lose money if the stock market goes down or a foreign currency collapses. The risk for employees involves the freedom to choose between risk and reward offered by such plans.

You may choose not to participate, believing you can get a better return on this money by investing it in other ways, such as real estate or stocks. Or maybe you feel intimidated by all the choices and the risks they represent.

Whether you're an investing wizard or an intimidated novice, remember that the best savings plan is the one that's easiest and few plans are quite as easy as a 401(k). As Amelia Earhart once said, "Adventure in itself is worthwhile." Think of participating in a 401(k) plan as an adventure! It's certainly worthwhile.

The Least You Need to Know

➤ Traditional company pensions are a thing of the past—today you must manage your own pension.

➤ Never pass up the chance to participate in a 401(k) plan.

➤ Always make the maximum allowable contribution—it will make a big difference in 20 years.

➤ Take advantage of a matching-contribution program if your employer offers one.

➤ Pre-tax dollars are the best ones to invest—you get 100% of your money instead of 78%.

➤ Never invest 100% of your retirement funds in the stock of the company you work for.

➤ Early withdrawal penalties are *stiff*—leave your retirement nest egg alone and let it grow.

Chapter 20

More Ways to Drive a Retirement Vehicle

In This Chapter

➤ Individual retirement account—the IRA

➤ Two types of IRAs—regular and Roth

➤ IRA du jour

➤ Looking through the Keogh

➤ Simple is as simple does—SEP IRAs

As we've said, the best way to save is through a vehicle that makes the process easy and painless. Ease is what makes most employer-sponsored retirement plans so worthwhile. But what happens to those of us who don't have access to this method of saving? The good news is that federal law provides for retirement plans you can set up for yourself.

Why would you choose to do it yourself?

➤ If your employer doesn't offer a retirement plan

➤ If you work for yourself (even if you're just moonlighting part-time outside a regular job)

➤ If you rely on income from other sources, such as alimony

These plans are designed to level the playing field for everyone who is saving for retirement, regardless of whether or for whom they work.

Self-administered retirement accounts come in three basic types: IRAs, Keogh plans, and SEPs. Each type offers you several options for investing. The main differences between them concern how much you can save, what kinds of tax benefits you receive, how (and when) you can use the money, and how complicated they are to administer.

Before we go much further, please keep in mind this caveat. The laws that govern IRAs and related retirement plans evolve continuously. What is deductible one year is no longer deductible the next. Income thresholds for deductibility and tax deferral seem to change with the seasons. So don't worry if you can't keep up with it—staying fully informed is not much easier for investment professionals, and that's what they get paid to do. For this discussion, we're going to stick with the basics. You'll want to consult your financial advisor for the latest information before making any decisions.

Individual Retirement Account

The individual retirement account, or IRA, was introduced to give an individual, whether she or he is self-employed or working for a small employer who doesn't offer a retirement plan, the same access to tax-deferred retirement benefits that employees of larger businesses often enjoy. First, let's consider a few fundamental differences between IRAs and employer-sponsored plans such as 401(k)s.

Flex Time

IRAs are more flexible than 401(k)s because, strictly speaking, you can open an IRA even if you're not working. For example, if your income primarily comes from alimony or rental property, setting up an IRA may be a useful way to shelter some of that income from taxes.

An IRA is also more flexible than a 401(k) plan. With an IRA, you are not required to make regular contributions, although you are limited to a maximum amount you can contribute in any year. (In fact, you don't really have to make any subsequent contributions after you open the account, although that's hardly the way to grow a nest egg.)

Make a Choice

IRAs and 401(k)s also differ in how you can invest your contributions. With a 401(k) plan, you are limited to the investment choices your employer offers you. With an IRA, you can consider a broader variety of ways to invest your contributions, including saving accounts, certificates of deposit (CDs), mutual funds, annuities, and individual stocks. Your financial advisor can help you pick investments that best suit your needs.

You are not generally precluded from contributing to an IRA and participating in a 401(k) plan at the same time. Consider enrolling in both if you can do it, and try to contribute the maximum amounts to both plans. This approach simply increases the earning potential of your contributions while providing you with valuable tax benefits.

Two Types of IRAs

There are two basic types of IRAs: the so-called traditional IRA and the Roth IRA, named for the U.S. senator who sponsored the legislation that created it in 1997. Each plan is designed for a different type of investor and a different purpose, and each has somewhat different features and benefits.

Anyone under the age of $70^{1}/_{2}$, regardless of income, can have a traditional IRA. Only people with under $100,000 in income in 1998 can have a Roth IRA.

Contributions to a traditional IRA may be tax deductible, depending on your adjusted gross income and whether you also participate in a company-sponsored retirement plan, such as a 401(k). In a traditional IRA, you are limited to contributing $2,000 or 100% of your compensation, whichever is less, each year. (The 100% figure may seem strange, but it allows people with very small incomes like students or those who work only occasionally to get the maximum benefit from opening an IRA—it's another way of leveling the playing field.) You and your spouse can each contribute the maximum amount tax free each year, regardless of whether you are both working.

With a traditional IRA, you only pay income tax on the money you earn on your contributions when you withdraw your earnings from the account. As with other types of tax-deferred retirement plans, if you withdraw money before you reach a specified age—age $59^{1}/_{2}$ in the case of a traditional IRA—you must pay any income taxes due on the money and a 10% premature withdrawal tax. However, the law provides for the waiver of penalties before that time if you withdraw the money to cover certain higher-education expenses, first-time home purchase expenses, long-term major medical expenses, or long-term unemployment expenses. You must begin distributing the proceeds of a traditional IRA at age $59^{1}/_{2}$.

The amount you can contribute to a Roth IRA depends on your adjusted gross income and whether you file a single or joint income tax return. In general, you can make the full $2,000 contribution if your income is a little lower and a partial contribution of less than $2,000 if your income is somewhat higher. Your accountant or financial planner can give you the current income thresholds. In 1998, the salary cap was $100,000.

Cash Cautions

Despite the publicity regarding the Roth IRA, not everyone can qualify to set one up. Both the size of your adjusted gross income and the type of tax return you file are considerations, and the exact numbers seem to change every year.

Pay the Tax Man Now Instead of Later

Regardless of the size, contributions to a Roth IRA are not tax deductible. This feature is one of the main differences between a traditional IRA and a Roth IRA and potentially one of the advantages of choosing a Roth IRA. Because you pay the taxes up-front (which means you're contributing after-tax dollars to a Roth IRA), you pay no taxes on the contributions or your earnings when you eventually withdraw the money, provided you keep your money in the account for a minimum period (usually 5 years) and you're over age 59 1/2, or you withdraw the money for a specific, authorized reason, such as a first-time home purchase, disability, or death.

Otherwise, as with a traditional IRA, you face a premature withdrawal tax for taking money out of a Roth IRA prematurely.

Unlike a traditional IRA, you also are not required to begin distributing money from a Roth IRA when you reach a particular age.

Cash Cautions

Through the course of your working career, you might end up owning several different retirement accounts. Unfortunately, tax laws make it almost impossible to combine them into one large account. Consult an expert.

IRA du Jour

Choosing the right IRA for your needs is a complicated business. Thanks to ever-changing laws coming out of Washington, keeping track of the individual features of each type of IRA and the differences between them is like aiming at a moving target. When it comes time to make specific decisions about what kind of IRA will work best for you, your accountant or financial planner can give you up-to-date information.

Looking Through the Keogh

A Keogh (rhymes with "Rio") plan is a self-funded pension plan designed specifically for the self-employed. (Small employers, such as self-employed professionals who are incorporated, can also set up Keogh plans for their employees.) A Keogh is a good retirement plan for people who have higher, stable incomes and need a way to maximize their tax deductions. This type of plan allows for higher annual contributions than you can make to an IRA or a SEP (described below). You can set up a Keogh using forms available through a bank, brokerage house, or insurance agent.

The basic mechanics of a Keogh plan resemble common employer-sponsored plans. A Keogh is most often set up as a defined-contribution plan, like a 401(k) plan, where you contribute a specific amount at regular intervals. With this choice comes two options. You can set up your plan as a profit-sharing plan, which allows you to set aside 15% of your earnings up to $22,500, or you can set up a money purchase plan. This latter approach requires you to commit to making a specific annual contribution (up to 25% of your self-employment income with a maximum of $30,000) or face a fine and/or penalty.

You may wish to set up both a profit-sharing and a money purchase plan if your income fluctuates too much to allow you to commit to a specific contribution. However, you are still limited to setting aside no more than 25% of your earnings up to a maximum of $30,000.

Wise Women Know

Although you can make your IRA contribution as late as April 15 for the previous year's tax period, earlier is better and early is best. For example, if you fund your IRA on January 10, 1999, instead of waiting until April 15, 2000, you get an extra 15 months of growth and compound interest. Over 10 or 20 years, the habit of early funding will make a dramatic difference in the size of your IRA.

The Old-Fashioned Way

A less common alternative to a defined-contribution Keogh is to set up your account as a defined-benefit plan. Like the old-fashioned employer pension plans, this approach provides you with a predetermined retirement benefit. You choose the amount of annual retirement income you want to receive (based on your previous earnings) and then set aside the amount needed to provide that income.

While a Keogh allows you to set aside more money than you could with an IRA or SEP, you may also be required to file special tax forms each year, depending on the size of the account.

Simple Is as Simple Does

When you look at the names of certain types of investments, don't be fooled by those that contain words like *simple* or *simplified*. That's usually a tip-off that the plan is anything but simple. Fortunately, with a simplified employee pension plan, or SEP plan, the name really means what it says.

A SEP allows you to set aside a greater share of income each year toward retirement than you can with an IRA. With a SEP, you can set aside self-employment income tax free, including part-time self-employment income you make while participating in an employer's retirement plan. The maximum annual contribution is 15% of self-employment income up to $30,000. SEP contributions are tax deductible.

A SEP automatically becomes a SEP IRA if you make the maximum SEP contribution and make an additional contribution up to the $2,000 limit for an IRA. Your accountant can explain why this may be beneficial in your case and how you go about it.

SEPs are easy to administer—for example, they don't require the same tax paperwork that a Keogh does—but with that simplicity come some limitations. For example, you cannot withdraw a lump sum upon retirement as a way to reduce taxes (e.g., through income averaging), the way you can with a Keogh.

You also can't roll a SEP into an employer's retirement plan.

Regardless of the type of account you choose, don't be intimidated by terms like *self-funded* or *self-administered*. While it's true that plans you do yourself come with a little more risk—after all, you're not a large employer being advised by a team of highly paid professionals—the risks are minimal compared to other types of investments and certainly nothing an accountant or financial planner can't help you handle.

And don't forget that with risk comes freedom. Don't underestimate the terrific feeling you'll get from watching your earnings accumulate, knowing you did it all yourself!

What Else Can I Do?

By now you've surely been inspired to grow your savings as much as much as possible through long-term growth vehicles like equity and bond funds. You've also fully funded a retirement plan by contributing the maximum annual amounts to a 401(k) plan or an IRA. But as you know, federal law regulates the amount of before-tax earnings you can contribute to these plans each year. If you can afford to save more than this limited amount, you may want to consider buying an annuity.

An annuity is a hybrid creature, offering both tax-deferred growth and a steady income in retirement. But these benefits come at a cost. An annuity is an insurance product, which means that a third party (the insurer) stands between you and your money. Paying that company to safeguard your investment costs money. And as you may know, insurance products typically carry the biggest commissions in the financial world. So you could pay handsomely for this investment.

Annuities are also relatively conservative investments, so you won't see as much tax-deferred growth as you would if you invested your money in stocks, bonds, or money market funds. However, costs and conservative performance are not reasons to ignore annuities. For those who want a minimum of risk and are willing to pay for it, an annuity can be a wise investment.

Inside an Annuity

To understand the mechanics of an annuity, consider the story of Jean Clemont, the French woman who lived to be 126 years old, making her one of the oldest people on record.

Madame Clemont lived for many years in a very desirable apartment. Relatively late in life, she was approached by a man who wanted the rights to her apartment after she died. He agreed to pay her a small sum each year for the rest of her life. Little did either of them know that she would live for many, many more years. Bound by his agreement with her, he continued to pay her the stipulated sum each year. He ultimately paid her several times the actual value of the apartment. Every woman's golden years should be so golden.

That's how an annuity works. You take an asset—in your case, not a desirable apartment, but accumulated savings—and you purchase an annuity. An annuity is a contract with an insurance company. In return for your money, the company agrees to pay you interest on your principal (this is when you see the tax-deferred growth). After a specified period, the company begins paying you a specified amount at regular intervals for a fixed period or for the remainder of your lifetime (this is the steady income you want). Depending on the type of payout you choose, you could continue to receive income for the rest of your life. Like Madame Clemont, you could earn a lot by living to be very, very old.

Inside-Out Insurance?

Basically, an annuity works like life insurance in reverse. With a life insurance policy, you make periodic payments in order to receive a lump sum later. With an annuity, you make one or more payments now in order to receive periodic payments later. Specifically, an annuity provides a way to turn accumulated savings into steady income once you retire.

The money you pay for an annuity is not tax deductible, which means you buy an annuity with after-tax dollars. But since you already paid taxes on this money, you pay taxes only on the interest you earn and then only when you begin receiving the payments.

Because annuities provide for tax-deferred growth, they typically are associated with retirement. The main reason you'd buy an annuity is to use your accumulated earnings to provide yourself with a steady income when you're no longer working.

How to Choose?

When choosing an annuity, you have a number of options that vary depending on factors such as how quickly you'd like your earnings to accumulate and when you would like to begin receiving payments. The two basic types of annuities are fixed-rate and variable.

Fixed-Rate Annuity

With a fixed-rate annuity, you receive interest on your principal and the accumulated earnings at a fixed rate, much the way you earn interest on a CD or the way you pay interest on a fixed-rate mortgage.

The advantage of having a fixed-rate annuity is that you aren't quite as vulnerable to fluctuations in interest rates. The disadvantage is that you may not always benefit when interest rates go up.

With a fixed-rate annuity, the interest rate is guaranteed for a period of 1 to 10 years. You decide for how long you want to receive the guaranteed fixed rate, taking into account such factors as the interest rate climate in the financial markets. For example, if the trend in interest rates appears to be downward, you may prefer to lock in a guaranteed fixed rate for a shorter period and then consider other rates and other guarantee periods when you renew your contract.

Variable Annuity

With a variable annuity, you invest your money in a variety of vehicles, such as equity (stock) and/or bond funds, and receive an interest rate that varies depending on the performance of those investments. If your variable annuity is invested mainly in stocks, for example, and the stock market is doing well, you earn a better rate of interest. But the opposite can also happen, and you could see yourself earning a lower rate of interest.

Obviously, with the variety of investment options and interest rates tied to their performance, a variable annuity is a somewhat riskier investment than a fixed-rate annuity is, since some investments inevitably perform below expectations. The rule of thumb here is to diversity your investments so you're not quite so vulnerable.

Other Bells and Whistles

In addition to the general features of the two basic types of annuities, you want to consider specific features that may help you decide which type of annuity better suits your needs.

Wealth Words

Contract Period—The time commitment required by an insurance company when you make an annuity investment. Your money is committed for a particular length of time. Should you withdraw the money early, you will pay a surrender charge.

Access to Funds

To pay for annuities, insurance companies invest your money and use the earnings on the investment to pay you interest. They make money for themselves by keeping the difference between what they earn and what they pay you (your bank does the same thing with your regular savings accounts). So, clearly, it's in the insurer's interest to see you leave your money with them rather than use it for yourself.

But since you may need access to your money after you've purchased the annuity but before the payments start (this is called the accumulation period), most annuities allow you to withdraw a percentage of the value of the annuity once a year without paying any charges. If you withdraw more than this percentage in a single year, you may face a withdrawal charge. A withdrawal charge on an annuity works the same as the premature withdrawal tax you pay for making an early withdrawal from an IRA.

Insurance companies also don't want to see you back out of your annuity contract. To keep your business, most annuities carry a surrender charge, usually a percentage of the value of the contract, which you would owe if you "surrendered" or abandoned the contract before payments began. This charge encourages you to stick with the contract until the payments begin (at which point you'd presumably feel less pressure to withdraw all your money).

The charge, sometimes as high as 7%, gradually diminishes each year, sometimes over the course of many years. As a result, you are subject to a higher surrender charge during the first few years of the contract (when the insurance company hasn't yet earned much from investing your money) and a lower charge the longer you stick with the contract. Of course, you won't pay a surrender charge at all if you leave your money in the annuity.

Cash Cautions

Are you tired of your annuity? Thinking about changing your investment? Careful! You can't just tell the annuity folks that you've changed your mind and want your money back. You will be subject to "surrender charges" and stand to lose up to 7% of your money.

Payout Options

You can also choose how you want to receive payments from your annuity. The method you choose depends on weighing the amount you want to receive against the certainty that you'll actually live to receive it all. A number of alternatives are available. Once you have completed the accumulation period specified in the annuity contract, you can receive the payments in a single lump sum. In this case, you would owe all the taxes due on your accumulated earnings (which is not always a bad thing, so talk to your accountant).

Otherwise, you can choose among four ways to receive the payments, each with its own benefits and drawbacks. Here are your options:

➤ Guaranteed payments for your lifetime

This option is self-explanatory. If you intend to live as long as Madame Clemont, you could do very well. The payout will continue for the rest of your life, even if you live long enough that the payments exceed the original value of the annuity. The risk, of course, is that you won't live to be nearly so old. Because an annuity is a contract, not an account, any money you were entitled to receive remains with the insurance company after your death, even if you have not received the full value of the annuity. Your heirs won't receive a thing unless they're named as beneficiaries.

➤ Guaranteed payments for a specified period

This option reverses the consequences described above. If you don't want to take the chance of leaving part of your estate to an insurance company, you can

205

choose to receive income for a specified period. The drawback with this option is that you could live for years after receiving your last payment, but without the full income you relied on. (Of course, if you've heeded our advice up to this point, you have money invested elsewhere, too.)

➤ Lifetime and limited payouts

This option may be the best of both worlds. You receive payouts for your lifetime, after which the beneficiary you name in the contract receives a payout for a specified period. This way you ensure that the remaining value of the annuity is not lost if you die early.

➤ Guaranteed lifetime incomes for both the annuitant (you) and the survivor (your spouse or other beneficiary)

This is the way to go if your savings need to support your spouse when you die.

➤ Guaranteed death benefit

With an annuity that provides for specified payments over the course of your lifetime, you want to make sure that your heirs get the remaining value of the contract in the event of your death. Most annuities come with a guaranteed death benefit. The specifics of a guaranteed death benefit vary depending on the type of annuity you buy.

If you have a fixed-rate annuity and you die before your annuity payments start, your beneficiary (whom you name in the annuity contract) immediately receives the contract value less any withdrawals you may have made. The main benefit of this arrangement is to keep this part of your estate from going through probate.

With a variable annuity, your beneficiary receives either the total amount invested in the contract, minus any withdrawals, or the current value of the contract, whichever is greater. This feature is great for protecting your heirs. They're shielded from the risk you took by tying your earnings to the performance of your investments.

You can also specify whether you want to receive payments monthly, quarterly, semiannually, or annually.

In the preceding chapters you've learned both how important retirement savings vehicles are, and how very simple they are to set up and fund. Once you've made the commitment to set up an account, devote that same commitment to making consistent deposits. Then sit back and watch your money grow!

The Least You Need to Know

➤ IRAs, SEP IRAs, Keoghs, and Roth IRAs are retirement plans that you can do yourself.

➤ The sooner in the year that you contribute to your IRA or other retirement plan, the better. Over the years, the extra time that your money is in the IRA will add up to many more dollars.

➤ Should you end up with several types of retirement accounts (from switching careers or being self-employed), you can seldom combine them into one big account.

➤ The laws regarding who qualifies for what plan and how much you can put into it change with great frequency—always make sure you have current information.

➤ Annuities offer both tax-deferred growth and a steady income upon retirement.

➤ The money you pay for an annuity is not tax deductible, but when you begin receiving the money, you pay taxes only on the interest you earn. (You already paid taxes on your initial payment.)

➤ Should you opt out of an annuity contract, you will be subject to a stiff "surrender" charge.

Chapter 21

The Best Thing to Grow— Long-Term Gains!

In This Chapter

➤ Starving the tax collector

➤ Another damned form? Schedule D

➤ Long term versus tax deferred

➤ Mutual of Oh My!

➤ A time to sell

➤ Passing it along

Every investor needs to be mindful of the tax treatment of success. No matter how patriotic a citizen you might be, it is your responsibility to minimize your taxes and pay only that which you must pay and not a penny more. In this chapter, we present what we believe is the strongest tax advantage available to any investor at any economic level. The long-term capital gains tax preference is the best and most straightforward tax benefit we can all enjoy today.

Starving the Tax Man

Simply stated, a capital gain is the difference between the money you paid to buy the asset and the money you receive when you sell the investment. If you meet the test of holding the investment for at least 12 months (or longer as we strongly recommend), the most tax you will pay on the difference (gain in your capital) is 20%. Furthermore, the ultimate tax shelter during your lifetime is long-term capital gains. How can this

Wealth Words

Capital gain—The difference between what you paid for an asset and the money you receive when the asset is sold.

be? If you buy something good and hold it your entire life, *you never* pay a tax on the gain! Your heirs *never* pay a tax on the gain. Of course, your estate will be worth a lot, and your heirs will pay an inheritance tax on the total, but *not* a capital gains tax on top of inheritance. As Jennifer's mother likes to say, "Why bother with seller's remorse? Just never sell."

Let's put this concept into a real case study so you will be more impressed. Anne has a client whose parent had the good sense to buy stock in Corn Products International (CPC) right after World War II. This investment was made in 1947 and cost $5,000. This sum was a lot of money at that time, but the growth would be just as impressive had the amount been $1,000. The original investment in Corn Products had grown to a value of over $250,000 in 1990. At that time, the client inherited the investment.

Chunks and Chunks of Stock

Anne's client still owns the same shares, which are now valued at more than $500,000. Not one dime of capital gains tax has been paid on this asset. It was included in the entire estate for the inheritance tax calculation, *but* during her lifetime, the purchaser had to pay taxes only on the dividend income. The enormous growth of this principal was never taxed. When the purchaser died, her son inherited the stock, and he has continued to own it in its undisturbed state. The position is worth more than $600,000 now, and the son plans to hold this asset and pass it on to his heirs intact, untaxed, and undisturbed.

Just Hold On!

What caused this enormous growth? CPC is the food products company that sells, among other things, Hellman's mayonnaise. The growth of the population, and the consistent production and consumption of this popular but very basic food product,

Wealth Words

Stepped-up cost basis—When you inherit stock, your cost basis for tax purposes is the value of the stock on the date of death, rather than the price that the decedent paid.

has been a great reward to the investor. As important as the success of the company is the discipline of the investor. She was a bright and patient investor, a terrific combination. A final component of the success here was that this capital grew completely free of taxation for a long period of time. The longer you can keep the principal and growth free from the erosion of taxation, the faster the dollars compound in your investment.

As a footnote, the original company, CPC, has since split into two companies, Best Foods (BFO) and Corn Products International (CPO). The client owns both positions, still intact. His stepped-up cost basis was appropriately divided between both positions, and no tax was paid. The positions added together are worth $600,000. Although the client had to review both companies after the original company divided into two separate companies, his investment decision was to continue to own both companies. The longer you or your heirs hold on to a stock, the greater the chance of splits or takeovers or acquisitions. You might end up owning stocks in many different companies thanks to one purchase many years ago.

Long Term Versus Tax-Deferred

How is the tax treatment of long-term capital gains different from the treatment of the tax-deferred investment tools we covered earlier? Whereas annuities and individual retirement accounts are good places to hold off the inevitable income tax, they never make it go away. The income tax will eventually be paid, whether you are alive to do it or your heirs have to do it. However, this situation is not true of investments that are growing and are subject only to long-term capital gains tax. By most measures, the long-term capital gains tax is the least expensive tax rate, currently 20%, versus the income tax rate most of us currently fall into, which is 28% and above.

To put this in perspective, there is no legal way around income and inheritance taxes. They erode your ability to accumulate wealth and pass it on to your heirs. Long-term capital gains are the ultimate method to build family wealth through investments. Compound interest will grow your wealth, but only if it is pure tax-free income. The return on good quality stocks on average has been twice the return on tax-free bonds. Therefore, the growth is twice as good for the long-term stock investor, over the compound income bond investor.

The Highest Returns

Another reason to rely on building your wealth in long-term stock investments is that they have the highest return to the investor. Combine the highest return with the most preferential tax treatment, and you are destined to be wealthier.

The True Cost

There are important numbers and terms to understand with long-term capital gains. You must keep a record of your cost basis. *Cost basis* is the amount of dollars you initially invest in the purchase of the stock. If, over time, you reinvest your dividends or simply buy more of the stock, you add those dollars to your cost basis. A stock split, however, does not affect your cost basis. You have more shares, but you did not have to invest more dollars to get them.

Wealth Words

Cost basis—The actual dollar cost you paid for all of your shares (including extra shares acquired through stock splits and reinvested dividends). Add up all of the shares and divide by purchase price to get the actual cost basis.

You also need to know the date of the original purchase and any subsequent dates on which you invested more dollars. This is not so true of the dates that your dividends were reinvested. The "core dates" are the ones that are most important. The IRS will not hold you to showing each dividend reinvestment transaction, but instead will allow you to lump them together.

File This, Too

Because you are monitoring these transactions on your computer, it is not difficult to keep track of your cost basis. You must also keep the trade confirmations you receive by mail from your broker. They should go in that file cabinet we keep pestering you to own!

In the unlikely event of an audit, the IRS might want you to present evidence of your cost basis data. The trade confirmations are your best evidence. If you lose an original document, the IRS will accept a copy, which your broker may be able to provide. But the best evidence is the original confirmation, so make every effort to save every confirmation slip you receive.

Another Damn Form?

When will you use this cost basis information? Some distant day, when you might have to sell this long-term holding, you will have to report your gain (or loss) on your taxes. Schedule D is where capital gain and loss activity is detailed. The IRS wants to know the date you bought and sold, the dollars you put in and took out, and the number of shares you have at the time of sale. It also wants to know the number of shares represented in this sale in case you are not selling your whole position.

Wealth Words

Schedule D—The tax form on which capital gains and losses are reported to the IRS.

Lest you think the concept of how many shares you have is an unimportant detail, Anne is astonished at how confusing this can be to bright clients. Suffice it to say, the following data—in order of importance—is crucial:

➤ You need to know the running total of all dollars invested, ever.

➤ You need to know the date of your original (first) purchase.

➤ You need to know the lump sum amount of dividend dollars you have reinvested automatically over the years. The dates of these reinvestments are not important.

➤ You need to know the date and amount of dollars you invested each subsequent time you purchased the stock.

➤ At the end, that is, when you might sell some or all of the investment, you need to know the total number of shares you have in the investment at the time of the sale.

Buying Into a Good Thing

To fully comprehend why this information is relevant, consider the following example. You bought 100 shares of an imaginary company, Agoodthing (AGT), 10 years ago, on October 1, 1988. The total cost was $2,000. At that time, you did not reinvest any dividends or purchase additional shares. The stock split 2 shares for 1 in 1992 (you now had 200 shares) and 2 shares for 1 in 1996 (giving you 400 shares). You got so enthused about the company after the second split that you purchased another 100 shares for $3000. Now (50 years too soon), you are forced to sell your 500 shares, worth $11,000, because your child got into Harvard. You have a long-term gain (more than a 12-month holding period) worth $6,000 (the sale price of $11,000 less the cost basis of $5,000). The tax is 20% of the gain, or $1,200.

This gain is the only capital gain you are taking this year and, therefore, the only entry on your Schedule D. The $1,200 gain carries from the Schedule D to your 1040. Don't worry, you will know where to put it, since the forms have it written right there and will tell you exactly which line to enter this number on in your itemized tax form. Short-term capital gains are taxed as ordinary income.

More Good Things

Many clients get hung up on what their cost per shares was, which becomes challenging to calculate after split activity. The exact number of dollars you invest, divided by the number of shares you have now, whether the origin of the shares is purchased or earned through split activity, is your *price per share*. At the time AGT was first purchased, the price per share was $20. At the time it was sold, the price per share was $22. Not too impressive until you remember that you once had 100 shares and now you have 500! Do not get hung up on following your stock by the price per share method. Just remember dollars in and, in the very distant future, dollars out.

If you were able to hold Agoodthing through your lifetime, let's say another 40 years, a few wonderful things happen. You have grown your wealth without any taxation eroding the growth. You die with the stock in your estate (and it's worth $50,000). What a good choice you made all those years ago!

Tax Time

Your heirs must pay an inheritance tax, which we discuss in the next two chapters, and then they plan to hold the stock during their lifetime. Their cost basis changes from yours. Their cost basis is now $50,000, and their date of acquisition is the date of your death. There are more details to this situation, but the point we are making is that your heirs now have a fresh stepped-up cost basis. What about the gain of $45,000? Does anyone owe a tax on that handsome sum of money? Only from the perspective that this investment combined with your others could cause an inheritance tax. There is no income tax. In this case, thanks to patience and dividends, there is not even a long-term capital gains tax.

Strong Performers

The news can't be all good. It can't be this easy. What is the risk of holding a company so long, in this plan for building long-term family wealth? You must be mindful of the performance of the company in which you have invested. Most good companies are managed for long-term performance and survival. The stocks of these companies go up in value as long as the company is growing its earnings year over year. The importance of diversification must always be balanced against the issue of taxation.

You do not want to give up principal by paying taxes for the sake of diversification. Look at it this way: Buy more of your good performing stocks, even if you have very few of them. You can continue to add new holdings as you save additional dollars.

Diversity

Do not sell stock for the sake of diversification alone. If you have good reason to doubt the future performance of your longest and most appreciated stocks, then you might need to make a sell decision. These kinds of decisions depend on all the variables at the time. A great guideline is that when in doubt, hold a good stock and focus on the power of long-term capital gains.

Mutual of Oh My—Look at This Tax Bill!

The same discipline applies to mutual funds that invest in a diversified portfolio of stock. If you have a fund, with decent performance and a large capital gain built into the position, think twice about selling and incurring the tax.

Mutual funds that invest in stocks have many benefits that are similar to owning the individual stocks directly. Funds also have two distinct advantages. One is immediate diversification of your investment dollars. The other is that the fund's professional managers might be able to produce a return that is superior to the return you might achieve on your own. We put a lot of *might*s in that sentence because mutual funds must look good every quarter. When you invest in a company on your own, you might embrace our suggestion to look at its performance for the long haul. Even if the professional money managers at the mutual fund want to have this longer-term outlook, they are punished by the mood of the shareholders. Shareholders are prone to think like the crowd.

Fear of Crowds

A distinct disadvantage of mutual fund investments is the aforementioned crowd mentality. The long-term disciplined investor is hurt in many ways by the undisciplined and foolhardy shareholder.

You see, fund managers must consider the investment value of companies they select on your behalf. If they could work with this as their only concern, we would all be fabulously wealthy.

Unfortunately, they must carefully consider the flow of dollars into and out of their fund. When the markets are going up, money floods into the funds, forcing them to scramble in search of stocks at fair prices, so that every dollar they have will be growing to contribute to the overall performance statistics of the fund. The reverse is true in down markets. As shareholders run to sell their fund shares, managers are forced to sell enough of the stocks they selected on your behalf to have the cash necessary to pay out to the lemmings. The lemmings are the other shareholders who lose their nerve.

This selling mentality on the part of the less-disciplined investor creates a self-fulfilling selling scenario in the stock market. The fund manager might not want to sell, but he or she is forced to raise cash to cover redemptions. Transactions made for these reasons have no bearing on the value of the stocks the mutual fund manager selected in the first place. In this scenario, the movement of the investors who do not have a long-term approach is harmful to the mutual fund shareholder, but not necessarily to the investor who actually owns the stock independently of a mutual fund. How can that be, since the stock went down in price for the individual stockholder as well?

Taxation Without Representation

The individual shareholder *still* owns the stock. The mutual fund shareholder no longer owns some of these good stocks, since the fund manager was forced to sell. The individual has not incurred a tax event. On the other hand, the mutual fund shareholder will get a capital gain distribution come October, November, or December; he or she will have to pay a tax even if the value of the mutual fund shares is not up by the same amount as the value of the distribution. This situation is true regardless of whether you automatically reinvest these distributions.

So, which is better for long-term capital gains: individual stocks or mutual funds? In weighing the risks of individual ownership versus mutual fund ownership, it comes down to a matter of which headaches you want to own. Secure enough education to make informed decisions, do your homework, and stand by your good decisions.

Even More to Gain

Here's a great story to illustrate the topic of long-term capital gains versus diversification.

An elderly couple sought to meet with a financial planner. This long-married couple had their entire life savings in four places. One place was their home, which they owned completely. They also had a substantial savings account at the bank. Finally, they had two and (only two) large stock positions: the local public electric utility and good old AT&T. They had slowly acquired these two stocks in dribs and drabs over the years and reinvested all their dividends. They came to visit the investment counselor because they were worried about having all their eggs in just a few baskets now that they were getting on in years.

The investment advisor genuinely understood their concern and suggested that they sell the two stock positions and diversify. She suggested several other excellent companies to invest in, and the elderly couple decided to take her advice.

But Then...

What is wrong with this picture? Everyone is acting in good faith, and making genuine investment suggestions. The elderly husband and wife are sincere in their concern about having all their eggs in one basket. The advisor is sincere in her suggestions that diversification is important. The investment advisor even suggested that the elderly couple consult with an attorney and accountant to secure their opinion.

This all sounds like they were on their way to a sound decision. Read on, and you will be surprised. The two big stock positions were sold, the couple bought into 10 other companies, and paid their capital gain tax. The following year, the new stocks went up approximately 15% as a collective portfolio. Then the husband and wife died within a year of one another.

And what happened next?

The three adult children, who were the elderly couple's heirs, contacted the advisor to inquire about dear old mom and dad's investments, in particular the AT&T stock and the electric utility stock that mom and dad had owned for all those years.

"Your parents wanted to diversify, and so we did," replied the advisor. "You mean they lost all that money on capital gains tax," the heirs protested. The advisor pointed out that the couple had nearly recouped the tax dollars in the year that followed and felt better being diversified. The heirs pointed out that unnecessary tax dollars were squandered and that their parents would never have made this move had they known they would avoid the capital gains tax by holding the original positions. The heirs further complained that the tax would not have been paid *and* that the original holdings were up the same 15% in value over the past year.

Do we need to tell you where this story ends? The heirs won some compensation and, needless to say, did not continue their affiliation with the financial firm. This is the power of the long-term gain and step up in cost basis upon death. Everyone, acting together and in complete agreement, left the heirs unhappy with their parents' decision. Please be mindful of this as you approach your investments and make the decision to be a long-term investor.

A Time to Sell

The converse of buy and hold until you die, pass it on to your children so they can hold until they die, and so forth is that sometimes it is time to sell the investment. Sometimes you can put your investment money to better use, for example, sending your child to college. Sometimes the company you own ceases to be worthy of investment. The product it makes is antiquated and no longer competes effectively with other companies. Look at a company like Woolworth. It used to be much more competitive in the world of department and variety stores. However, unlike Sears, Woolworth did not remain competitive and has lost out to newer stores like Wal-Mart. This is not an endorsement of either, but merely a note that for several decades it was fine to own Woolworth, but the company did not remain competitive or worth holding over the long haul.

Another example of a company that changed when necessary is IBM. After dominating the computer industry for 7 decades, it hit a huge obstacle and stumbled in front of our eyes. IBM was forced, by the success of a little company named Apple Computer, to realize that people would prefer to use millions of small computers that are linked together by software, rather than huge machines.

Up until that time, IBM believed that the world would be run by large "super" computers and that all the worker bees in the world would use dumb terminals that connected them to a big IBM mainframe. IBM, which had been an unstoppable stock investment for decades, tumbled to half its value when the company announced the error of its ways. Long-term investors were truly tested, but those with discipline were ultimately rewarded. Investors who studied the situation, decided to hold, and perhaps even purchased more still have their highly appreciated shares *and* have not paid a tax yet on their capital gains.

Passing It Along

Since you have embraced the "buy and hold for the long term" philosophy, let's discuss another reason you have to keep track of your cost basis. You might decide that you want to help your kids now by passing along shares in your highly appreciated stock each year.

This is a good and appropriate thing to do in many cases. Let's put that aside for a minute and discuss the tax ramifications of that choice. When you give a gift of stock *during* your lifetime, the recipient also receives your cost basis. Put another way, when the recipient sells that stock, they must pay a 20% tax on the gain since your date of acquisition. This is not necessarily a bad thing. But contrast this to waiting until you die, when your children would get the same shares with a stepped-up cost basis. As you can see, the planning of gifts during your lifetime is not always simple.

Keeping Track

This points out another reason why you need to keep track of your cost basis. What did you pay for that AT&T stock 20 years ago? How much money have you reinvested from dividends? If you do not know, how will you be able to share this important information with your children? The IRS will let you create a reasonable estimate, but we only want you to know that, in this age of computers, you should not find it a burden to keep track of these important details.

Now that we have you focused on long-term family wealth and have started using startling terms like *heirs,* it is time to move on to more serious topics. In the next two chapters, we discuss the importance of wills and estate planning.

The Least You Need to Know

➤ By holding assets long-term and passing them on to your heirs, you stand the best chance of avoiding capital gains tax.

➤ The longer you can keep the principal and growth free from the erosion of taxation, the faster the dollars compound in your investment.

➤ Long-term investments have the highest return to the investor.

➤ It is important to keep track of when you first purchased a stock and the original purchase price.

➤ Although holding a stock for the long term is optimal, you must still make sure that the company is a strong one with good management in place. Sometimes the world changes.

Part 6
Everybody Dies—
Why Not Have a Plan?

Not the most pleasant of topics, but one that you must confront to make sure that what happens after you are gone is what you want—not what a court-appointed administrator or the IRS wants.

Wills, estate planning, and the high cost of health care can all affect (positively or negatively) not just the money you leave behind, but the people you leave behind as well. Please don't skip this important section. The information here can make a great deal of difference in your own peace of mind.

Chapter 22

Where There's a Will, There's a Way

In This Chapter

➤ Will I? (die, that is)

➤ Intestate and other bad trips for your heirs

➤ The designated hitter

➤ Psst...look in the top left hand drawer

➤ The philanthropic life

We've tried to present a great many facts and figures in this investment book. Many of them were rosy—all about how your money can grow because of investing and compounding interest. Some were cautionary—the facts and figures on options trading, for instance. Well, we have yet another fact to share, one that is uncomfortably grim yet of which we are 100% certain. The fact is, you are going to die.

Will I?

Die? Will I? Yes, you will. And speaking of wills, we're awfully glad you brought it up! Yes, you will die. And yes, you will need a will.

Ah, we can hear you now—"But I am just getting started with my financial investing, I really don't have anything to leave to anybody. Why should I bother with a will?" Why should you bother? Don't you like to be in charge of your life? And don't you think you should be in charge of your death, too?

Wills have always sounded so mysterious, so very like something from *Perry Mason* or *Murder She Wrote*. Exactly what's *in* a will? Here are the major provisions of a good will:

➤ A revocation clause—Revokes any previous wills you may have written

➤ A family status clause—States your marital status, your spouse's name, and the names and birth dates of your children

➤ A payment of necessary expenses clause—Authorizes your estate to pay for your funeral

➤ A bequest clause—Where you get to give it away

➤ A residuary clause—Gives away any property not specifically given away elsewhere in the will

➤ A payment of taxes clause—Authorizes your executor to pay any and all taxes that come up

➤ An executor clause—Names an executor for your will

➤ A guardian clause—Specifies who will have guardianship over your children (should the other parent not be living)

➤ A property guardian clause—Oversees the distribution of money and property to your minor children

➤ A children's trust clause—Should you opt to establish a trust for your children

➤ A signing clause—Where you and your witnesses validate the will with your signatures

➤ An affidavit clause—Where the truth and validity of the will is affirmed

Can You Do It Yourself?

Hmmm…sounds like a bunch of legalese. Are there books to help you sort this out, computer programs you can use, or real live people to take on the task? Yes on all three counts.

Nolo Press, the well-known self-help legal publisher, has a book that is continually updated as the laws change—*Nolo's Simple Will Book* by Denis Clifford.

The same folks also have a computer program called Willmaker that you can use to create your own will. "When our first child was born my husband, Pete, and I, finally sat down to think about wills. We decided to do it ourselves using Willmaker software," says Laura Lewis of Lafayette, Colorado. "All you have to do is answer self-explanatory questions, and the form is pretty much filled in. It is very easy to update after the birth of each new child."

But Should *You* Do It Yourself?

Well, although you can do it yourself, many legal experts strongly advise against it. Steven D. Strauss, author of *Wills and Trusts*, cautions that the money you save by preparing your will yourself will be gobbled up in the first 5 hours of probate if you do it wrong.

Does it cost much to have an attorney do a will for you? That depends entirely on how complex your estate is. A basic will drafted by an attorney should cost just a few hundred dollars. But if you hire a big-gun estate-planning specialist to handle your very complicated financial affairs, the fee can run into the several thousands.

Cash Cautions

For just $20, you can buy a book on writing wills; for just $60 or so, you can buy a computer program to help you do it. What a smart way to save money! Maybe, maybe not. The money you save by drafting a will or living trust yourself will be quickly gobbled up if you make even a minor mistake.

Post This Warning

Here's an example of the pitfalls of handmade wills:

Cindy spent several weeks nursing her dying aunt. Just a few days before her aunt died, Cindy helped her make a will (using a fill-in-the-blanks form) that left her estate to her sister, Cindy's mother. The will was notarized. But as the hour of death approached, the aunt changed her mind. She decided to leave $30,000 each to Cindy and her brothers and sisters, and she wrote out these instructions in her own handwriting and attached them to her will with sticky notes. And then she died, content that she had provided for those she loved in the manner that she wished.

So, who got the money? Yes, the aunt's sister, Cindy's mother, inherited the estate, as per the original will. And what about the little yellow notes granting money to the nieces and nephews? Not a penny.

So what is the alternative to doing it yourself (or dictating it to your niece at the last moment)? Ask around and get a recommendation for a good estate attorney. Remember some of the suggestions from Chapter 5, "Can I Get Some Help With This?" on how to find good "dance partners"? This would be a perfect time to put some of those ideas into action.

Intestate and Other Bad Trips for Your Heirs

What happens if you die without a will? The legal term is *intestate*, and a person is said to have died intestate if he or she does not leave a will behind or some other kind of valid estate-transfer document.

What does this mean to the people you love, the folks you have left behind? In layman's terms, they're screwed.

Wealth Words

Intestate—Someone has died "intestate" if he or she leaves behind no will or other valid estate-transfer document.

Regardless of all the hopes and dreams you had while you were alive—that your sister should have your favorite china tea pot, your children would go to live with your best friend, and your beloved heirloom Persian rug would go to a museum—your money and stuff is now pretty much in the hands of the state. And it is the state that will make all of the cozy and loving decisions that you hoped to. Wow, won't they do a *great* job?

Here are some of the scary things that will happen if you don't leave a will behind:

➤ If you aren't married, have no children, and your parents are alive, guess who gets the cash? They do, regardless of how long you've been living with a faithful lover you adored.

➤ If you aren't married, but do have young children? The court will appoint a guardian for your minor children. Who knows who they will pick? The children will get your money.

➤ If you aren't married and have no relatives? "Thanks for the donation," says the state in which you reside. Your loving circle of friends and favorite charities will be out in the cold, and the state will add your money to its coffers.

Kinda creepy isn't it, letting the "state" have so much control...a bit like an Orwell novel. And that is what you will leave behind if you don't leave a will behind: one big, tangled, scary Orwellian novel.

Wills are especially important for couples who live together. No matter how long and how loving the relationship, if you die without a will your money will go straight to your living parents. And can you trust them to graciously give it to your partner?

Have we got you so concerned that you are reaching for a pen and pad to start writing out a will this minute? Might work, depending on where you live. A handwritten will is legal in about 30 of our 50 states. And even if it is legal in your state, problems might occur from a will that you composed yourself because of fuzzy interpretation of your bequests. Silly as the language of the law can sound to us, there is no mistaking its usefulness here. If you write that you want to leave everything to your sister Ann and her children, do you mean that it should go first to your sister and then to her children when she dies? Or that they should all get equal portions right away? Who knows?

Wealth Words

Holographic will—A handwritten will.

Better to prevent misinterpretation and consult a lawyer. You worked hard for your money, and you should be 100% certain that after you go, it goes where you meant it to.

The Designated Hitter

So you write a will and then you die. You've done your part, but who picks up the ball from here? An executor, that's who.

An executor is someone that you hand pick to carry out your wishes after you are gone. To see that your bequests are properly bequeathed. To alert your creditors to your unfortunate passing. And the executor has certain legal powers over your estate, as well. For example:

➤ The power to exchange, mortgage, lease, buy, and sell real estate. This activity usually occurs when the estate needs to sell property in order to settle unpaid debts.

➤ The power to hire an attorney, an accountant, a real-estate agent, or any other professional whose help is needed.

➤ The power to settle claims with your creditors (pay your debts) or resolve claims on behalf of the estate (get money from people or organizations that owe money to you).

➤ The power to borrow money, should it be needed to pay taxes or creditors.

➤ The power to make investments on behalf of the estate.

Yikes, that is a whole lot of power for one person! Who should you choose? Needless to say, choose someone you can trust to wield that power in the best interests of your heirs.

How Do You Choose? Who Do You Choose?

Most often people choose either their spouse or one of their grown children to serve as executor. You should also let that person know that you intend to name him or her executor. This job requires a great deal of time and responsibility, and not everyone will feel comfortable assuming the mantle. It is entirely possible that your chosen person might decline the offer. Wouldn't it be better to ask that person yourself and have him or her decline, rather than have your designee decline later when you are, uh, not around to choose a replacement?

If you don't name an executor in your will, or if the person you choose ultimately says "no thanks" after you pass away, then what? The court will appoint someone for you, likely not a friend or relative, but someone affiliated with the court.

Wealth Words

Executor—An executor is the person you appoint who is responsible for carrying out the wishes in your will.

Wise Women Know

Probate can take 2 years and gobble up 8% of the gross value of the estate. Pick an executor you trust, but also one who is located geographically near you—he or she will end up in court a time or two. You don't want your estate to have to pay for all those plane tickets to fly an out-of-state executor to a court appearance.

Psst...Look in the Top Left-Hand Drawer

So, you have a will! Mazel tov! Where are you gonna keep it? In a safe-deposit box? Your lawyer's office? The glove box of your car?

"Please don't leave it in your safe-deposit box at the bank," says attorney Steven Strauss. Why not? Because when you die, the bank *seals* your safe-deposit box. You do not want your heirs to have to go through the difficulty of getting it unsealed just to get at your will.

The best advice is to keep it at home—the original copy, that is. Give a photocopy to your attorney or your executor.

How many copies do you need? One for yourself, one for your executor, and probably one for your lawyer (if you used one). Remember, you keep the original.

Cash Cautions

Go ahead and make photocopies of your will. But *don't* make more than one original, signed copy. Why not? Because if the court knows that there is more than one original signed copy of your will, it will hold up the start of probate until all of the original copies are found.

Ch-Ch-Ch-Changes...

Changed your mind? Changed your life? Changed your financial circumstances? Then change your will. Don't draw up a will as a single, unmarried woman in her early 20s and then ignore it for the next 20 years. Marriage, divorce, children, property, investments, all manner of things might have happened in the meantime. If you now have two children and a loving husband, do you want all of your money to go to your best friend—the only person you could think of 20 years before? Or worse, what if you still have a will that bequeaths all to your *ex-husband*? If you get hit by a car before changing your will, he will inherit.

You need to check your will with every major change in your life; make sure that it is still appropriate and that it still accurately reflects what you want to happen to your money after you aren't around to spend it.

The Philanthropic Life

We were surprised to read recently that, according to the *Wall Street Journal*, although in 1997 individuals, foundations, and charitable institutions gave a whopping $143.46 billion away, *proportionally* fewer households gave than in past years. And this was despite the big, instant fortunes created by the rising stock market.

So when divvying up your money and your stuff, don't forget the many deserving charitable organizations that would love to be mentioned in your will. Who knows, perhaps they are even more deserving than some of your own family members. And depending on how much you donate, you might end up immortalized on a brass plaque somewhere. Graduates of women's colleges should pay special attention to their alma maters in their wills. Research shows that many times the husband's college will be remembered in a will, but not necessarily the wife's college. Many women's colleges are (ahem) underendowed as a result.

But, as you no doubt know from opening your mail every day, a mind-boggling number of organizations are looking for your help. If you are not already an active contributor to a favorite charity, how can you decide which one(s) to remember in your will? Here are two Web sites that can help:

➤ www.bbb.org

The Better Business Bureau Web site includes a Philanthropic Advisory Service.

➤ www.give.org

Sponsored by the National Charities Information Bureau, this Web site lists (and rates) some 400 nonprofit organizations.

Well, did we do it? Did we convince you that, regardless of your age or financial circumstances, you need to be thinking about a will? That you need to be working on your will right now? That you *need to have a will?*

In our next chapter, we move on to the really sticky part: actual estate planning. Believe it or not, how you leave things behind in your will after you are dead can actually destroy relationships among the living. Read on to learn how to avoid that dire outcome.

The Least You Need to Know

➤ You must have a will, or the state will decide who gets what.

➤ You can do it yourself with the help of books or computer programs, but chances are good that a small mistake will foul things up after your death. Talk to an attorney.

➤ A simple will drawn up by an attorney costs a few hundred dollars. It costs into the thousands for a more complicated estate.

➤ Make sure that the person you name as executor is up to the job—it is demanding and time-consuming.

➤ Never keep the original, signed copy of your will in your safe-deposit box, as it will be extremely difficult to access after your death.

➤ Don't overlook charitable contributions in your will. It is a chance to give a lasting memorial to yourself (and to help the world).

Chapter 23

Estate Planning and Living Trusts

> **In This Chapter**
>
> ➤ Your will—distribution or retribution?
>
> ➤ Ruling from the grave
>
> ➤ Deciding who gets what
>
> ➤ Five steps to estate planning
>
> ➤ All a matter of trust
>
> ➤ Gee, thanks for the tax bill, Ma!

Now that we have pestered you about preparing a will—and you are getting started on one *right now*, aren't you?—what are you supposed to put in it?

How on earth are you going to make all those frightening decisions about who gets what, and why?

Your Will—Distribution or Retribution?

Every estate-planning lawyer can tell you hair-raising tales about what has happened to friends and family in the wake of a will reading. Some folks leave happy, and some leave utterly destroyed. Why does what is in a will have the awesome power to make the heirs feel either great or suicidal? Because all too frequently it is interpreted as your very last statement on how you feel about the people in your life.

Cash Cautions

Even a seemingly fair and benign statement like "my estate is to be divided equally between my three daughters" can open the door for years of sibling wars over who gets what property and how much various heirlooms are worth.

"Did mama really ever love me?" a grown man might think to himself as he listens to a lawyer announce that the man's sister is to receive a greater share of the estate. "Did he think I was a total idiot?" a widow might think, hearing for the first time that her husband has designed an elaborate estate plan that deprives her of the ability to control the money she has inherited.

Mother Always Liked You Best

Relationships between siblings can be forever destroyed simply because of uneven distributions (or even the *perception* that the distribution is uneven!). We talk more about how to try to prevent this from happening in the upcoming section on goal setting.

Ruling From the Grave

Not only can many of the relationships you leave behind be damaged or destroyed, but your heirs might be made to feel that you are, uh, still around somewhere calling the shots!

Wise Women Know

The decisions you make in your will can either help to heal wounds between siblings or drive them apart forever. One elderly woman, concerned about her unmarried daughter's need for a place to live, bequeathed to her alone the house that the family had lived in for several generations. Once she'd inherited it, she promptly banished her older brother from it, threatening to call the police should he ever step foot on the property. He was never again allowed in the house he had loved his whole life. Every summer he parks a large motor home at the very edge of the property and camps there for a week or two.

If you attach lots of stipulations to your bequests, it may well seem that you are loathe to actually lose control. "I leave $150,000 to my daughter Jane, if she can maintain her weight at 135 pounds." "To my stepson Michael I leave $75,000, provided that he successfully completes an alcohol-abuse program." Bequeathing houses that must be lived in and never sold or tying up money in trusts that can't be touched until your heirs are well into their dotage will cloud your heirs' ability to remember you with fondness and love.

Wealth Words

Conditional bequest—A bequest that is made only after certain conditions are met.

Five Steps to Planning an Estate

How can you avoid the drastic situations we've described above? Start by developing a plan that includes the goals that you have for your estate and what you'd like it to do for the people in your life. "An estate plan is a family plan and a financial plan, a safety net and a dream launcher," attorney Steven Strauss reminds us.

There are five essential steps to successful estate planning. Those steps are

➤ Formulating goals

➤ Creating a solid inventory

➤ Deciding who gets what

➤ Working to minimize the financial impact

➤ Choosing which of the estate-planning options will best accomplish your goals

Sounds like a lot of work? Yes, but don't forget our words of warning—the way you plan your estate will forever have an impact—both financial and emotional—on those you leave behind. Planning an estate is a lot of work, but it is worth the time. Let's get started with that first step.

Formulating Goals

To repeat the quote from Steven Strauss: "An estate plan is a family plan and a financial plan, a safety net and a dream launcher." Beautiful ideas. Are these goals you should invite your heirs' involvement in? Yes, particularly if you are planning a bombshell like an uneven inheritance. Invite your grown children to sit down and go over your plans with you. A safety net? You might learn that your children are well positioned and don't need a safety net. A dream launcher? You might learn that your son dreams of owning a photo-developing franchise and secretly plans to do that with any money he should someday inherit. Why not investigate the implications of giving him the money early, so his dream needn't wait until you are gone?

And about that uneven distribution? You might as well break the news now so that they can hear your reasons directly from you instead of from a sober-faced attorney. And then you can try to work through the issues while you still have a chance to participate, rather than leaving them alone on earth to slug it out among themselves.

What are the needs and desires of your family members? Are there charities that you would really like to help? A good friend who you'd like to remember for his or her friendship over the years? You need to examine all of these things when deciding just what the goals are for your estate. And those goals will in turn help steer you toward other estate-planning decisions.

Taking an Inventory

Okay, now get yourself a pad of paper and a pen and make a list of all the assets (accounts, investments, property, and so on) you actually own. If you followed our instructions on record keeping earlier in the book, this step should not take much time. You know just where to find this information, don't you? (Most of your major assets should be listed on the worksheet you made when you calculated your net worth.) Don't forget to include your great-grandmother's silver and those antique end tables that you bought years ago. Oddly enough, sometimes the smaller, more sentimental items cause the biggest struggles among heirs! By the way, if you decide to involve an attorney in your will-making or estate-planning decisions, a complete list of your assets will be one of the very first things he or she asks for.

Wealth Words

Beneficiary—A person or organization to whom you leave money or property in your will.

Deciding Who Gets What

Now that you know what you have to give away, how are you going to decide who gets it?

Estate attorney Ian McPhail of Carmel, California, recalls with fondness an elderly client who came to be known as Miss Cups and Saucers by his staff. A well-educated woman who'd never married, she lived in a tidy white house by the sea filled with a library, antique furniture, jewelry, and several sets of china and silver she had collected over the years. They were her treasures, and she agonized over just what should go to whom. And every few months, she would come into Ian's office to change her will, revising which set of teacups would go to which friend or relative. "She obviously treated these treasures as dynastic items that would change the life of each beneficiary who received them," he remembers. "I hope the beneficiaries appreciated all her care and thoughtfulness."

Should you describe each precious item in your will and allot it to someone special? Or should you let your children, friends, and family decide among themselves after you are gone? Once again, a family meeting can be a great place to air these kinds of concerns and try to devise a system that will work when you are not around to supervise it.

Larger items should be dealt with individually in your will.

When it comes to property, you must decide whether to bequeath the property itself (and in what percentage shares if you are leaving it to more than one heir) or to direct your executor to sell the property and divide the proceeds in the manner you dictate.

Minimizing Taxes

As the old saying goes—only two things in life are certain: death and taxes. And we hate to be the ones to tell you, but taxes will follow you to the grave! Or they will follow your heirs, anyway.

For many years the first $625,000 of an estate (or an estate that was smaller than $625,000) was not subject to estate taxes. This figure is due to the rise in increments of $50,000 over the coming years, so that by the year 2006 the first $1 million of an estate will not be subject to taxes.

When the value of an estate exceeds the $625,000 limit, federal estate taxes kick in at a rate of 37%. And that's not all. All states but Nevada have death and inheritance taxes, too. A frightening problem to leave for your heirs to deal with.

So how do you minimize death taxes? Both through careful planning and some generous pre-death gifts.

Now, we realize that most of you reading this book are years and years away from confronting the idea that you don't have much time left. And we also realize that by the time yours is running out, the laws will no doubt have changed significantly. But here are a few strategies to consider:

➤ You can give away $10,000 per year, per recipient, tax-free. Friends, family, neighbors—the government doesn't care whom you choose. It can be a powerful way to pass money along.

➤ Use a trust.

Wise Women Know

Although the first $625,000 dollars of an estate has been slipping by without estate taxes for many years, the limit is about to rise. Great news for baby boomers whose parents own houses that rose dramatically in value during the '70s and '80s! By the year 2006, the number will be raised to a cool $1 million. Now if we can all just encourage our parents to live that long...

Maybe a Trust?

The fifth basic element of estate planning is examining the various ways to pass along your estate. Now that you have clearly established the goals for your estate and have a clear picture of how much your estate is worth, you must examine all the possible choices. One popular choice nowadays is a trust.

Wealth Words

Taxable estate—The portion of the estate that is subject to inheritance tax after the current exemption level is passed.

Probate is a public affair. And a will is a document that anyone can gain access to. After Jackie Onassis's estate passed through probate, a smart publishing fellow in New York saw a unique opportunity for a book. He published it as *The Last Will and Testament of Jacqueline Kennedy Onassis*. So even a fiercely private woman like Jackie O lost that dignity in death. Be careful what kind of secrets your will reveals...

All a Matter of Trust

Quite an active industry has sprung up in the last few years to convince ordinary folks that what they *really* need is a trust. Companies that want to sell you on the idea that a trust is the only way to go if you plan to leave your heirs any reasonable sum are holding seminars in hotel rooms across the country. But is a trust for you?

Sometimes trusts can be the right vehicle; other times they are a waste of your money and can cause real headaches and legal tangles for your survivors. As Jack W. Everett, the author of *The Truth About Trusts*, advises: "Be wary of trust mills. Use a qualified estate-planning attorney to prepare your living trust. There is no such thing as a "standard" trust; your needs and desires are different from everyone else's. And make sure you meet with your attorney as many times as necessary to make sure that both you and your attorney fully understand *your* trust."

So what are these trusts, anyway? The word *trust* conjures up all kinds of old-money associations, from trust fund babies to country club denizens. But what exactly is a trust?

A *trust* is a legal arrangement that transfers ownership of assets to a trustee, who manages these assets for your beneficiaries. Many types of trusts are available, and each one is designed to reduce income taxes and estate taxes and to meet specific estate-planning needs. Here are three different types:

➤ Qualified terminal interest property trust—Popularly known as a QTIP, this type of trust qualifies for the unlimited marital deduction by leaving any amount of property in trust to the surviving spouse. This money is not taxed until the surviving spouse passes away.

➤ Revocable living trust—This type of trust generates income while you are alive and provides for professional money management when you die or become incapacitated. It is quite flexible and not subject to probate.

➤ Charitable remainder trust—This trust is a way to make a tax-advantaged gift while you are still alive. When you place your property or asset in a charitable remainder trust, you get an immediate tax deduction as well as the income from that trust during your lifetime. When you do die, however, the remainder of the trust goes straight to the charity you designated when you established this trust.

➤ In addition, testamentary trusts, generation-skipping trusts, and a veritable treasury of other trusts are available.

Wealth Words

Charitable remainder trust—This type of trust involves signing over an asset to a charity while you are still alive, taking a tidy tax deduction, and then receiving the income from that asset. Once you have died, however, the remainder of the trust belongs to the charity.

Depending on your circumstances, trusts really can be the answer. But to make a fully informed decision, we urge you to speak to an estate-planning attorney.

Gee, Thanks for the Tax Bill, Ma!

According to Merrill Lynch, Elvis is dead. The glossy brochure that Merrill Lynch hands out to clients, "The State of the American Estate," uses Elvis's estate as an example of how quickly the money can disappear without proper estate planning. Here's what happened to his money:

➤ Elvis left a gross estate worth more than $10 million.

➤ About one third of that money ($3.7 million) went to settle outstanding debts.

➤ After the debts were settled, $6.3 million remained. Federal estate taxes; Tennessee and California inheritance taxes; and fees for attorneys, executors, and administrators ate up 56% of this sum.

➤ Of the original $10 million, Elvis's heirs inherited $2,790,799—just 28% of what he'd left.

The Elvis story is a fairly dramatic example of what can happen after you're gone. On behalf of your heirs, take the time to investigate just what type of estate planning is best for you and your situation. Don't leave your loved ones with little more than a big tax bill.

Update It!

Your net worth will no doubt increase in the coming years. Many other things about your life situation will change as well. We want you to make a will and an estate plan now, according to your current circumstances. But do not imagine that you can leave it at that. Every few years—or whenever a dramatic change happens in your life—you will need to review your will to make sure that it still does the job. Keeping your will up-to-date is a grim task, but one that will help the people you leave behind know how much you cared.

The Least You Need to Know

➤ The decisions that you make in your will affect your heirs' relationships with each other forever.

➤ Bequests that come with stipulations or conditions attached can also leave a bad taste and tarnish your memory.

➤ Estate planning is five simple steps: developing goals, inventorying, deciding who gets what, trying to minimize taxes, and deciding whether a will or trust is best.

➤ The first $625,000 of an estate is not subject to estate tax. This figure is due to rise over the years, and by 2006, the first $1 million of an estate will escape taxation.

➤ Trusts are being actively marketed nowadays, but are really not suitable for everyone.

➤ If you choose to use a trust, have an estate-planning attorney do the work.

➤ Poor estate planning robs your heirs—Elvis's estate was $10 million, but his heirs ultimately received only $2.8 million.

Chapter 24

Keeping It All in the Family

In This Chapter

➤ Building the old family estate

➤ More ways to drain your estate

➤ Who would you rather give the money to?

➤ Further strategies for hanging on to money

➤ Take your lumps

➤ Are your heirs worthy?

Heavens, are we still on this same topic? How much do you really need to know about what could happen to your money after you are gone? Quite a bit, actually.

Throughout this book, we have urged you to build up your net worth. And after all that work, we don't want to see it dissolve into thin air. Ashes to ashes, cash to dust...no thanks!

Building the Old Family Estate

The purpose of another chapter on estate planning is to give you more of the ground rules about how to pass along to your heirs as much of the money you have saved as possible. First, let's examine exactly what the government defines as your estate. The ingredients are as follows:

➤ Anything you own in your own name, including life insurance and retirement benefits

➤ Half of what you own jointly with your spouse—for example, your home or joint accounts

➤ Your share of anything you own in common, such as property you own with business partners

➤ Assets in trusts and custodial accounts for which you are the trustee or custodian

➤ Everything you own jointly, with anyone except your spouse, unless you have proof the other person helped pay for it

After your heirs add up the value of the preceding items, they get to pay the following:

➤ An inheritance tax, which are state taxes paid by your heirs, those people you designate to inherit your assets. The tax is based on their share of the inheritance and their relationship to you.

➤ A federal estate tax is due for every dollar in value of your assets that exceeds $625,000 (at the time this book is written). However, certain deductions and expenses can be subtracted from that total number.

➤ Legal and court costs, commonly referred to as probate costs, can be due. If someone contests the will, or makes a claim against your estate that is disputed (for example, someone might claim you owe him or her an unpaid debt), your heirs can anticipate court costs and legal fees. Even when there are no disputes, the court and your executor are often allowed by law to charge your estate for the supervision of its closing.

Once again, we will point out that anyone who even considers dying without a will should ask this question: Do I want to decide, or do I want the court to decide for me? If you die without a legal will in place, you are telling your heirs and the world that you wanted the court to decide for you. Please readers, do any of you really want the court to decide who your heirs are, what part of your money they get, and when in their lives they get to receive this money? You must *at least* secure a will to keep as much of your money in the family as possible. However, a will is the very least you need to do to keep your money in the family.

Tantalizing Trust Techniques

In Chapter 23, "Estate Planning and Living Trusts," we discussed the importance of estate planning and the value of the living trust to you and your family. We need to focus more on how you can best keep your nest egg in the family. The living trust, which will save your family probate fees, is only the tip of the iceberg. Other trust techniques go beyond the living trust to save your family from paying unnecessary inheritance taxes. As we've mentioned before, as this book is being written, any person can die and leave $625,000 exempt from any inheritance tax to his or her heirs. This number increases by $25,000 per person or $50,000 per married couple each year through the year 2006, at which point it is $1 million.

What Married Folks Do

What we have not mentioned yet is that every married couple should provide for the marital deduction trust at the first death in the couple. Other names for the marital deduction trust are the AB trust, bypass trust, marital exclusion trust, spousal deduction trust, and unified credit trust. No wonder people get confused. The use of several names for the same thing is naturally very confusing (might there have been lawyers involved?). The point is that you must set aside the allowable amount—this year it is $625,000—so that after the first spouse dies the remaining spouse has use of the money, but not *ownership* of the money. What the heck does that mean?

Who Would You Rather Give It To?

If the surviving spouse retains the entire estate, inheritance tax free, then the family (especially the heirs) pays an estimate of more than $200,000 in unnecessary taxes at the second spouse's death. That's a lot of money, and who would you rather give it to: your heirs or the government? Keeping this money in the family is important from other perspectives as well.

Trusts rely upon a very important component in a family, trust in one another. By definition, if a family seeks to avoid the probate process, and the probate fees that must be paid for "court supervision" of the settlement of your estate, it must trust that the heirs can be trusted to implement the instructions in the trust. The word *trust* is key.

Keeping it in the family can also mean the following: Trusts are very private, and wills are, by necessity, very public. Wills must be filed at the county recorder. The deceased person's death is literally posted, and the assets and liabilities of the estate are available for public scrutiny. If you want your family assets to be private, a trust is the only way to accomplish this desire. Are you wondering who could possibly be interested in the particulars of your estate when you die? Do not kid yourself; the curiosity seekers are out in droves even if you aren't Jackie O.

We've touched on some of the other trusts that can help to keep your assets in the family: a qualified terminal interest property (QTIP) trust, a charitable remainder trust, and now the unified credit trust. After you have done everything possible with trusts to keep the money in the family, there are still more sophisticated techniques you can learn about and seek advice on. Among these creative and legal techniques are family foundations, charitable lead trusts, and granter-retained trusts. You would be well advised to cultivate a relationship with an attorney who specializes in this estate-planning area of law.

Choose Wisely

A word of advice on choosing an attorney: You might want to consider someone your own age or even younger! You do not want to outlive the attorney who drew up your plan unless you relish the thought of cultivating this kind of close, personal relationship several times in your life.

Naturally, these kinds of things cannot be planned perfectly, but age should be balanced with experience when you select an estate-planning attorney. Lest you be too concerned about attorney's fees for a good estate plan, remember that the fees you pay while you're alive to get the proper documents in place are far less than the taxes and, in most states, probate fees you will sacrifice without the proper plan.

Further Strategies

After you have diligently done all that you can to avoid unnecessary taxes, you can employ some additional strategies to preserve as much inheritance as possible for your heirs. The first thing to know is that inheritance tax is due and payable exactly 9 months after the date of death. This fact is true regardless of whether a will or a trust is in place when you die. In addition, the tax is payable only in dollars; it cannot be paid in kind. Put another way, your heirs cannot ask the government to accept a corner of the family farm—they have to sell the corner and pay with cash. They cannot give the government some of that old family holding in Disney stock—they have to sell the stock to pay the tax.

Government Bailout

The government will loan you the money, but the rate of interest it will charge makes a pawnshop look like a great deal. Banks will not lend you the money to pay the government. Therefore, the better people are at amassing wealth in their lifetime, the more carefully they have to consider a solution to the inheritance tax problem.

Irrevocable Life Insurance Trust

Finding the cash to pay the inheritance tax may not be a serious problem if the estate is composed largely of readily saleable assets. But a very serious problem can develop when the larger part of the estate is illiquid, as in a family farm, a family-owned business, or even a very good stock that happens to be down on its luck during the time frame in question. Not to worry—a very solid solution is available. The irrevocable life insurance trust can save the day.

Here's how it works: You establish a trust that is intended to hold only a life insurance policy. The policy can be on one person's life, or on two in the case of a married couple. Life insurance on one person is either term or whole life. Life insurance on two people is called second-to-die insurance, appropriately named in that it pays money to the trust when the last spouse dies.

The trust is irrevocable in order to put the insurance policy (and, more important, the proceeds paid when the last spouse dies) outside the estate that is being measured for inheritance tax. Voilà! Lots of cash available, just when your heirs need it, outside your taxable estate in a trust that instructs the trustee to pay the tax with this money. Very clever, very efficient, and not to be ignored in a good estate plan.

Intricate Matters

The intricacies of this kind of strategy are not to be ignored either. Please research this strategy, contact an attorney, and be certain you get different bids on the insurance policy premiums that would be paid into the trust. Insurance companies, investment firms, and some private counselors provide competitive bids for these types of insurance policies as well.

Government Generosity

Even your government, in an unusual moment of generosity, included some relief to the estates that are actually composed largely of a family business or a family farm. Starting in 1998, heirs to family-owned businesses and farms are entitled to an extended credit exemption. This exemption, plus the unified credit exemption, may not exceed $1.3 million. Before you get too grateful, consult an attorney regarding the complex qualifying requirements for this special exemption. We mention it only to provide encouragement to those of you whose family owns a family business or a family farm.

Take Your Lumps

Over and above the irrevocable life insurance trust, another important and actually relatively simple estate-planning tool that many of us can use is to take a lump-sum distribution from our IRA account on the eve of our death. In as much as it is possible to anticipate your death, this strategy can mean very serious tax savings to your heirs. Although this move is counterintuitive to a lifetime spent trying to delay, defer, deny, and in every legal way possible avoid taxation, this time taking the tax hit actually makes great financial sense. Surely we jest? We have spent this entire book telling you to minimize taxes; do we now want to turn that strategy on its ear? Yes. Bear with us and read on.

The assets in most IRA or IRA rollover accounts have never been taxed—you still owe taxes on the money in them. A Roth IRA is a special case, so if you have a Roth, skip forward two paragraphs. When you die, the first tax paid on the IRA is the income tax. Then, unfortunately, the entire value of the IRA at the date of death, including that part on which your heirs have already paid income tax, is included in the calculation of the total value of your estate.

Let's say you accumulate $600,000 in your IRA rollover before you die. This amount is misleading because only approximately $400,000 is really yours. The government is due income tax worth about 200,000 of those dollars. And you thought that money was all yours—tsk, tsk.

Because of income tax, only about 70 cents of every dollar you grow in value, or earn in income, is really yours; the government inevitably owns 30 cents of that dollar. However, when you die, the full value of the IRA is added into your entire estate, not the IRA value after income tax. Essentially, you are paying inheritance tax on money that you pay to the IRS as income tax. How can this be? Take this injustice up with your government.

For Immediate Distribution

How can you avoid this pain and bill? If you have any advance knowledge of your demise, take a full distribution of your retirement asset. At least the income tax is then OUT of your estate before your date of death. Your inheritance tax will then be calculated on the dollars that remained in your estate *after* the income tax is calculated.

Meet the Players

Perhaps with these various trusts we are discussing, we should define our terms and the players involved in any trust:

> ➤ There is always a *trustor,* the person(s) who creates the trust. This character gets to establish the rules in the trust.

> ➤ There is always a *trustee*. This is the character who actually runs the trust. By the way, the same person may be and frequently is both the trustor and the trustee.

> ➤ Finally, there is the *beneficiary* (or beneficiaries) of the trust. The only right of the beneficiary is to sit back and receive whatever benefit the trustor defined for him or her and in whatever manner the trustee decides to implement the wishes stated in the trust.

Wealth Words

Revocable trust—A trust whose contents can be modified by the person who set it up.

Irrevocable trust—A trust whose contents, once established, cannot be modified in any way.

Blind trust—A type of trust whose contents are managed without the knowledge or input of the benefactor.

If the trustor creates a revocable trust, then the trustor can modify all aspects of the trust until he or she or they die. The trustor still controls the assets and pays the taxes of the trust. Assets can be transferred into and out of the trust freely. The assets of the trust are taxed as part of the trustor's estate.

If the trustee creates an irrevocable trust, no changes can be made after the trust is established. The trustor loses control of the assets. The trustee is now in control. Usually, the trustor and trustee are *not* the same people in the irrevocable trust. The trustor cannot benefit from the assets of the trust. Gifts into the trust are limited to $10,000 per beneficiary, per trustor, per year into the irrevocable trust. The trust must pay any taxes due each year. You may be able to avoid estate taxes with the irrevocable trust.

Trusting Blindly

Have you ever wondered what a blind trust is? You might have heard of a government leader owning a blind trust. A *blind trust* means that the person who deposited her or his assets into the trust has no information about or influence on the decisions the trustee makes for investments in the trust. Clearly, the word *trust* is imperative here, since you are *blindly* giving control over to your trustee to handle your dollars on your behalf. The trustee cannot report any of the parts to you, only the sum of the parts. Government officials put their money into blind trusts to separate the decisions they make from their financial interests.

Probate Means Prove

The textbook definition of *probate* might read as follows: Probate is a legal process that validates your will and authorizes the person you have named in your will as the executrix to carry out your wishes. Everything transferred by your will is subject to probate. The Latin root of probate is *probare*, which means "to prove."

What assets avoid this process of "proving" your money should go where you stated it ought to go?

➤ Any assets that are held jointly with rights of survivorship, such as bank accounts, investments, and real estate pass to the joint owner (surprise: by right of survivorship!).

➤ Death benefits from retirement plans or annuities are directly payable to a surviving designated beneficiary.

➤ Insurance benefits paid directly to a beneficiary instead of to your estate avoid probate.

➤ Assets distributed to your beneficiary from a living trust also avoid probate.

Wealth Words

Probate—The court procedure in which the validity of a will is proven, during which time executors might be appointed, heirs identified, and debts paid.

Avoiding probate does *not* mean you avoid estate taxes.

Take a Pass on This One

Here's a big mistake we suggest you avoid: Do not, we repeat, *do not,* own your own life insurance policy. If you do, the insurance benefit must become part of your estate, providing even more dollars on which your heirs will pay inheritance and estate taxes.

You can assign ownership to someone else, have them actually buy the policy (with money you provide to pay the premium), or set up a trust to own the policy. When you leave money or property to charity, the value of those gifts decreases the value of your estate. Although this form of generosity does not pass assets on to your heirs, it passes a lovely legacy on to them.

As this group of three chapters proves *ad nauseam*, you can never be over-informed about estate-planning techniques. You don't have to obsess about this topic, but you do need to get your basic plans and documents in place; then take them off the shelf and inspect them periodically.

Many Roads, One Destination

You've learned about many estate-planning techniques that you can use alone or in various combinations. Each of us has to deal with unique circumstances, and therefore we make different selections from the same menu. But we all share the same goal, which is to keep as many of our assets as possible in the family.

Worthy Heirs

The preceding material brings us to the most important point in this chapter: You must invest time raising worthy heirs. None of this information on wills and estate-planning techniques matters if you have concern about the worthiness of your heirs. Clearly, we do not want to sound too judgmental—only you can determine what constitutes a worthy heir.

Over the years, Anne has seen countless heirs come into family money. And every time the ending is different.

Unless you devote time and thought to coaching your heirs about how money can be a positive instrument in their lives, your thoughtful plans to pass as much as possible through to them can backfire. Some people say, "I am gone, and therefore it won't matter too much to me." Others would roll over in their graves if they knew what was happening to their carefully shepherded wealth.

Cultivate Worthy Heirs

Perhaps the most important part of your work is to cultivate worthy heirs. Our advice here is simple: Include your heirs in your plans, with as much clarity and openness as possible. Tell them your hopes and dreams for how this money might serve them. Develop a family money philosophy together—decide what money is for and what it is best spent on. Encourage your potential heirs to ask questions and be open with you about how this money might serve them, when and if it becomes theirs. Teach them how to manage the money they might inherit.

The cultivation of worthy heirs is more rewarding than the creation of wealth.

The Least You Need to Know

➤ Passing family wealth from generation to generation requires careful estate planning.

➤ Inheritance taxes are due exactly 9 months after the date of death.

➤ Your heirs can borrow from the government to pay inheritance taxes but at a high rate of interest. Banks will not loan money for this purpose.

➤ Establishing an irrevocable life insurance trust is one way to help your heirs pay inheritance tax.

➤ If you know that your death is approaching, consider cashing out any remainder in your IRA (and paying the income tax due) so that your heirs won't have to pay both income tax and inheritance tax on that money.

➤ Your estate can avoid probate, but it cannot avoid inheritance tax.

➤ Make sure that your heirs have the same philosophy regarding money that you have—develop a family money philosophy.

Not Really Dead, Only Mostly Dead

Your Most Expensive Week

Imagine the most expensive week of your life. What would it be? Paris, perhaps? A suite at the George V, dinners at the Ritz, a visit or two to Chanel or Hermes? Sorry, but chances are that the most expensive week you will ever spend might be your last. It may well be your final stay in a hospital. Despite all you've heard about health care reform, it still costs tens of thousands of dollars to survive an illness of any duration.

A Most Serious Business

Most people neglect one very vital area of financial planning—the part where you plan to become very sick some day. No matter what our age, we all seem eager to ignore these preparations. Perhaps it's our desire to ignore that which we cannot control or our acceptance that ultimately our health is in the hands of providence. Could it be that we are practicing denial and following our feathered friend, the ostrich, by burying our heads in the sand? The harsh financial reality of sudden and severe illness has a sobering effect on all of us.

We believe that your first step towards properly preparing for the end of life is to secure a signed copy of a power of attorney for health care. The best person to ask about this important document is an attorney. If you find an attorney who specializes in estate planning, she or he can reinforce the importance of this legal document.

If you hope to avoid legal service altogether, you might check at the business office of your local hospital. The staff usually has preprinted, fill-in-the-blanks forms that ask you a series of questions to help you determine your wishes and record them for your agent. Gee, that really stings for many aspiring authors and actors out there—here you are on your sickbed, and you finally manage to get an agent? No, we're talking about a different kind of agent.

When you sign a durable power of attorney, the agent is the person you assign the legal right to make decisions on your behalf. Choosing an agent is a very serious decision. This person will make life-or-death decisions for you when you cannot make those decisions for yourself.

Sign Here, Dear

It is important to note that the laws vary from state to state. We cannot cover the particulars for all 50 states in this book, but we can convey the universal concept that you *must* put some thought into exactly what your wishes would be for your care if you were suddenly thrust into a life-threatening situation in the hospital. After you consider your feelings in the matter, study your state's laws. Do they allow you to have a voice in your care? Do they allow you to appoint an agent to act on your behalf if you are unable to do so? If the state in which you live allows this, it certainly wants you to record your wishes in writing. What kinds of documents are legally acceptable to ensure that your wishes will be implemented?

Wealth Words

Durable health care power of attorney—A legal document that authorizes your chosen representative to make health care decisions on your behalf.

Do not rely on the "good judgment" of health care professionals. They are trained to preserve your life at any cost. Saving lives is their mission, as well it should be. Do not rely on your family members to know what to do, and how to do it. They have probably *never* confronted this situation before and will face a lot of emotional turmoil, so you need to relieve them of the stress of guessing your wishes.

You Need a Plan

When you know how much say your state allows you in these matters and what method you must use to convey your wishes so they are legally acceptable, implement your plan.

The final and most crucial step in this process is to discuss your plan, decisions, and the location of the documents thoroughly with the person you have appointed to be your agent. Most people forget this very important step. In fact, for many people, just thinking about this eventually is a challenge, and talking about it is even more formidable. You must get past these barriers. One of the best gifts of love you can give to your friends and family is to convey your wishes in an open, straightforward manner.

Free to Be

As we like to say, once you have all the documents that deal with your death and illness complete, then you are free to live!

Consider the following scenario: Anne has a client in her early 60s and in apparently adequate health. This woman, Joyce, has two reasonably well-adjusted and thoughtful grown children who hold their mother's best interests at heart. Suddenly, and quite unexpectedly, this client became very ill and needed to spend 2 weeks in the hospital; 1 of those weeks was in the intensive care unit. This client had the best medical insurance she could buy, but it had a $50,000 cap for costs incurred in any 1 year.

She had considered the durable power of attorney for health care, but had not yet actually completed one. Joyce had told both of her children her wishes and considered herself more prepared than most for an event like this in her life. This story has a happy ending: The client recovered and was discharged from the hospital.

But That's Not What She Told Me!

Unfortunately, Joyce's children underwent considerable stress in the process. At several points, the children disagreed with the manner in which the hospital was caring for their mother. They were particularly distressed at the use of restraints in the intensive care unit to inhibit their mother from interfering with the tubes attached to her to provide her care. The children were allowed to voice their opinion, but had no written document demonstrating their authority to do so.

This situation is very frustrating. Furthermore, the children even disagreed over the lifesaving measures their mother wanted taken. Each child had a different recollection of what mom had said she wanted. So you see, you must put your desires in writing. This document plays a crucial role in helping you and your loved ones survive an extraordinary health event.

Write It Down!

While all's well that ends well in Joyce's story, her children were left with some sobering realities. They realized that although their mother had told them the same wishes, they interpreted their mother's words differently. Although their versions were very similar, they were not identical. Such disparity would be less likely had the words been in writing. While they both wanted to follow their mother's wishes, it was not clear who should step forward as her advocate.

In any case, we hope you get the point that even with everyone working in the patient's best interest, the most loving gift you can give to your heirs is to express your wishes clearly. It is best for everyone, especially you, to remove all the ambiguities *before* the crisis. After all, even with all this work completed in advance, many variables and obstacles remain for you and your family to face.

Get a Good Agent

Now that we have persuaded you that having an agent is a wise idea, consider who might make the best agent. Most married people name their spouse first, but you must consider a strong second in line as well. What if you and your spouse are involved in the same accident and arrive at the hospital *non compos mentis*?

Now that is a big, scary-sounding expression—what exactly does it mean? *Non compos mentis* has its roots in Latin and means "not legally sane." This does not mean to imply we are all insane when we arrive at the hospital. Incapacitated, not of sound mind, or unconscious are other conditions that trigger the use of a health care power of attorney. If you are unable to make your own decisions and advocate for your own point of view (after all, you are the patient and entitled to a voice in your care!), you need to appoint someone who will be your spokesperson.

Wealth Words

Non compos mentis—A legal term that describes a person who is mentally incapacitated and unable to make decisions on his or her own behalf.

Trust Us on This One

All of this involves trust. If the list of people you trust to this degree is too short, or nonexistent, it is time to cultivate this level of relationship with others. Not because you need them when you are ill, but because you need this level of trust with others in you life while you are alive and well!

This whole area of our book is delicate, and the financial impact might not be readily apparent. Most of us toil our whole lives with the implicit or explicit goal of amassing enough money to support ourselves until we die. Many of us hope to pass money along to our heirs, and short of being able to meet this goal, we at least do not want to pass our debts along to our heirs.

The reason we are devoting so much of this book to this topic is twofold:

➤ First, paying attention to this particular legal area of your life will leave a happier legacy for your loved ones.

➤ Second, we all spend so much time saving, investing, and building our nest egg that conservation of these dollars is frequently overlooked.

As we opened this chapter, we reminded you that the most expensive days of your life are not likely to be spent on an exotic vacation—they are typically your last days spent in the hospital.

Setting Limits

A durable power of attorney for health care does not eliminate all this expense, but it can set some limits and provide everyone working toward your recovery with invaluable guidelines. It also relieves your health care professionals of having to make the decision on their own. Crisis health care is not the only instance where you are not really dead, but only mostly dead. As many of us are aware, we often outlive our ability to really take care of ourselves and end up living in nursing homes. Sometimes, we end up needing in-home care for some period of time to assure even a reasonable quality of life.

Unfortunately, this area of life is another in which we practice the fine art of denial and play ostrich with our heads stuck firmly in the sand. Even when we might make plans, as our ability to implement our well-laid plans slips away, the people we trust to help us might not make the same kind of decisions we would. Again, careful consideration of your wishes and even more carefully committing these thoughts in writing prove invaluable in saving your money.

Run It to the Limit!

You can always take the point of view that you want all your money spent, and you would like to be allowed to die when your last dollar runs out. Granted, this seems like an easy plan, but even this one is very tough for anyone to implement for you if you do not put it in writing! We hope you are seeing the common theme here: that you need to spend some of your healthy time thinking about your wishes. You need to find out what your state allows. You need to dedicate your thoughts to writing. Finally, you need to bring your trusted agents in on the plan, *before* the event or decline. Once you do all this, you are free to *live*!

Let's look at another example: Amy, a woman in her middle 70s. Both she and her husband (while he was alive) had carefully made plans for their old age. They had very little confidence that their children, two grown daughters, could be of help. Therefore, they brought a corporate or professional trustee on board with their documents, so they would have the means to be taken care of without involving their daughters. After her husband passed away, Amy grieved so deeply that it affected her health. Her children (much to Amy's surprise) stepped up to the plate to try to help her. The children had always been self-serving and, frankly, too immature (even in middle age!) to be of much help with their parents' care before. Yet, here they were.

The daughters were very attentive, and many fences were mended during this time of caring for their mother. Within a year, though, their mother died quite peacefully.

During this time of decline and reconciliation, their mother appreciated their help. She even provided what financial assistance was necessary to her daughters to facilitate their help. For example, one daughter had considerable airfare costs to travel to be with her mother from time to time. Her mother gladly picked up the cost of travel. Amy never changed her original plan to have a professional trustee oversee her estate, nor did she ever intend to do so. Her daughters were both unhappy and amazed that even after the reconciliation, their mother thought they needed professional supervision of their share of the estate.

This story is important to demonstrate that you must make your best plans while you are of sound mind. Even during the reconciliation phase, emotional differences were being resolved. The daughters' abilities to make good investment decisions did not change. The mother and father had put considerable time into their original plan, and emotional healing did not change the logic of their original plan. Even though the daughters were disappointed, it was not their decision to make. They had to respect their parents' decisions about their estate. If these plans had not been put in writing, the reconciliation might have altered the way a court would have decided.

Amy's Plan

Although Amy did not want her daughters to have her money outright, neither did she want it squandered on nursing home and hospital bills. Instead, she wanted prudent in-home care. She wanted enough care to ensure her comfort, but absolutely no heroic intervention. Because she had stated her desire in writing and appointed a professional trustee, her wishes were implemented.

For those of you who think you might eventually end up in a nursing home, it is a valid choice. Be mindful that as the laws currently exist, you have to drain all of your personal assets, until you cannot afford to provide for your care, before the government will take over your care.

Long-Lived Women

We told you earlier in this book that women, fortunately and unfortunately, live longer than men. The realities of our care in aging are more profound. If you hope to leave your heirs any of your hard-earned and carefully invested money, you *must* make plans.

Many people work under the assumption that when the time comes, they can just give everything they have to their kids and thereby show that they do not have the means to support themselves. They then hope the government will take over the costs of their old age care.

This plan is flawed in that the government reserves the right to take a 64-month look back at the value of your assets. If you gave it away, the government wants it back!

Therefore, you need to craft your plans more carefully. In this area, you need to consult an attorney who specializes in eldercare. It would also be helpful to attend adult education classes on this topic. Many health care organizations, insurance companies, and investment firms offer relevant classes and seminars. Surprise—they all have a reason for helping you!

➤ Health care organizations want you to plan so they do not have to fight with your family about who is responsible for the bills.

➤ Insurance companies offer a product, called long-term-care insurance, to make some of your problems disappear. Be very careful before you purchase this type of insurance. There is a wide disparity in policies. If they sound too good to be true, they are, and while many of them are good, many are not worth the paper on which they are printed.

➤ The investment firms offer the same insurance, but they have one other important reason for helping you understand your options here. They have watched while many a client's hard-earned and carefully grown nest egg is wiped out by lack of planning.

Cash Cautions

Sorry, but you can't fool Uncle Sam very often. Aware that some elderly folks had given their assets to their children in order to preserve the family's money and still qualify for government-provided health care or nursing homes, the government changed the rules. Now, before picking up your bills, the government examines your financial dealings for the previous 64 months to see whether you gave away any valuable assets.

Be warned that this area of the law is evolving quickly as our population ages. Make sure you are investing your time in current and up-to-date information. The most important message we hope to convey in this chapter is that the worst plan is no plan at all. If only you take the time to sort out your feelings and make your plans, you will live free of the worry of what might happen!

The Least You Need to Know

➤ You can build up a fortune over your lifetime, only to see it drained away by health care costs at the end of your life.

➤ Should you be mentally incapacitated for any reason, you really should give a trusted person durable power of attorney for health care questions. Make these arrangements before anything happens to you.

➤ Make sure that your children understand exactly what your wishes are, too.

➤ If you choose your spouse as your agent, choose a back-up person as well, in case both you and your spouse are injured together.

➤ You might choose to go ahead and spend all of your money on a long hospital stay. It's your money, and you can decide how to spend it.

➤ Nursing homes can quickly eat up your family's money.

➤ Before granting you nursing home coverage, the government will examine your finances and personal affairs for the previous 64 months to see whether you gave away any major assets to make yourself poor enough to qualify for government assistance.

Chapter 26

Believe in Yourself!

In This Chapter

➤ More women of Wall Street

➤ In good company

➤ Major reasons to invest

➤ Best strategies for beginning investors

➤ Hanging on when the going gets tough

➤ Yes, you can!

➤ Watch your money grow

Congratulations! You just read an entire book on investing. It might have been your first investing book, or it might have been your fifth, but the fact remains that *you read the book.*

Are you surprised by your behavior? Don't be. You are in very good company: the company of smart women who are taking charge of their financial lives and assuming total responsibility for making their money grow through investments.

More Women With Money and Power

Remember all we told you in Chapter 2, "Gosh, Will They Let Me In? Isn't Investing a Boy's Club?" about how many powerful women there are on Wall Street and throughout the world of finance? Allow us to cheer you and your investment efforts on with a few more examples:

➤ Sheryl Kwiatek Pressler—As chief investment officer, California Public Employees' Retirement (PER) fund, Sheryl Kwiatek Pressler manages billions of dollars on behalf of retired state employees.

➤ Darla Moore—When Darla Moore married mega-investor Richard Rainwater, he stepped aside and let her run the show. As president of Rainwater Inc., Darla Moore is sometimes described as "corporate America's most feared female activist" for her aggressive raiding techniques. *Fortune* magazine recently named Darla as one of the most powerful women in the country.

➤ Carly Fiorina—Featured on the front cover of *Fortune* magazine as *the* most powerful woman in American business, Fiorina made her mark at Lucent Technologies by taking the company public in what turned out to be the biggest, most successful IPO in U.S. history.

➤ Abigal Johnson—Surely you recognize the name Fidelity Investments, one of the nation's largest fund companies. Fidelity, with $600 billion in fund assets, is a privately held, family-owned company, and Abigal Johnson is the heir apparent to take over when her father steps down. At 36, she maintains a fairly low profile in the investment world.

Imagine, if we just added up the money that *these* women alone control—it's a hundred times more than Bill Gates has his hands on, girls!

Wise Women Know

Women's faces are cropping up more and more in the advertising of financial services and investing. Wait! Who's that in the television ad with the ubiquitous Peter Lynch of Fidelity? Why, it's Lily Tomlin!!! Now, if a large mutual fund company decides to feature Lily Tomlin in its ads, just who do you think the company is trying to reach? Could it be you?

In Good Company

There is no reason for you to feel alone as you learn more and more about money and investing. There is no reason for you to feel freakish if you find yourself fascinated by the high-stakes world of money. Does Darla Moore think she's a freak as she leads the stockholders' charge on yet another company? Somehow, we doubt it.

In mapping out this book, we have tried to follow a logical progression. The steps we all took together were:

➤ Understanding and mastering personal money-management techniques

➤ Learning about investing and how to take the steps into the market in the way that best suits our needs

➤ Making long-term financial plans for ourselves, our families, and our heirs

Back to the Beginning

Let's revisit some of the points we'd like to leave you with before you close the book and wander off to begin your extraordinary life of investing.

➤ In Chapter 1, "What, Me Worry?" we tried to jolt you out of your safe cocoon and gave you some startling and grim facts and statistics about what happens to most women in the face of divorce, widowhood, or retirement. And we hope you got the point—you are on your own, honey. Take charge of your financial future now.

➤ The pump-up chapter, Chapter 2, opened your eyes to all of the many women who are already out there making investment decisions on a huge scale day in and day out. So don't you hesitate for a second to take charge. Not only are women perfectly capable of handling these decisions, but we are currently being targeted by all of the different arms of the financial world. They know how much money women control, and they want us to come and invest it!

➤ So you were ready to invest, but weren't sure just how much you really had? We helped you unscramble your nest egg in Chapter 3, "The Money Under Your Mattress." You've got to get a handle on all those different accounts before you can clearly assess your next money move. Chapter 4, "Junk Mail and Other Stuff You Will Receive," gave you a better way to get all of your mail under control: We told you what to toss, what to save, and for how long.

➤ Lest we'd already overwhelmed you, in Chapter 5, "Can I Get Some Help With This?," we introduced some of the professionals who'd love to help you with your financial life. We think you should understand as much as you can about all of the aspects, but if you want to call in the pros, don't be ashamed.

➤ The four chapters in Part 2, "I Owe, I Owe, It's Off to Work I Go," were pretty harsh looks at what most of us are consumed by—debt. We hope that you received our subtle message—*stay out of debt! Credit cards are poison. Quit squandering your money on silly stuff.* Ah yes, a very subtle message...

➤ And then we jumped into the big stuff with Chapter 10, "The World Is Your Rolex Oyster." The stock market was revealed and explained at last. Chapter 11, "More on the Market," took you deeper into the world of the stock market. Then we moved on to other types of investing—the bond market and mutual funds.

➤ Once you had a handle on investing, you realized that life would quickly become more complicated. So we outlined several ways to help calm the waters—by using central asset accounts (Chapter 14), booting up your computer and using the great investing and financial software available (Chapter 15), and utilizing the tremendous information available both online and in old-fashioned newspapers and magazines.

➤ In case you were feeling lonely, we told you all about investment clubs. A great way to spend time with other investors, learning about the market together, and making your money grow at the same time.

➤ And then it was on to the rest of your life. Returning to our theme from Chapter 1 about what happens to most women upon retirement or widowhood, we examined basic retirement planning.

➤ Part 5 examined many different retirement vehicles, everything from 401(k) plans to annuities.

➤ And in Chapter 21, "The Best Thing to Grow—Long-Term Gains!" we described what they are and explained why you want them!

➤ The last few chapters (which you have no doubt just read) are based on one grim statistic—that 100% of us will die. Why not start planning now so that you can pass on as much as you can to the people that you love? It is *never* too early to plan your estate.

Major Reasons to Invest

And here we are, having gone full circle. Do you remember all of the best pieces of wisdom from earlier in the book? We know you took notes, underlined here and there, and notched the top of a page or two. But why don't we just repeat some of the things we feel strongly about.

➤ *Why you must begin to invest now*—Charles Schwab sums it up best: "The riskiest investment of all is to take no risk and not invest." Regardless of where the market is this week or next, regardless of how much (or how little) money you can invest, you must begin now. There is no perfect time; there is only right now.

➤ *The stock market has historically delivered the greatest returns*—Sure, there are many other ways to grown your money, but investing in the stock market has consistently beaten the returns on everything else. Even Beanie Babies.

➤ *Pay yourself first*—Paying yourself first is the simplest, yet most powerful, investing lesson you can learn. Instead of worrying about where the extra money will come from to invest, if you consistently remove 10% of your paycheck and put it into investments, you will never miss the money.

Please take the information that you learned in this book and act on it. Your financial future depends on the steps you take *now*.

Those are the three top reasons to invest, but what are the three best strategies for beginning investors? After 15 years as a stockbroker, here is what Anne suggests:

➤ Pay attention to what is going on around you. If you and all of your neighbors are raving about a new store that is publicly traded, check out the stock. Keep your eyes open for investment opportunities in whatever field you know best—probably the one you work in. Of course, you know who the market leaders are, what the long-term prospects are for this business segment, and which direction the industry is headed. Act on your knowledge; put it to use.

➤ Don't buy in haste and repent at leisure. Don't invest based on what you overhear at a cocktail party, or worse yet, what a telephone-soliciting broker tries to pitch to you. Do your own research before you buy; make up your own mind.

➤ Forget about timing the market; there is no "best" time to get in. Always make investments with the idea that you will own these stocks for years and years to come.

Hanging on When the Market Gets Tough

It is glorious when the stock market continues to rise and rise. But when the market falls or when it gyrates or when it hits a "correction," it can be terrifying for investors. And there is no predicting the future—during the time that it took us to complete this book, we went from an all-time market high (on July 17, 1998, to be exact) to a period of severe market swings. In the past few weeks, as we wrote the words to urge you to invest for the long term and stand firm in the face of uncertainty, the market has been up almost 250 points one day, only to fall steadily downward again immediately after. Kind of exhausting; not only are we drained, but our own portfolios are down.

Wealth Words

Market correction—A sharp decline off a market high. The market average must fall at least 10% to be considered a market correction.

So what do you do? How do you handle these wild swings? Here are a few pointers on how to hang tough in the midst of market turmoil. Remember, you only *lose* money if you sell!

Understand that over the course of your portfolio's life, the market will sometimes go up and sometimes go down. But if you stay in for the long run, history is on your side. Remember the example of IBM stock we gave you? It was an unbeatable blue-chip stock until it tanked. Investors who panicked and sold then lost out. Not only did the stock regain and then some, investors who *added* more IBM to their portfolios picked up some great bargains.

Watch the market, but don't watch too closely. If you have researched a stock, believe it to be a strong stock, and invested in it with the intention of holding on to it for years and years, spare yourself the heartache of watching the fluctuations that occur during the course of the day. Of course you should be aware of what is happening with the stocks you own, but if you concentrate on the minutiae, you may well sell long before you should.

Don't get too focused on the immediate value of your portfolio and plunge into despair the minute its value drops. Do not sell. If you sell, then your portfolio is definitely worth less and you have lost money. But if you just sit tight, chances are it will rise again. Plenty of people who were stock market millionaires in the summer of 1998 slipped from that vaunted status just a short 6 weeks later. But, as long as they didn't sell off their portfolios, chances are that they will again become market millionaires in the coming months or years. Learn to think of your portfolio as "down." Never beat yourself up about how much money you had last month or last year. You are temporarily down and will be coming back up again soon!

Always keep focused on the fundamentals of a company. If you examined the company thoroughly before you bought the stock and decided it was a good, solid company, why is it any less solid if the stock price slips a bit? Will people still pay their phone bills? Yes, so why worry about your AT&T stock? Do you still go to the grocery store several times a week, and don't you have to wait in a long line? So why worry about your Safeway stock? Hmmm…even though the market has fallen, your car (and every one else's) still needs a tank of gas every week. So should you worry if your stock in the Mobil Corporation is down a bit?

Yes, You Can!

Can you build real wealth on your own by investing? Yes, you can! Can you build a retirement fund that will see you through your golden years? Yes, you can! And can you trust yourself to make important decisions about money even though you are…gasp…a woman? Oddly enough, even in the twilight of the twentieth century, many women out there still feel the teensiest bit unsure that handling money is a proper thing to do.

Don't you let anyone make you feel that you can't manage your finances! Do not doubt your ability to handle money, do not doubt your ability to handle investments—just get out there and do it!

Teach Your Children Well

As mothers, we all try hard to teach our children what they'll need to know to live successful lives. But all too often, the topic of money and finances is not broached. Why? It's an embarrassing, taboo topic in many families. Some parents think that children shouldn't know too much about a family's financial situation.

Why should this be? Why shouldn't we want our children to learn about money management and investing from an early age? Buy them a few shares in McDonald's instead of taking them for a weekly Happy Meal. Kids are bound to take a personal interest in the stocks of companies they know, for example, Toys 'R' Us, Disney, and Tootsie Roll Industries.

Wise Women Know

As you expand your own knowledge of the financial world, don't miss out on the opportunity to teach your children. Anne's children are still too young to understand what she is doing on her computer, but Jennifer's 4-year-old, Julian, has begun to display an interest. "Can I play Toy Story on CD-ROM?" he asked her as she sat checking stock prices. "Not right now; mama is looking at how much things cost. It is a good time to buy this." Julian nodded seriously, "Okay, you buy it, and we'll go and pick it up from the store. Then can I play Toy Story?" Well, maybe next year he'll get the hang of it...

So as you embark on your mission to learn more about investing, bring your children in on the mission, too. Explain the financial pages to them. By describing it out loud, you will also be inscribing it in your memory. It's a great way to learn.

One topic that we haven't really touched on yet is husbands. Can we talk about men? As you grow more knowledgeable about investing, strike up a financial conversation with your significant other. Money is an incredibly fascinating topic, one with something new to discuss every day (every hour!). Don't miss the chance to talk about money with your man.

And We Want You To!

In the last few hundred pages, we've tried to give you a solid understanding of the basics of investing. But please do not let your financial education end with this book. Go on and learn more; the world of money is endlessly exciting! It's energizing! And—literally—the world of money is *empowering*!

We might have mentioned somewhere in this book that both authors, Anne and Jennifer, are graduates of Mills College, a small women's college on the West Coast. Spending 4 years (graduating in different classes) in an environment filled with other smart women gave both of us the opportunity to develop self-confidence. We both feel strongly about empowering women with the knowledge and financial tools to make our own investment decisions—and to prosper as a result. Women have long been the home-builders; now, let's all become wealth-builders! We owe it to ourselves, we owe it to our children, and we owe it to our husbands and loved ones.

The Least You Need to Know

➤ Women are everywhere on Wall Street, and they handle huge sums of money.

➤ The stock market has historically turned in the greatest growth for investors.

➤ Paying yourself first, putting 10% of your paycheck aside to invest, is an easy and painless way to build wealth.

➤ There is no "best" time to get into the stock market; get started now.

➤ Hold your investments for the long term. Don't get caught up in what is happening on an hourly basis, or you will be tempted to sell.

➤ Stay focused on fundamentally sound companies and fundamentally strong markets.

➤ Take every opportunity to teach your children about money and investing.

How to Read a Company's Financial Report

Five months after you buy General Gymshoe, a thick envelope shows up in your mailbox. You open it and find what looks like at first glance a mail-order catalog on steroids. Beautiful professional shots of all kinds of shoes, really cool graphics and holograms, and the familiar General Gymshoe logo. What is this thing? What do I do with it? Has Gymshoe's marketing department gone mad?

You've just received your first annual report. Now what?

What Are These Reports?

The true purpose of annual and quarterly reports is to provide to investors the financial data they need to assess the company's performance. Publicly traded stock companies are required by law to produce an annual report, along with quarterly reports showing basic financial performance.

That is indeed their legal duty. But something else becomes quite clear at first sight—company reports are also marketing documents, particularly the annual report. They are marketing the company's shares to individual investors like you as well as to larger, more powerful investors like mutual funds.

It's Show Time

The first part of most annual reports is the fun part. It is where the company gets to show off its products, its employees, its factories and facilities, and its trucks and airplanes. These pictures and story lines are all very professionally created, posed, and captured on film. This isn't to say they are false or fictitious, but almost any firm is going to present itself in the best possible light. The first few pages of an annual report give you an idea of the company's personality and the look and feel of its products in the marketplace. But often there is more.

Some companies that produce a complex product or deal in complex markets use the annual report to show and explain their products and services. For those not familiar with the soybean oil industry, for example, the Archer Daniels Midland annual reports go into great detail about where soybeans come from and how they're processed into myriad products. For those not familiar with B-STDX broadband packet switches, the Ascend Communications annual report describes their function and shows how they fit into a complete product line. You, as a diligent owner of a company, should probably make it a point to know some of these things.

These front sections often include important data on market size and market share. Market size is, for example, the dollar value of all soybean products sold in the United States. Market share is, for example, the percentage of those products that are sold by Archer Daniels Midland. Readers are also likely to find information on the contribution of different product lines to revenue and profits, geographic breakdowns, and recent years' trends. Want to find out how much of Philip Morris's business comes from selling tobacco products? Check the annual report.

The Positive Spin

Usually near the beginning of both annual and quarterly reports is a management discussion. The top officers in the company provide a one- to two-page summary of the company's results and plans for the near future. The summaries are worth reading and are often entertaining, but remember these are a company's top-paid executives telling the world about their accomplishments and hopes for the future. Rarely will there be a negative comment. If there is, watch out!

And Now, the Numbers

It's far beyond the scope of this book (and especially this appendix) to turn you into a crackerjack financial analyst.

Yes, there are lots and lots of numbers—and many footnotes, which lead you to still more numbers. Not exactly light reading material for the beach.

Among the many financial worksheets, there is always an income statement and balance sheet. The income statement (sometimes called the "Consolidated Statement of Income" or "Consolidated Statement of Operations") shows revenues, expenses, and net income before and after taxes, and finally, net income per share for a given time period. The balance sheet is a snapshot of assets, liabilities, and net worth (partly owned by you!) at a given point in time.

There are many things to look for on both of these statements. For starters, it is worth looking at trends. Check the comparisons: quarter to quarter, same quarter last year, and year to year. Check and see that things are moving in the right direction, at least. For example, if a toy company sells fewer toys in this year's Christmas season than it did in last year's, you want to know why.

Incoming...!

The income statement shows sales, costs, and profits. The following items are worth a closer look:

➤ Revenues, or sales—Are they increasing or slowing down? What is the percent increase? Is the rate of increase slowing down?

➤ Gross margin—This item is revenues minus "cost of goods sold." That is, it is what the company makes on every widget produced before marketing, administrative, and the ubiquitous "other" expenses. Gross margin is money that came in from sales minus the cost of making the product. Margins are less controllable than these other discretionary expenses and are a good indicator of market position, competition, and potential market saturation. Does the company have a commanding market position, control of prices, and solid profit and profit growth prospects in the future? Not if its gross margin is shrinking. Note: You should measure margin as a percent of sales. Profit margin is therefore equal to profits divided by sales.

➤ SG&A—This acronym stands for selling, general and administrative expenses. If these expenses are increasing as a percent of sales, either (1) expenses are out of control or (2) the company's markets are getting tougher, requiring greater investments and expenditures to achieve the same results. Growing SG&A as a percent of sales can spell trouble.

➤ Net income and earnings per share—This figure is the so-called bottom line. Earnings per share, or EPS, is the denominator for the widely used price-to-earnings (PE) ratio (share price divided by EPS). Naturally this number is important and should be tracked over time. The PE ratio is one of many numbers you can use to determine whether your stock is expensive compared to other stocks.

➤ Extraordinary gains and losses—More and more companies are choosing to bury their mistakes and take onetime write-offs for "restructuring"—closing, resizing, or getting rid of unprofitable operations and assets. These charges are tacked on to normal net income and can produce wildly distorted bottom-line figures. For investment analysis, it is usually best to overlook these one-timers unless a company has the bad habit of incurring write-offs every year! Similarly, big gains (such as gains from selling pieces of the company), while nice for the corporate treasury, don't mean much for the investor.

A Balanced Approach

Like the income statement, the balance sheet has some gems in it and some numbers the average investor can probably overlook.

➤ Cash is king—A good indicator of a company's financial health is its cash hoard (which often comes in the form of "marketable securities"—liquid short-term investments). Growing cash is a good sign; very lean cash or declining cash balances are usually a bad sign, absent of extraordinary events. A company with a *very* large cash hoard—billions and billions—may also raise eyebrows. Is it getting ready to make an acquisition (diluting share value)? Has it no productive way to invest its assets? Why doesn't it want to invest in itself? If a company doesn't want to invest in itself, why should you?

➤ Accounts receivable (A/R) and inventory—A/R would seemingly be considered a good thing—isn't it nice when someone owes *you* money? Well, nice to a point. If A/Rs are expanding and your company is in an industry where its customers aren't doing well, (for instance, your company sells products to the steel industry), it might be time to switch investments. Likewise, growing inventory (unsold products) is a bad sign—business may be slowing down, and future sales may be stunted by discounting necessary to move (sell) an inventory glut (all those unsold products). Like gross margin and SG&A, these numbers should be looked at as a percent of sales—that is, growing inventories are okay if sales are growing at a faster rate. In this case, *productivity* is increasing (it's okay to make more stuff if you can sell it).

➤ Liabilities—You don't like to owe money, and at a certain point it is also bad for a company. Although the acceptable amount of debt varies greatly by industry, your main concern should be that debt isn't growing too rapidly, measured again as a percent of sales.

➤ Shareholders' equity—Shareholders' equity includes items such as common stock, preferred stock, additional paid-in capital, and retained earnings. What it all really means is the amount of "net worth" that you share with other stockholders. Don't worry too much about how much each category contains—that's all stuff for accountants. Take a look at the total and particularly the trend. Growing shareholders' equity is a good sign.

Great, But What If I Don't Own the Company?

Don't fret—it is still easy to get an annual report. You don't have to buy a share and wait for the next issue. Simply contact investor relations, or some other department with a similar title. You can find the address by looking at company profiles online, or look in *Standard & Poor's*, *Moody's*, or *Value Line* in the local library. (Reading some of these publications can be an education in itself!) Simply send a postcard with your name and address. You'll be surprised how little time it takes for you to get your copy! Companies love to spread their image and acquire new investors, and first-class postage or even overnight-shipping expenses are seldom spared.

The Daily Dose: How to Read the Financial Pages

Now that you've become a savvy investor and manager of your own finances, you've probably come to realize that your newspaper-reading priorities have changed. You can still read the Lifestyles section first, but somewhere in your daily read you now need check out the financial pages. Yes, the ones with all those little-bitty numbers from top to bottom. Not only will you be able to better manage and track your investments, but you will look more sophisticated at the corner Starbucks! Sooner or later, as your financial fortunes grow, we predict that the daily intrigue will get the better part of you, and you will "check the numbers" first thing when the morning paper hits your breakfast table.

Do I Need the *Journal?*

Every newspaper carries a different "mix" of business and financial data. With a few sad and surprising exceptions, the great bull market of the '80s and '90s and the vastly grown field of savvy individual investors have driven most daily newspapers to carry improved and more complete financial sections.

You generally do not need a financial newspaper such as the *Wall Street Journal* to track your investments. Sure, you will get more—and more complete—information about what's happening in the business world from the *Journal* than from a local paper (as well as very interesting coverage of non-business topics), but a good daily paper and an occasional trip to the Web should suffice. However, if you're actively trading equity options, commodities, or other more sophisticated vehicles where a close, daily vigil is vital, it's time to subscribe.

What's the Recipe for a Good Stock Page?

Most adequate daily investment sections are three or four pages long, sometimes longer. If your paper squeezes half a page of numbers alongside 6 column inches of business news, and its dwarfed by the furniture store ads or squeezed between "Garage Sales" and "Men Seeking Men," it's time to search for another resource.

All the News Fit to Print

A good investment section in a daily paper should give some basic national and international business news. Some of this news should be about business and the economy in general. Some of it should be about specific companies. If the only companies that appear in your paper are local companies, you should get another resource (unless you have chosen to hitch your future only to "Stocks of Local Interest").

The Averages

Your business section should contain key market indicators. Almost all contain the venerable Dow Jones indexes: the Dow Jones Industrials, Transportation, and Utilities averages. Your paper should also publish the NASDAQ composite index and the S&P 500. Many also carry the New York Stock Exchange indexes, although these largely mirror the Dow. Give your paper extra credit if it reports indexes from key international markets (Japan, Germany, United Kingdom—the more the better).

What are these indexes? They are weighted-average composites of a group of chosen representative stocks from their category. Think of them as shopping baskets of stocks. Individual price moves are weighted according to the amount in the basket (some companies are more important than others, so they have a greater effect on an index). The number you see is a composite total weighting of all the individual values. These indexes are widely used to track overall market moves, filtering out the "noise" of individual stock moves.

The Dow Jones Industrial Average (DJIA) is the one you'll hear about the most. The DJIA has 30 "industrial" companies (if you'll for a minute consider American Express and JP Morgan as industrial). The 30 are considered the bellwether indicators or reflectors of the performance of all American companies. For the most part, unless you're particularly interested in technology or small emerging companies, the Dow has served well. For techies and *avant garde* investors, the NASDAQ index will attract more attention.

The Market Summary

A good paper will include market highlights—sort of the evening-newsbreak summary of the more exciting individual stock achievements (and disasters) of the day.

Market highlights include the "most-actives list," a listing of NYSE, NASDAQ, and sometimes American Stock Exchange stocks that were the most actively traded issues for the day. Certain stocks—for example, COMPAQ, Philip Morris, Intel, and Microsoft—are regulars on their respective lists. But when General Gymshoe hits the list, something's going on, good or bad, that's driving investors, especially institutions, to make some moves. Time to find out more.

The most interesting part of market highlights is the "price percentage gainers" and "price percentage losers" section from each market. Here are the top stocks by price move in a given day. Finding your stock on the "gainers" list can be one of the most uplifting feelings in all of investing, sort of like having your boss gush over your latest piece of work. Conversely, a trip to the "losers" column can leave you heartbroken, especially on the NASDAQ exchange, where the big losers usually lose 20% to 40%, sometimes more, in a day. Your stocks probably won't be on these lists too often, but it's fun to watch the action.

Another important indicator is the "advance-decline line." Somewhere your listing will probably show how many stocks were up for the day and how many were down. This line indicates overall market *breadth*—how closely the market as a whole follows the movements of the elite few in the averages.

There is also a "new highs, new lows" list of stocks reaching new 52-week high or low prices (great if you have a stock with a new 52-week high!). Stocks on the 52-week low list can be bargains if all else is right. When the new lows greatly outnumber the new highs, especially over a period of time, look out! There's a lot of stuff here for the technical-trend people, but these indicators are also good for a high-level understanding of what's going on.

The Listings

A good stock-listing page will have lots of numbers on it.

Watch out for the less-than-one-page newsprint savers some papers try to foist on you. These "composite" listings probably exclude two-thirds of the market, and, after all, you wouldn't want to fly an airplane with a mask over two-thirds of the windshield, would you?

Individual stock listings should occur in separate sections for NYSE and NASDAQ stocks.

A stock listing that shows only the closing price is okay but certainly leaves room for improvement. Good basic listings will show volume and price movement during the day. Better listings will provide more relevant information about the stock itself, such as dividend rates, yields, and the PE ratio. The best listings show price-movement ranges over the past 52 weeks. You might want to buy a copy of the *Wall Street Journal* once and keep it, just to see what the professionals use and to compare the best listings in the country with the listings you get.

Reading From Left to Right

The following example is what you find in the most complete listings. The *Wall Street Journal* uses this format.

52 weeks					Yield		Vol					
Hi	Lo	Stock	Sym	Div	%	PE	100sNet	Hi	Lo	Close	Chg
25	15	GenGymshoe	GYM	.24	2.2	16	301	23	21	22	+1/8

➤ 52-week pickup—The left-most three figures tell you what happened during the last trading year. The small *s* is good news if you're an owner. It means the stock split its shares during the past 52 weeks. If you're a shopper, not an owner, the *s* is also possibly good news: The company management has had strong enough thoughts about the company's growth—hence the stock price growth—to execute the split. The high for the year (adjusted for the split) is 25; the low is 15.

Considering today's closing price of 22, the stock is doing fairly well right now. If you're a shopper, be aware that the stock was a better deal in the past ($15). But if everything's right, perhaps it's time to buy. On the other hand, if everything is *not* right and you're trading so close to the 52-week high, it might be time to sell.

➤ What's in a name?—The name of the company is abbreviated so it can fit into the 11 or so characters allowed. Usually the name is recognizable, but sometimes not. Following the name is the ticker symbol under which the stock trades.

➤ Yield signs—Most papers show an indicated annual dividend rate for companies that pay dividends. Better papers also divide this rate by the stock price to get the current "yield," or annual percentage rate of return. Watch for little letters after the dividend rate—they can convey such things as omitted dividends (bad!) or extra or stock dividends (good!). Consult the symbol lists printed in the front of every newspaper's stock section.

➤ PE ratio—Here's the famous price-earnings ratio. This most basic ratio indicates a company's profitability relative to its stock price. A lower PE indicates better value (a cheaper stock), but you need to look at the underlying trends! See Chapter 10, "The World Is Your Rolex Oyster."

➤ Turn up the volume—Here is the daily trading volume, usually with the final zeros deleted. The 301 means that 30,100 shares changed hands during the trading day, which is fairly low volume. To get to the most-active list normally requires trading at least a million, often more, shares. Watch for big spikes in trading volume.

➤ The prices—Listed now are the daily price movements of your stock. Here the high trade for the day was at 23. Pity the poor gal who paid that much, because the stock closed trading at 22. Likewise, three cheers for the savvy investor who bought at the low price of the day, 21.

➤ A change for the better—The last column is where the eyeballs of the experienced stock-listing reader usually go first. It tells you whether the stock went up or down and by how much. This number is simply the difference from the previous day's price. For example,

➤ Eighths? Sixteenths? Even smaller fractions on the NASDAQ? These numbers are price fractions, fractions of a dollar. $\frac{1}{8}$ of a point is $\frac{1}{8}$ of a dollar, or 12.5 cents, $\frac{1}{16}$ is 6.25 cents, and so on. This system provides a language for those in the know. Actually, the "eighths" trading system dates from when market records were kept on paper, instead of computers, and where sign language was used on the trading floor to make trades. You have eight fingers, setting aside your thumbs to indicate "buy" or "sell." Sixteenths, thirty-seconds, sixty-fourths, and even smaller fractions evolved from the need to fine-tune for the huge trades being executed today. U.S. markets are glacially evolving toward the decimal system used by exchanges abroad (and our own monetary system) for centuries. Stay tuned. Change is guaranteed.

Glossary

Annual report—A firm's annual statement of operating and financial results.

APR—Annual percentage rate on a loan. This number is the total of all the financing costs such as interest and loan origination costs. A low interest rate charged every month adds up to a higher APR. Use the APR number to compare loan offers.

Asset—Any possession that has monetary value (can be bought or sold).

Beneficiary—The person or organization who receives money or property from a will.

Blind trust—A trust whose assets are managed without the knowledge or input of the benefactor.

Bull market, bear market—A bull market is a long period of time when stock prices are on the rise. A bear market is a long period of time when stock prices are on the decline. Either kind of market could last for months or even years.

Capital gain—The difference between what you paid for an asset and the money you receive when the asset is sold.

Central asset account—An account, with a large brokerage house, that includes checking, debit or credit card, margin loans, all investment accounts, and mutual funds in one numbered account with one monthly statement.

Charitable remainder trust—This type of trust involves signing over an asset to a charity while you are still alive, taking a tidy tax deduction, and then receiving the income from that asset. When you die, however, the remainder of the trust belongs to the charity.

Commission—The fee charged by a broker or brokerage house to process a customer's stock purchase or sale.

Conditional bequest—In a will, a rule that a payment to an heir is made only after certain conditions are met.

Cost basis—The actual dollar amount you paid for all your shares (including extra shares acquired through stock splits and reinvested dividends). Add up all the shares and divide by the purchase price to get the actual cost basis.

Credit—An arrangement whereby you borrow money to make a purchase.

Credit limit—The maximum amount that you can charge on a credit card. The maximum amount that you can owe at any one time.

Day trader—Someone who jumps in and out of a stock on a daily basis, hoping to eke out a profit on the daily movements in price.

Dealer markup—The amount that a dealer adds over and above the manufacturer's suggested retail price.

Default—To fail to make payments on a mortgage, credit card, or loan.

Depreciating asset—A possession that loses value with age and use.

Discount broker—Unlike a full-service broker, a discount broker like Charles Schwab won't give you any advice on what to invest in. It is up to you to do the research, make your own decisions, and then call the broker when you are ready to place an order.

Dividend—A portion of the company profits paid out to the company's shareholders.

Equity—The money that you pay into an investment.

Interest—Payment for the use of borrowed money. When you put money in a bank, you are literally loaning your money to the bank. The bank will use your deposit to make investments, hoping to make a profit.

Investing—Using money to purchase securities, property, or anything that will increase in value or produce income.

Investment club—A group of private individuals who pool their money and invest on a monthly basis in stocks that they have chosen for their long-term growth potential.

Irrevocable trust—A trust that, once established, cannot be modified in any way. *To revoke* means "to take away." An irrevocable trust cannot be taken away.

Liabilities—Debts and other financial obligations.

Load funds—Mutual funds that charge either to buy into the fund or to leave it.

Margin call—When you borrow to buy a stock ("buy on margin"), you may have to pay more money to retain the stock if it declines in value. A margin call is the announcement that you must pay what you owe.

Market correction—A sharp decline off the market high. The average must fall at least 20% to be considered a market correction.

Matching contributions—A program whereby some employers will match dollar for dollar an employee's contributions to a retirement plan, up to a certain maximum percentage.

Money market fund—A type of mutual fund that can serve as a savings and checking account with a higher than normal interest rate. It typically requires a $5,000 minimum balance and allows you to write only a limited number of checks per month (usually three).

Mortgage—To give a bank or lending institution a claim on property as security for the payment of debt on this property.

Mutual fund—A portfolio of securities managed by professional managers. Investors buy shares in the fund, and when the value of the stocks the company owns goes up, so does the value of the shares in the mutual fund.

Negative net worth—When you owe more money (liabilities) than you are worth (assets).

Net worth—Total assets minus total liabilities.

No-load funds—Mutual funds that charge no transaction to buy in or out, but do charge an annual fee to own.

Online trading—Buying or selling stocks, bonds, or commodities via a computer plugged into a network, usually the Internet. Individuals engaged in online trading typically do so without the help of a full-service stockbroker.

Payroll deduction—Money that is taken from your paycheck before it is given to you. The deductions are listed on your pay stub.

Probate—The court procedure in which the validity of a will is proven, during which time executors might be appointed, heirs identified, and debts paid.

Proxy—A proxy form authorizes someone to act in your stead—in this case to cast a vote at a shareholder's meeting.

Real-time quotes—The most up-to-date information on the trading price of a particular stock. Not to be confused with delayed quotes, in which the information is sometimes 15 to 20 minutes old and may already be outdated.

Revocable trust—A trust that can be modified by the person who set it up. *To revoke* means "to take away." A revocable trust can be taken away.

Schedule D—The tax form on which capital gains and losses are reported to the IRS.

Status symbol—An item that the owner hopes will help him or her project an aura of wealth and success.

Stock market—The method, and the venue, in which shares of stock are traded.

Street name—When the stock certificate is held in the name of the brokerage house rather than the individual client. This system simplifies trading.

Tax code—The body of law that covers taxes. The codes are identified by a system of numbers and letters, hence the 401(k).

Taxable estate—The portion of the estate that is subject to inheritance tax after the current exemption level is passed.

Index

281

J-K

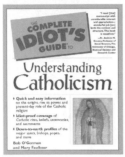

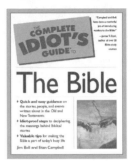

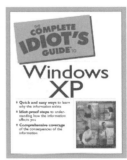